The art of Table dancing

The art of Table dancing

Escapades of an Irreverent Woman

by DC Stanfa

ORANGE FRAZER *PRESS*
Wilmington, Ohio

ISBN 1-933197-09-9
Copyright 2006 DC Stanfa

Additional copies of *The Art of Table Dancing: Escapades of an Irreverent Woman* may be ordered directly from:
Orange Frazer Press
P.O. Box 214
Wilmington, OH 45177

Telephone 1.800.852.9332 for price and shipping information.
Website: *www.orangefrazer.com*
DC Stanfa can be reached at: *www.dcstanfa.com*

Jacket design: Jeff Fulwiler
Cover photo: Tom Schonecker

Library of Congress Cataloging-in-Publication Data

Stanfa, Denise Marie., 1959-
    The art of table dancing : escapades of an irreverent woman / by DC Stanfa.
       p. cm.
    ISBN 1-933197-09-9 (alk. paper)
    1. Stanfa, Denise Marie., 1959- 2. Toledo (Ohio)--Biography. 3
  Women--Ohio--Toledo--Biography. 4. Catholic women--Ohio--Toledo--Biography. I.
  Title.

F499.T6S83 2006
977.1'043092--dc22
    [B]   2005058983

For my father and mother, Denny and Gloria Stanfa. Dad, you taught me to be patient with God, and with people—especially those who think they are God. And Mom, you help me see what's so funny about the drama.

Also, for Sandy Heshley who never stopped laughing. We can hear you all the way down here, you know.

ACKNOWLEDGEMENTS

I AM GRATEFUL TO THE following people: All the men who didn't call. Without them, this book would not have been possible. And The One who finally did. Tom, you saved me from death-by-cynicism.

Sherry—the real writer in the family, who understands why writing isn't as fun as reading. You talked me down off the bridge when I felt like jumping and showed me what needed to be tossed from the bridge (and the page) to make it all better.

My friends and family, for your love, encouragement, and patience with my self-focus—which was at its extreme during the evolvement of the manuscript. Some of you are in the book, as in real life: Lori, Sheila, Amy, Robin, Janet, Sue, Jamie, and Karen. For the sake of condensing stories, that otherwise would have been twice as long, I had to edit out other important, real characters who were there along the way: Connie, Kimba, Knize, Rocks, and Hesh-Dog to name a few. Thanks, girls, for helping incite the riots.

The writers I've met, especially the unpublished. I learned something from each of you. Some authors who've helped, and inspired me: THE Sweet Potato Queen—Jill Conner Browne, Bill Fitzhugh, John Kachuba, Steve Kissing, Tim Bete, and Robert Parish.

Tom Cox, for letting me first stick my neck out at www.stickyourneckout.com

Ann and Ralph, for home-owner support. Thanks for everything, especially getting the squirrels out alive.

Barbara Cox, the best unpaid therapist around.

My support groups: The Hashers of SCH4. On, On! My favorite audience, the patrons and staff at Anderson Township Pub—where everybody knows your name and what you did last night—but keeps their mouths shut, anyway. Thanks for encouraging my antics.

Doctor Paul Baker, and everyone at Baker Family Chiropractic—for getting me back in front of the computer after the dancing.

Susan Dudek, my cul-de-sac conscience.

My customers. For making the day job not seem like work. My employer, Packaging Corporation of America. Ditto.

Finally, Cori. Do not attempt to do any of the things I did—other than finishing college, and staying strong. My message to you, and your generation, is to get past all of the milestones, no matter if they fall on you. You can find humor in most of it (if you look really hard, later). There is life after high school. Don't shorten your stories. Leave that to God and the editors.

CONTENTS

Introduction   xi

Chapter 1   Nunsense   17
Chapter 2   The Unfair   32
Chapter 3   Driving Lessons   47
Chapter 4   Strangers On The Bus   61
Chapter 5   Question Marks In The Sand   85
Chapter 6   Gidget Goes To College   107
Chapter 7   Put-In-Bay   128
Chapter 7¹/₂   No More Fishy Parts   140
Chapter 8   Nuthin' But A Cardboard Box   145
Chapter 9   Picture This   158
Chapter 10   Fleetwood's Chicago   175
Chpater 11   Beach Therapy   189
Chapter 12   Just Shoot Me   208
Chapter 13   Revenge And Make-Up   224
Chapter 14   Just Shoot Me Again   234
Chapter 15   Zen And The Art Of Table Dancing   240
Chapter 16   A Fling With Gravity   258
Chapter 17   Hashing It Out   270

Epilogue   283
About The Author   287

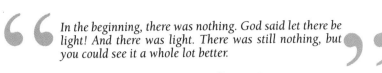

In the beginning, there was nothing. God said let there be light! And there was light. There was still nothing, but you could see it a whole lot better.

—Ellen DeGeneres

INTRODUCTION

I T HAS BEEN SAID THAT WHEN YOU DISSECT all the books and films ever produced, you ultimately discover that there is really only one basic story: that of sin and redemption. In an attempt to prove otherwise, I challenge you to look very, very hard in this book for any redemption. Not to say you won't find a religious thread, but if this book were a sweater, it would be like that miniscule stray strand of yarn on your sleeve that you barely notice until it begins to unravel, and you try to fold the sleeve under, because you like the sweater, but eventually you know you can't knit it back together, so you give it to the Goodwill. Which is a charitable act. So there, I guess, is the redemption after all. Which means I've failed to invent any story other than the only one that already existed.

If you choose to read on anyway, you should know that my own story of sin (and arguably redemption) often takes place in fun and unusual locations, like tropical beaches and the tabletops in bars—particularly upscale establishments, when it clearly wasn't condoned (there were no Coyote Ugly-type bars back then). However, as I began writing of these experiences,

I realized my behavior began—as behaviors tend to—during my childhood. My mother would tire of my moping-about-sighs-of-boredom and say, "Go entertain yourself." So, I did. Later, during a particularly miserable experience called high school, I realized that if I also entertained others, I just might make a new friend or two. I decided to write about some of that stuff, too.

In the midst of life's dramas, the phrase "someday, we'll look back at this, and laugh," is rarely consoling at the time. Even more rarely is it ever true. I vowed to change that, at least for some of the painful events of my life. I'm not saying that the stories in this book aren't true—fundamentally they all are. Many just weren't funny at the time. So, in writing this book, I have combined my ever-hungry ego with my lapsing memory, and created a remake of a stale film biography. I call it the Streisand Touch (not to be confused with the Streisand Effect, which is about Barbra filing a lawsuit that backfired, resulting in negative publicity).

This is the Streisand Touch at work: As the new producer, you recognize that the old movie just had a bad director and a worse editor. Some actors you'd like to replace, and the script needs a re-write. Now, we can re-shoot the scene where you desperately begged your old boyfriend, Joe, not to leave you for The Stripper, and you cried over him for days when he left. Through the gauze-covered lens and the new million dollar lighting, we replay the scene, where this time you realize that Joe (replaced by a more attractive actor) can't give you what you need in a relationship (a return phone call), and you sensitively let him down, telling him he'll find someone else. It's just a slightly altered point-of-view on the original, from a much longer lens. No bad close-ups, either, and the camera angles always favor your good side.

If you want to push further, and really turn the original horror show into a comedy, go for the *Funny Girl* Gamut. Instead of million-dollar lighting, you just need to use fun-house mirrors for your rear-views, and smoke something illegal. (Just kidding about that last part. That only worked in the '70s). *Silence Of The Lambs* can become Shari Lewis and Lamb Chop, if you just use some imagination.

I believe we each have the ability to reinvent our lives. When ego meets memory, ego should win. We can become better-intentioned people, more heroic, smarter. We can justify and minimize our weaknesses, as well as our character flaws, just like we would those of a new lover.

Maybe that's where the redemption lies.

If not, it still makes for a helluva better story.

The art of Table dancing

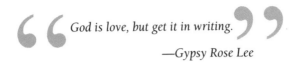

God is love, but get it in writing.
—*Gypsy Rose Lee*

N U N S E N S E

IT SEEMS QUITE NATURAL TO RUN FAST, furious, and far away from that which frightens you. In grade school, that retreat was initiated with a four-letter synonym for fear: NUNS. I've spent the subsequent decades of my life being the furthest thing from a nun I could figure out to be. Except maybe a prostitute or a Protestant. Anyone who knows me will tell you:

"DC Stanfa is the furthest thing from a nun that I know."

That makes me feel safer.

My friend Karen, also raised Catholic, told me that when she was young she used to pray to God,

"Please don't make me a nun."

If you are Catholic, you already understand the desperation of her plea. For the rest of you, whom I'll most likely meet in hell some day, let me explain.

Among the other myths and legends of grade-school religion class (such as only Catholics get into the real heaven; the others may just look in over the fence), we were taught that if we were meant to become a nun or a priest, we would personally be called upon by God to do so.

Inasmuch as the idea may repulse us, we would have a vision or an epiphany, and we would have to answer God's "call." Of course, all this proves to me is that God is a man, since He hasn't called. Being a typical woman, I'm still waiting. At age 40, and after a child, a failed marriage (to a non-Catholic, of course), and many other flawed and failed relationships, it could still happen. Any day now the God-phone could ring and *poof,* I'd get "THE CALL," and The Catholic Church would never be the same. First I'd clear up some confusing rules. Eat meat on Fridays? You bet. Slim Jims and beef jerky for everyone.

If I were in the sisterhood, the 7th grade sex talk would finally be taught by someone who actually experienced it— someone from a different 'hood. I might even bring pictures. How about that ever-so-touchy contraceptive controversy? Chapel veils? No. Other head coverings? Yes.

I could be wrong, but it's pretty safe to say I'll be running from nuns and other Catholic icons until they become extinct. Which could happen. That whole celibacy thing isn't quite the draw to the order that it used to be.

SIXTH-GRADE RELIGION CLASS IN 1971 AT ST. PETER'S was as predictable as a Disney cartoon, and for me, just as believable. The stories seemed outlandish even to imaginary me. Entire world floods? I just could not buy the idea that only one guy, Noah, saves all living species on a homemade boat. Even the Titanic couldn't have warehoused all that fauna and flora. Who were they kidding? How 'bout the Jonah guy, who survived being eaten and lived in the belly of a whale? A wooden puppet, maybe, but a man? I don't think so.

On one particularly gloomy October Toledo morning, I was daydreaming, as usual, during class. Gazing out the window into the overcast sky, I could see that the permacloud was settling once again into northwest Ohio as it had done all eleven years of my life. The sun might outsmart it for a few odd days during the winter months, but the drabness of the permacloud was pervasive over Ohio moods until it lifted in late spring.

Luckily, in my daydream, I was on a sunny beach in Malibu with John Cowsill of the Cowsill family singers. (The Cowsills were the inspiration for The Partridge family TV show, except they were a real family and could really sing and play instruments). I was picturing me as part of their album cover come-to-life.

"The topic we've been discussing, Denise, is Adam and Eve. Maybe you could tell us why Eve wanted to eat the apple," said Sister Susan, instantly transporting me back to the classroom.

I was conditioned to come to attention when I heard my formal name instead of my nickname, DC. By this formality, I could always tell what degree of trouble I was in at home or school. When the middle and last names were used, I might as well have bent over for the paddle.

"She wanted to have the forbidden knowledge that Satan, disguised as a snake, had promised her," I replied.

The nun was stunned by the accuracy of my answer,. and I went back to my daydreaming. In *this* daydream I was in the basement of the college's University Hall, in the dim, musty, slate-smelling corridor, which was the geology lab and offices. I was watching a guy with a ponytail polish brightly colored rocks.

This daydream was a replay, a montage of many real life hours spent the past summer in that same lab with my two sisters. Our mom worked at the University geology department as a part-time secretary. My sister Lori was a year older than I was and the source of my nickname. She was just learning to talk when I was born and pronounced Denise as "DC." My other sister Sherry, two years my junior, was named after Shari Lewis, the ventriloquist and puppeteer of Lamb Chop (a puppet who, as far as I knew had *never* been in the belly of a whale).

Although we were old enough to stay home by ourselves,

19

we went once a week to work with my mom while she did the payroll. Then we'd go swimming at the Lucas County Recreation Center.

The geology lab was pretty cool. So were the graduate students who worked there, although my Dad said he thought they smoked left-handed cigarettes. They taught us all about rocks and fossils. We even started our own collection. When the grad students weren't around, we read books about the planet.

One book had illustrations of evolving man. The one where he starts out all crouched over, ape-like, knuckles scraping the ground then over a series of drawings Cro-Magnon becomes Homo Sapiens. This college knowledge however, didn't jibe with the Church's Adam and Eve gig. Was this knowledge *the* forbidden fruit? I wanted to know. So now, back in class, I took a bite. I mean, I raised my hand and asked Sister Susan a loaded question.

"Sister, scientists have found fossilized remains proving that man evolved. How do Adam and Eve fit into all that?" I asked with a self-satisfied smile. This bite was going to be good.

Sister Susan was the youngest nun at St. Peter's. In her mid-20s, she was the founder and lead performer at "Guitar Mass." She picked a few kids from our class to sing with her and I was one of them. She was pretty cool, for a nun. She never hit us or made us kneel in the corner like the rest of them did.

Sister Susan paused at my question, put her rosary in her top desk drawer, and stood up slowly before answering.

"Denise brings up an interesting point, one that the Church has a definite opinion on. We stand by the word of God, which tells us that Adam and Eve did exist. However, some modern theologians have tried to resolve the seemingly opposed explanations by merging God's creation of Adam and Eve with the theory of evolution."

"Adam and Eve were monkeys!" Jeff Sanecki, the class clown, shouted, scratching his underarms like a gorilla.

"No, Jeffrey," Sister Susan interjected firmly. "What I am saying is that *if* man *did* evolve over the centuries, once he evolved to the point of discerning right from wrong, God placed a soul in him. Obviously God was responsible for all of creation, but Adam and Eve were claimed as God's own and made in God's own likeness. God's gift of love and the lesson about evil could have been learned in many ways. Some theologians, outside of the church, view the serpent in the Bible as symbolic. The time period over which this took place, and whether Adam was made from earthen clay or Eve of Adam's rib, can also be viewed symbolically."

That did it. Sister Susan wasn't only the sweetest nun, she was the smartest. Her brief monologue resolved this and many other biblical tales for me. *Symbolic, yeah, like the parables Jesus told.* There was truth and symmetry in the idea, and it made perfect sense to me.

BY SEVENTH GRADE, LIKE MOST 12-YEAR-OLDS, I knew everything. I had moved up a grade but traded down considerably on teachers. In her mid-50s, about five feet tall and just as wide, Mrs. Nader was no Sister Susan. She was also *not* a nun. She was what the church referred to as a lay teacher. That meant she was not a nun or a priest, who were the "not-laid teachers." The running joke was that she had as many Chins as the Chinese phone book. Sitting through her dry classes was itself an act of penance.

One afternoon she led us through the barren religion-lesson desert for what only felt like forty days. At one point she introduced Cain and Abel as Adam and Eve's sons.

"Mrs. Nader," I asked, "if we were to view Cain and Abel symbolically, could they represent two nations or two races of people that battled one another?"

"What on earth are you talking about, young lady? Like I said, Cain and Abel were brothers, the sons of Adam and Eve. These are biblical facts. What are *you* suggesting?"

Drawing a deep breath, I bit once again into that forbidden fruit.

"What I'm suggesting is that a lot of the Bible stories cannot possibly be true. I mean if there were just one Adam and only one Eve their kids would have to marry each other and that would be incest, right? So, there has to be another explanation."

I looked over at my best friend, Sheila Hart, who was doing her best to stifle a laugh. My trouble-making always amused her.

"You'd better have an explanation for that blasphemous, disruptive comment," Mrs. Nader screeched, as she waddled, like a duck with a hemorrhoid, to my desk. When I was within reach of her stubby arms, she shot out her open-palmed right hand to box my left ear.

"Maybe that will help you get rid of your pig-headed ideas," she snorted.

The embarrassment stung more than the actual blow. Getting smacked in the head in front of my classmates wasn't the cool outcome I'd hoped for when I began my debate of the doctrine. So, I decided to use my trump card, which was a higher authority than Mrs. Nader: one of Jesus' own brides, Sister Susan. Nuns are considered the "Bride of Christ" when they take their vows. This is symbolically, I'm sure, since that is one marriage that will likely never be consummated.

I confidently launched into my explanation,

"Last year, Sister Susan said that the Bible can be viewed symbolically since there's evidence of evolution. She told our class that maybe, after men and women evolved, God put souls into them and called them Adam and Eve. I was just taking the idea further...that God put souls in many races of people at one time and they battled one another, like Cain and Abel."

I was unprepared for the vehemence with which Mrs. Nader faced such heresy.

"Blasphemy and lies! You are a liar and I'll prove it. Sister Susan would never teach such nonsense. What do you say we go next door?"

Mrs. Nader picked me up off my chair by my hair, literally, not symbolically. I was pissed off momentarily but looked forward to Sister bailing me out.

Boy, Mrs. Nader sure was going to look like an idiot.

Sister Susan's class was in the middle of a spelling test when we flew into the room. "Articula…" She stopped just short of the t and got wide-eyed in the not-so-pleasant surprise kind of way.

Mrs. Nader buzzed with indignation like a big fly that had been interrupted from feasting on a cow carcass. To amuse myself, I pictured a gigantic fly swatter slapping her up against the chalkboard, jiggling all her chins. Heads popped up from desks and eyes stared. Mrs. Nader had a firm grip on my Peggy Fleming hairdo. I knew I was skating on thin ice.

"Sister, I'm sorry to interrupt," Mrs. Nader blasted self righteously. "But this is extremely important. This blasphemous creature has dared to defy the word of God, and more important, question the Catholic Church's teachings. She has also told a terrible lie about you. So I brought her in here to apologize to you."

"But I'm not lying," I said.

I didn't realize then that the opening statement for my defense would also serve as my closing argument.

"What did she say? What lie did she tell about me?" asked a stunned Sister Susan.

"She said that you spoke against the traditional Adam and Eve story. She said that you believe there's even evidence of evolution. She said that you told your class that The Bible could be viewed SYMBOLICALLY!" Mrs. Nader spat with remnants of spittle clinging to two of her chins.

Sister Susan made brief eye contact with me and became very still. Someone in the back row dropped a pencil. Someone else coughed. The butterball turkey at the end of my hair finally had butterfingers and I slipped out of her hair-hold on me.

Sister is probably taking a moment to gather her thoughts so that she can explain it as eloquently to Mrs. Nader as she had to me.

"I have no idea what you're talking about," said Sister Betrayal.

A surge of blood rushed from my heart to my head and I couldn't catch my breath.

"Of course, I believe as the Church does and teach the traditional Bible stories," Sister Nail-in-my-Coffin said, as she slid her hands up opposite sleeves of her habit, signaling that she was finished with this little drama.

Mrs. Nader spouted with superiority, "O.K., Little Miss Liar. What do you have to say for yourself? How about an apology to Sister for this awful thing you've done?"

I looked at Mrs. Nader, then at the class, and finally at Sister Susan before I spoke.

"I am very, very sorry that one of us is lying."

THERE WAS A POPULAR BUMPER STICKER in the late sixties that said simply, QUESTION AUTHORITY.

Yeah, but don't believe their answers.

You'd think I'd have learned my lesson from the evolution incident and quit rocking Noah's Ark. However, being an ark-rocker from birth, I determined that certain *other* people needed to learn a thing or two, and if there were any vessel in need of a good rocking in the early 1970s, it was the Catholic Church.

Just ask my mom, Gloria.

Gloria Stoll was raised in the Lutheran faith by her German immigrant parents. To prevent having a mixed marriage, she converted to Catholicism after she married my dad, Denny Stanfa. Mom tried to do the Catholic thing, but there were some "issues" that pissed her off. I inherited this sensibility. Mom was a bit of an ark-rocker herself, and she was responsible for the first of many major Stanfa family disturbances at St. Peter's Church and elementary school.

In those years, St. Peter's did not have uniforms. The rules of dress, however, were every bit as strict as the rules of conduct. No skirts or dresses above the knee for the girls and, even when it was ten below zero, and even though we had mandatory outside recess, no slacks were allowed. Among the families at St. Peter's, my family was on the lower side of the income scale, and although Mom occasionally shopped at thrift stores, we'd never been busted for, or embarrassed by, our attire. (Unless one counts Sherry's innocent admission to our higher-income friends that her boys' ice skates came from Goodwill.) On the contrary, Mom usually dressed us like little dolls, and because we were so close in age, she even dressed us alike for some special occasions.

On the special occasion of the first day of school, 1967, Lori, Sherry, and I were dressed in matching red, white, and blue outfits. I'm certain we were the inspiration for the Brady girls. Lori was a fourth grader, I was in third, and Sherry was in her rookie year of the brain-spanking that was Catholic school.

Sherry was a product of the rhythm method of birth control, which was the only method not considered a sin by the Church. This method was second only to the let's-get-drunk-and-do-it-on-prom-night-and-cross-our-fingers method.

At about 10 a.m. on yet another dreary Toledo morning, a secretary from the parish office came to Sister Francis's room and asked for me. I was escorted to the principal's office, for the first—and definitely not the last—time, and found that my sisters were already in her office. Everyone looked somber and Sherry looked as if she'd been crying.

Oh my God, I thought, *something terrible must have happened,* and I began to imagine a horrible accident where we became orphaned.

Our principal was Sister Anita. Sister Anita, AKA "Big Red," as she was known behind her back, was sitting behind her desk, blinking her flaming red eyelashes and fiercely fingering her clicker, a hand-held device nuns used in church to get someone's attention or direct movement. Stand, sit, kneel. There was a lot of that.

Big Red was the most surly nun to ever inhabit a habit. She was six feet tall with shocks of fire engine red hair visible around her head before it disappeared into her veil. Fear alone brought her victims to their knees.

God forbid if you were caught with your hands in your pockets, or talking in line, or any number of the heinous crimes punishable by Big Red's law. She was the Principal pain in my ass throughout most of my malformative youth. Under her iron rule I was beaten down and had arisen so many times that my knees were shot and my classmates revered me as a martyr for the misgoverned.

Big Red ran a dictatorial regime, and I led the resistance. Each time I defied her, she seemed to grow stronger in her determination to break me down.

"All right, girls, which one of you is going to explain to me why you've chosen to disregard the dress code today?"

Looking down at my hemline, I thought, *it is a little too much above the knee.*

"I've already called your mother to come get you and dress you more appropriately before bringing you back to school. What do you call those ugly things, anyway?"

"They're called culottes," Lori said, with a bit of cockiness in her voice (for a 9-year-old).

Big Red moved around her desk toward us. This mountain of a woman was holding back, repressing thirty-five years of sexual needs built up inside her like hot lava inside a volcano. That churning lust transformed into anger. A violent eruption was imminent, and we were the villagers of Pompeii.

Mentally, I was picturing Big Red as being the only Nun that God didn't *really* call. She was actually the devil's sister and *she* called God, to tell *Him* how it was going to be.

"Well, it's obvious to me they are shorts hidden by flaps. But not so well hidden, are they? Who taught you to be so sneaky?"

"I didn't know culottes were a sin, Sherry wailed. "My mom dressed me."

"Oh, I see," said Sister Chief-Prosecutor-Judge-and-Jury through tightly clenched teeth.

Then we saw Mom, Gloria-you-can-call-me-Glo.

Glo, with her cute blonde flip and black-and-white culottes. She looked at her girls and then Sister Anita. She knelt down and put her arms around Sherry.

"Why are you crying?"

"Sister Anita was yelling at us and telling us we look ugly in these outfits," Sherry boo-hooed from the safety of mom's arms.

"I was not yelling!" Big Red yelled.

"You've said or done *something* to upset a sweet 6-year-old who is wearing a darling and perfectly decent outfit I picked out!"

Mom was a foot shorter than Big Red but could stand up to her better than anyone I'd ever seen.

"Mrs. Stanfa, if you need a copy of the dress code, I will get it for you. These culottes are by no means acceptable. In fact, I find them *in*decent."

Mom simply glared at her and shuffled us out of there, biting her tongue. Just as we were outside Big Red's office, she shouted back through the doorway.

"What on earth do you or the Catholic Church know about fashion, anyway?"

I get my insolence from my mother's side.

On the way home we had quite a discussion about standing up for what was right and wrong. Mom said the Church didn't know it all and to never be afraid of Sister Anita, or anybody else, for that matter. She was our Mom. She'd stand by us.

Glo drove us to the A&W Drive-in for an early lunch.

"Do we have to go back today?" Lori asked.

"I'm certainly not in the mood to iron more clothes today," was Mom's rational response.

I'm not saying the great culottes caper of '67 gave the Stanfa girls license to rock the ark, but, with Mom behind us, we boldly seized many opportunities to throw in an oar and attempt to paddle in a different direction. On occasion, we even got a few friends to paddle with us.

By THE TIME LORI WAS IN EIGHTH GRADE, she'd earned her own nickname from Big Red—"Ring Leader." Ring Leader decided she was too cool to belong to Girl Scouts any longer and convinced most of the troop to quit with her. Several of them even burned their membership cards, on school property. As for me, halfway through seventh grade Mrs. Nader was still calling me "pig-headed." It had been months since the Sister Betrayal/evolution episode, but she just wouldn't let it go.

It was early March and I was in religion class one afternoon, actually paying attention for a change. Mrs. Nader was out sick, and Father Boyer was teaching. We had a different "lay" sub for the other classes that day.

Father Boyer was new at St. Peter's and very energetic. Our other priests were as old and about as lively as the church statues, but without the priest uniform he might have been handsome. I wondered what he'd look like in a baseball uniform.

Father Boyer was wrapping up the lesson, which was about making God-guided choices in our lives.

"By the way, are there any of you boys who would like to serve Mass for me? If so, please raise your hand, I have a sign-up sheet."

Hands went in the air, including mine. Father called on me, assuming I had a question.

"Yes, Father, why can only boys serve Mass? Why can't girls be servers?"

"Well, uh, what is your name?"

"Denise, but everybody calls me DC."

"Well, DC, I'm not sure there is a strict rule on the matter.

It's just that, traditionally, only boys have served. Are you saying that you would like to?"

"Yes, Father, very much."

He put his finger to his chin, a sign I read as DEEP THOUGHT IN PROGRESS.

"If you are sincerely interested, I'd be happy to get you some instruction and you can serve Mass for me."

Jaws dropped, including mine.

A few days later, I was sure the entire planet was talking about DC Stanfa, the religious pioneer and soon-to-be-saint, the first girl server in the Catholic Church. It was just after noon recess and Sheila Hart and I were making weekend plans, which included a skating party Friday and a sleepover at my house on Saturday, when Mrs. Nader returned to the classroom from her lunch. As Mrs. Not-by-the-Hair-of-my-Chinny-Chin-Chins huffed and puffed her way down the aisle directly toward me, I knew that once again, I was in trouble. So when she shot a stubby arm in the direction of my head, I was ready for it. She was going for an ear-box or perhaps a hair-lock.

Either way, I ducked, and put my hands in front of me in a pseudo kung fu defense.

"It's all your fault! You impudent, pig-headed yippie!"

I wasn't sure of the definition of some of the words Mrs. Nader was using, but she was making her point. The point was: Once more, I'd done something terrible.

"You're coming with me. I've had it with you!" she screamed. "You want to serve Mass? Let's see what Sister Anita has to say about this. Who do you think you are?" She grabbed my left wrist and pulled me behind her as she waddled toward the door.

"Never in my life have I had a disagreement or argument with a clergy member. But, now because of you...."

Her sentence trailed off into the deep recesses of her chins as we snaked our way down the hall toward the principal's office.

Mrs. Nader was panting and sweating so hard she could barely get the words out.

"She's all yours. I've had it with her. I don't want this troublemaker in my classroom any more." With that, Mrs. Nader exited Big Red's office, and I was left at her lack of mercy.

Big Red's blazing eyelashes were batting so fast that they were certain to burst into flames any second. When they didn't, I just prayed for spontaneous combustion of any kind.

"Little miss showoff," she said.

She folded her arms across her chest and drummed her fingers above her cloaked elbows, fluttering with indignation, fanning the only fire in the room, which was my funeral pyre.

"You're a real big shot, aren't you? Just like your sister The Ring Leader. Well nobody thinks you're cool. Do you know that the other kids talk about you behind your back? I've heard the boys talking about not liking a girl who wants to serve Mass, like a boy. Is that what you want, to be a boy?"

One slap, two slaps.

Not by her hand but by her words.

What was she saying? The other kids say bad things about me? The boys think I want to be a boy? Oh, my God.

I started shaking. It couldn't be true. I was popular. Everybody liked me, didn't they?

Oh, I get it, she's messing with my mind like they do when you're in a P.O.W. camp. It's part of the brainwashing.

I tried to be brave, but part of me capsized with self-doubt.

Do the kids really talk about me?

Cast into the sea of adolescent emotion, I began gasping for breath. I felt the familiar throat tightening, that I'm-about-to-cry pharynx sensation. I fought back hard.

I will not let her see me cry. She cannot make me cry, that's what she wants.

And then the tears came.

"Kneel down," instructed Big Red, pointing to a spot on the hardwood floor.

I obeyed, cautiously looking about for any weapon she may have.

"Pray for forgiveness for your impudence. Pray for help for your ignorance. Pray for Mrs. Nader and what trouble you've caused her and most of all, pray for the cleansing of your blackened soul. You'll not get into heaven with these sins you continue to commit."

If she only knew the sin I was committing in my head as I mentally stuck pins in a red-headed Barbie doll dressed in a nun's habit. Mental voodoo, transferring my ever-so-real pain by inflicting imaginary pain on Big Red. The psychic release provided me momentary peace and cosmic clarity. I knew that my ideas were too far ahead for the Catholic Church. They'd be stuck for centuries to come. If I lived through the penance session in Big Red's office, I was going to get a new religion.

Maybe I'll go see if Father Boyer wants to start one with me.

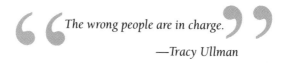

The wrong people are in charge.
—Tracy Ullman

THE UNFAIR

THERE ARE MANY UNCERTAINTIES IN LIFE. Even after more than forty years of living it, I often struggle with choices. Coffee or tea. Kick-boxing or yoga. Hit the snooze alarm or not. Then there are some pretty clear-cut rules that *do* make sense. Do floss. Do pass on the left. Don't eat anything that falls on the floor (unless it is chocolate and no one is looking). Don't pick a fight or your nose, unless you've really considered what you might be getting into.

Like most 12-year-olds in 1972, I'd attained a moderate amount of wisdom from various sources: church, school, home, the neighborhood, and the reading material Mom and Dad kept hidden under their bed. But there comes a time, usually in adolescence, when the most important things to know you learn yourself—the hard way. When you do learn them, it is your humanitarian obligation to pass along such truths to the rest of mankind. So let this be known. Please pass it on. Tell it to your children and your children's children. Make it part of the genetic code and the universal mind. This is the imperative: Never, never, never work for a man named Turtle.

It was late summer. My best neighborhood friend, the more exuberant of twin sisters, swung, standing up on the backyard swing-set.

"Donny Welch says that they're setting up over at the fairground, you know, rides and games and stuff. He says they're hiring kids to work there. Wouldn't that be fun?" Lee leaned back on the swing to gain momentum and height.

"What kind of jobs?"

"Oh, I don't know, like selling ride tickets, I guess."

She must have sensed I wasn't sold on the idea.

"Donny says the jobs pay up to three dollars an hour!"

"Wow, that's more than twice what we get for baby-sitting, and no dirty diapers. The fair lasts five days. If we get three dollars an hour for, let's say, eight hours a day, oh my God, that's over a hundred dollars! Think about what we could buy with a hundred dollars!"

As I shouted those words, my mind was calculating the enormity of the numbers and picturing a crisp one hundred dollar bill in my hands. I was aware that the five-dollar-a-week allowance I earned with daily chores divided down to about seventy-five cents an hour, which was peanuts compared to the wealth that awaited me at the fairgrounds.

Lee was my age, but she always seemed much older. With her confident style, she could get into and out of just about any situation. She had a natural look, a thick brown mane of hair, a smooth complexion, and she would never need cosmetic camouflage for zits or orthodontics while I would require both.

We rode our banana-seat bikes out to the Lucas County fair grounds to investigate our possible employment. I'd gotten a ten-speed the previous year but had recently stripped the gears, so the going was slow.

There was no official hiring process at the fair. We just wandered the fairgrounds while food booths, rides, "carnie" games, and exhibits were being set up. That's when we encountered our boss-to-be, Turtle, and his family.

Lee and I watched as the five-foot-two character stood on a ladder hanging enormous, stuffed St. Bernards around the inside perimeter of a game booth where milk bottles had been stacked, pyramid style, on small tables. The stuffed animals were more than half his size. Stains decorated his T-shirt like tie-dyed dirt and sweat. His black, slicked-backed pompadour glistened with Brylcreem. He turned his head in our direction and stepped down from the ladder.

"You hiring?" Lee asked Elvis's shorter, ugly brother.

He grinned a black and white checkerboard set of teeth at us. "Can you bark?"

The words fell out of his mouth as if they might take a few more teeth with them. Consistent with carnie tradition, Turtle had a high tattoo-to-teeth ratio.

Lee and I were confused by his question.

"I mean, do ya'll think ya can yell loud enough for folks to wanna play these 'ere games?"

A petite blonde woman who'd been blowing up balloons at the adjacent booth and a little boy who'd been tacking them to a corkboard stopped to listen to our conversation. Turtle pointed in their direction.

"In this 'ere game, ya gotta bust balloons for prizes."

"Step right up and break a balloon for a prize," Lee quickly auditioned.

"That's the idea, little lady. How 'bout your friend?"

Nervously, I reached into a basket near the front of the other booth and picked up a well-seasoned softball.

"Knock over the milk bottles and win a prize," I said, lacking Lee's volume and confidence. This caught the attention of the little boy who walked over and took the softball from me.

"No. Ya cain't just knock 'em down, ya gotta knock 'em all off the table to win the BIGGEST PRIZE ON THE MIDWAY!"

This kid looked about 10 years old. But his excitement was convincing.

I nodded in approval.

"This is my boy, Ike. You can call me Turtle, and my old lady over there is Betty."

Betty's hair reminded me of the color of a Lay's potato chip bag, and it was so over-teased and over-bleached I was sure the texture was probably a lot like a potato chip.

"How much will you pay us?" Lee asked, after we'd completed our side of the introductions.

"Three dollars an hour if you can start tomorrow."

"It's a deal," Lee said, shaking his grimy hand.

"Be here at 9:30. The fair opens at 10."

"That was unbelievable! It was almost too easy to get hired, I mean, considering our ages," I said to Lee.

We sat on a picnic table at Dairy Queen where we'd stopped on the ride home. Pleased with our new career paths, we were celebrating our good fortune over peanut buster parfaits.

Lee shrugged and gave me a raised eyebrow.

"Yeah, well, it is the day before the fair and he probably wanted to make sure he had some help. The job seems pretty easy too. All we have to do is, like, stand around and talk to people."

By 9:30 A.M., THE FAIRGROUNDS HAD REACHED a steamy 80 degrees and the pungent stench of the contents of the 4-H barns loomed heavily over the Midway. My elephant leg bell-bottoms were sticking to my butt as a result of the bike ride, and I'd caught the hem in the bike chain along the way. That act of gracefulness tore my jeans and caused the chain to come off its track, par for my course. Lee had the chain fixed in no time. Her control over all situations was definitely contagious. Still, I had a gut feeling that it was going to be a long day

Lee must have read my mind. As we ambled past the Tilt-A-Whirl and the Freak Show featuring Gorilla Woman, Snake Man, and Lobster Boy, she speculated out loud,

"Wonder how late we'll have to work? Probably until five or six, don't you think?"

"Yeah, I'm sure there are other people working nights."

As we arrived, Turtle's boy, Ike, was gingerly working on stacking the milk bottles. Turtle approached us with money aprons and instructions.

"One throw is fifty cents, three for a dollar, both booths. Ya break a balloon, ya git the small prize. Break another, and ya can trade up. Six trade-ups will git ya to the big prize. Betty and I will replace the balloons and git the prizes after the dart throws. And Ike, only Ike, will set up the milk bottles. Get it?"

"Sure," Lee said.

I nodded.

"Got it?" Turtle asked, directing the question to me.

"Yeah."

Like, don't have a cow, man.

"Good!"

The only other person I'd known to use the 'Get it?-Got it?-Good! training method had been a visiting priest who spoke to our seventh grade religion class at St. Peter's earlier that year, and emphatically taught us sex-ed with the basics that he himself lived by.

"Boys, girls, hands off," he said. "Get it? Got it? Good!"

I wondered what common denominator these two unlikely counterparts had experienced to share such a methodology.

As prospective patrons passed, Lee barked out a convincing invitation to play. My own bark was more like that of a small dog. A Chihuahua, perhaps. But it didn't take a whole lot of vocals to convince people to play the milk bottle game. The prizes and the simplicity of the game were the draw. Knock five bottles off the table and win a stuffed dog bigger than your car trunk. It wasn't like taking candy from a baby; it was more like taking money from a person shoving the money in your face.

After about four hours in the blazing sun and an apron full of cash, I hadn't had one customer win this simple game. Oh, there were a few that knocked them down. One or two that actually succeeded in knocking a few off the table, but never all five. Then Ike would "set 'em up again." I was beginning wonder if anyone would ever win.

While Lee and I grabbed a quick corn dog for lunch, she said, "This is pretty fun, huh?"

"At least you're giving away some prizes,"

I was a little mopey but kept my suspicions to myself. Lee, however, must have been having her own doubts.

"I guess that milk bottle thing is harder than it looks."

As the day wore down, so did we. I was beginning to wonder where our replacements were, so I asked the boss.

"Are you for serious? This is an all-day gig."

"Well, I think our parents are expecting us back," Lee interjected, overhearing our discussion. "We can't ride our bikes home in the dark."

She sounded so reasonable.

"All right. Stay until 7:30. I suppose we can handle it after that."

On the bike ride home, I was almost too exhausted to peddle. But we'd been paid in cash. Three dollars times ten hours added up to thirty dollars each.

"Four more days of this kind of money and we'll be rich," Lee assured me.

I nodded and simultaneously spit some gnats out of my mouth. We rode in silence, conjuring up what wondrous items we might buy. I mentally spent $3.99 on a sealing wax set with a peace symbol stamper I'd seen at Wicks-N-Sticks. I also envisioned a cerebral purchase of some round, wire-rimmed glasses with interchangeable, colored lenses from J.C. Penney. All that, and I still wouldn't have to break the hundred dollar bill I was going to get.

Maybe I'll even open a bank account. The money at the bank earns more money by just sitting in the account.

I pictured big things, like a plane trip to see the ocean.

The next morning as I was getting ready to meet Lee, my Mom called from work,

"Is everything going alright with the fair job? You mentioned that this guy, Turtle, was a little weird."

"It's okay, Mom. Sorry I was too tired to talk when I got home last night. I didn't realize that standing on my feet all day in the heat would be so, uh, hard."

"Well, I don't like you working so many hours. I think there are laws about how many hours kids can work."

"Mom, I gotta go. I'll be careful and we'll try to get off a little earlier tonight."

I was getting antsy and didn't want to be late. As I hopped on my bike, it crossed my mind that Turtle might not care much about child labor laws, or many other laws, for that matter.

The day was as steamy as the day before. Being a veteran carnie, I at least had the intelligence on the second day to wear shorts. As I had not yet bonded with my fellow carnies, I could only fathom a guess at the collective intellectual level. I did, however, strike up some conversation with Ike during lulls in the softball throwing business.

"So where are you from?"

"Cain't pacifically say. Last year I went to school in three places, Kansas City, Knoxville, and Birmingham. 'Course, I was born in Gary, Indiana."

He wasn't a bad looking kid, considering he was spawned from the loins of Turtle and Potato-Chip Hair. Regardless of the bizarre upbringing he might have had, Ike was pretty well-mannered and seemingly well-adjusted.

"Have you always been in this business?"

My line of questioning was like rowing an anchored boat; you go through the motions but there's little doubt where you'll end up.

"As long as I can remember. Really ever since Daddy got out," Ike replied.

"Out of what, or, I mean where?"

"Joliet, you know, prison. He got paroled when I was four. I was born while daddy was still in."

The boat had broken free of its anchor and I was really getting somewhere. Little Ikey was most likely the product of a conjugal visit I didn't want to picture.

"Oh really? What was he in for?"

"Bad checks and other stuff."

Bad checks didn't set off alarms. The other "stuff" worried me just a tad.

Just as things were getting juicy, a 60ish woman and her two grandkids interrupted us to play for the big prize. After we'd relieved them of about eight dollars of grandma's social security money, I felt a twinge of something I recognized (like any good Catholic would) as guilt.

"So, what's the deal, Ike? Why hasn't anybody won?"

I really was not expecting the answer I got.

" 'Cause it's rigged thataway."

I was as surprised by my naiveté as I was by his answer.

"Yeah, I figured that. But how?"

"Well, ya see these bottles are weighted down here at the base and if ya set 'em up jist right," he demonstrated the job he'd perfected, "Ya jist cain't knock 'em all off the table."

"Cool," I lied.

"When Daddy sees us getting a little slow like this, he'll have me set 'em up different so somebody can win and tote the prize around the Midway to drum up more business. But we never give away more than a prize a day."

Quickly processing his confession, and being fairly certain that rigging a game was a crime, I was aware that I had now become Turtle's accomplice. I was working for a con artist.

Man, what were Mom and Dad thinking when they let me get a job at the fair? Didn't they know what kind of people I'd be dealing with? Maybe I inherited my naiveté.

I grabbed Lee for our guess-what's-on-the-stick lunch and blurted out the story between bites.

"Bummer," she concluded.

"Lee, I can't keep doing this."

I chewed on the idea of theft and a piece of mystery meat, neither of which I was able to immediately digest.

"He's ripping people off and I'm helping."

Mom and Dad would be proud. Their investment in Catholic school tuition was paying off nicely; instead of field trips, we go on all-expense-paid guilt trips.

"If you're going to quit, then so am I, but we can't quit in the middle of the day. Turtle might get mad and not pay us."

Lee's reasoning seemed sound to me.

"Okay, but we're not coming back tomorrow."

IT WAS ALMOST EIGHT WHEN WE HIT THE ROAD for home and I was ready to relax.

"Boy, I could use a dip in a pool."

With that in mind, about three-quarters of the way home, we stopped at a city park and hopped the fence to have ourselves a private pool party. I took a moment to remove my Beatles watch and macramé belt. Shoeless, but otherwise fully clothed, we loitered in the shallow end, too tired to take full advantage of the entire pool we were trespassing in.

"So we're working for a convicted felon." Lee muttered with a combination of amusement and angst. I sat on the edge of the pool, drip-drying myself and smoothing out three folded ten-dollar bills, the damp spoils of a very disturbing day.

"It's getting dark. We'd better get going. I want to talk to my parents about this, because maybe we should report him to the police," I said, unsure of what our next move should be.

"Yeah, but first let's get out of here before someone reports *us* to the police."

THE MORNING WAS OVERCAST AND COOLER, MAKING the formerly pungent fairground air a bit more breathable. As we passed the ferris wheel, the operator pursed his lips and then made some sort of sucking sound.

"Gross," I cringed. "What is that, a carnie mating call?"

Lee didn't seem to hear me over the screams of a dozen ferris wheel riders imprisoned in their swinging cages. We had once again jumped into the genetic pool of carnival people. And what a shallow pool it was. Obviously most of them couldn't read the NO DIVING sign.

We entered a little building at the far end of the grounds. This was the office of the Lucas County Fair Board. Lee's parents and mine had decided the previous night that this was the right thing to do. Our plan was to turn in Turtle, then go enjoy the fair. A middle-aged woman with cat eyeglasses and a huge beehive greeted us from behind a countertop.

"Can I help you?"

Her voice purred a doubtful, anticipating arrogance. We'd interrupted something she was eager to get back to. From the looks of the man and the woman on the cover of the Harlequin romance novel she slyly tried to cover with one clawed hand, it involved heaving bosoms. She was an old cat who'd been sitting on the hot tin roof too long.

Lee was our spokesperson and she began, pointing a guilty finger at me.

"We're working at the fair and the game she's working at is rigged."

"What do you mean, rigged?" Beehive Woman asked.

Alert now, she narrowed her gaze at Lee and furrowed her brow.

"I mean it's impossible to win," answered Lee.

"What game are you talking about?"

"It's the knock-down-the-milk-bottle game with big stuffed dogs as prizes," I explained. "I've been working there for two days and nobody's won. The guy we work for, Turtle, well, he's an ex-con and his son sets the bottles up a certain way so they won't go off the table."

There.

I'd told her the whole story.

"Young lady, these people are licensed and they abide by all the rules and regulations of the governing board. I'm sure you're mistaken."

"His kid admitted it," I argued.

"All right, I'll have someone look into it next week when the fair is over. Right now, we're just too busy to answer every little complaint."

She cut off eye contact with us, patted the top of her hair-sprayed tower (quite a reach for her short pudgy arms) and picked up her book. Pawing the cover with her well-manicured claws and adjusting her glasses she tuned us out in favor of the hot promise of her paperback.

As Lee led the way out of the building, I was still numb from shock at Beehive's indifference.

"Bullcrap," Lee said. "This is not fair."

The fair is not fair, and the fair smells like bull crap.

I was amused by the pun. My mind played ping-pong with the words. Beehive Woman was digging a hole in the sand to insert her head, a very deep hole. Lee's words were getting louder, which brought me back to reality.

"If they're not going to do anything, we are. Do your shorts have pockets?"

"Yeah," I answered, glancing down at my fringed jean-shorts with front and back pockets.

"Okay. We've been sweating our asses off for two days, so he can make hundreds of dollars, and all we have to show for is sixty bucks. I mean, he didn't, like, even pay us for overtime. We deserve more!"

I knew what she was suggesting.

"So what you're saying is that because he's cheating, it's okay to steal from him? It's not exactly Robin Hood, unless we're going to buy pagan babies."

I was mixing Catholic school maturity with the Stanfa family sarcasm.

Lee gaped at me. Her dropped jaw closed around her question.

"What the hell are pagan babies?"

Although it was an excellent question for a non-Catholic, I answered in total disbelief of her ignorance.

"Foreign Orphans. We save money to adopt them to get them baptized, and we can name 'em too."

"Weird."

It hadn't dawned on me until that moment, but it *was* weird. I briefly wondered if the Church actually used the names that we came up with because our class, led by my irreverence, produced a few doozies. For all I knew, there was a child toddling around Africa, answering to the name Crosby Stills Nash Young.

"So we stash a few twenties, you know, to make up for the money we would have made the next couple of days, and then we'll take off at lunch. What'ya think?"

Stealing from an ex-con. Good idea or bad? Sin or justifiable robbery?

I pictured the hundred dollar bill being snatched out of my hands by an angry God.

"What if he catches us?"

Lee had already thought this through. Man, she was smart.

"We'll do it very carefully, like when he goes off to the bathroom or to get a Coke or something and when Potato-Chip hair is blowing up balloons."

43

As we approached the games, Turtle yelled at us. "Yer late."

We quickly grabbed the money aprons he threw our way. Lee was giving him the middle finger behind her back.

My first patrons were a great-looking, muscular guy about 20 and his cute dimpled, blonde-shagged girlfriend. He was intent on winning her a St. Bernard.

After dropping five bucks and coming closer than anyone yet to knocking the bottles off the table, I tried to talk him out of a bigger loss.

"You know, this is really hard, I mean REALLY hard to win."

"He can do it. He's a pitcher at Bowling Green State," said his girlfriend.

Great, now I'm taking money from a starving college student.

I walked over to Ike who'd already reset the bottles and was picking his way through a funnel cake.

"Couldn't you set them so he can win? Please?"

"Naw. We gave one away last night after ya left. Business looks good so far today. Besides, daddy has to say when."

The handsome pitcher reluctantly retired after forty-five throws and $15 and I wanted to be traded to another team, fast.

As Pitcher and Dimples slunk away, I felt desperate enough to plead their case to Turtle. Unfortunately, he was already walking behind the booths toward the small family trailer.

Opportunity lost or opportunity found? I glanced over at Lee, who, thinking ahead of me, already had her hand in her money apron. Her eyes cut toward the dartboard to make sure Betty was busy replacing balloons, and she was. Lee's hand left the apron with deftness and dived smoothly into her front pocket, depositing the pilfered cash.

Merely considering the seventh commandment made my heart beat faster. Before I could think through the justification of the deed, my sweaty hand closed around several reasonable facsimiles of dead presidents who were slyly exhumed to the nearest pocket of my shorts. While Ike was happily juggling softballs, I was unhappily juggling emotions.

By noon I had pocketed three twenties. Lee and I plotted our escape plan at the lemonade stand.

"We're not leaving until I find that baseball player."

I had told Lee about him and his embarrassment in front of his girlfriend. She laughed, not understanding my intent.

"DC, he's too old for you, and besides, he has a girlfriend."

"I just want to give him back his money."

"That's cool, but we have to stay far away from the Turtle family. They're gonna be pissed off when we don't come back from lunch."

We zigzagged around the midway in search of the baseball player, avoiding the games of little-or-no-chance *and* our recent employer. I imagined the baseball player being so grateful to me for giving his money back he'd pick me up in his strong arms and hug me. Then maybe he'd go knock out a few more of Turtle's teeth, with a softball.

After an hour of sincere but futile effort, Lee suggested, "How about if we go on a few rides. Maybe we'll catch up with them in line somewhere."

It seemed like another good Lee idea.

"Want to ride the Bobsled first?" I asked. Then I noticed her eyes had gotten as big as ferris wheels.

"Don't spaz out, but Turtle sighting! He's over at the lemonade stand."

She started backing away from her spot, then turned and ran. I followed her all the way to the other side of the midway. We gasped for breath in front of the Freak Show. Grotesque, cartoonish paintings depicted Gorilla Woman, Snake Man, and Lobster Boy in their absurd habitats.

"Wanna duck inside here and hide for awhile?" I suggested. With a guilty glance at her, I pulled out some of my ill-gotten Turtle money to buy tickets.

There are many uncertainties in life. This was not one of them. There comes a time, usually in adolescence, that you have to experience some things for yourself.

My first glimpse of Snake Man was hardly startling, as he appeared to have a severe case of psoriasis. I'd seen worse in my doctor's waiting room. Gorilla Woman was hairy, but not scary. She sat calmly in a chair, puffing on a cigarette as she spoke to the audience. She introduced us to her husband who appeared normal, except that he didn't have any teeth—which in the carnie world may have been normal, relatively speaking.

"Nothing a few bottles of Nair couldn't take care of," Lee said as we exited the Gorilla cage/stage, and moved over to the Lobster Boy viewing area. I immediately had a sick feeling in my stomach and my face felt flushed when he showed us his hands and feet. His fingers and toes were deformed and fused together, which made them look like real, horribly malformed appendages—unlike the painted rendition of a boy with bright red, snapping lobster claws for hands. I looked away from the stage, searching for an exit.

What am I doing in here? This poor boy has a birth defect, and I'm paying money to gawk at him like he's a zoo animal or something.

"Hey, let's get out of here. You know Turtle has to have gone back to the games by now. He's a little short-handed," I said.

"Talk about short-handed—man, how does he tie his shoes, or eat, or do anything?" Lee was staring in painful amazement at Lobster Boy.

Lee and I barely talked on the bike ride home. I didn't know what was going on in her head, but if I had any guilt about stealing from Turtle, it was nowhere near the shame I felt gaping at the freak show. Some things in life are just unfair.

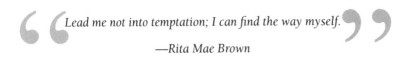

Lead me not into temptation; I can find the way myself.

—Rita Mae Brown

DRIVING LESSONS

IT WAS THE FIRST SUMMER OF MY RECOVERY from the brain-spanking of parochial elementary school. After eight years in the perpetual dunking booth of holy water, I'd seriously considered continuing my ecumenical imprisonment, since most of my friends were going to attend the all-girl Catholic high school. Much like a child raised by wolves, it felt safer to remain in the pack rather than face the wild jungle of puberty alone. The good news was that fate had other plans for me. The bad news was that fate had other plans for me.

The story unfolded after the eighth-grade graduation ceremony. My best friend, Sheila Hart, and I snuck away to the church parking lot while everyone else was herding into the church basement for the reception. Crouched down next to a new, brown-on-brown 1973 Buick, I lit a Parliament, took a drag, coughed, and passed it to Sheila.

"No way. Big Red is *not* leaving St. Peter's to be Principal at St. Cecelia," I exhaled in disbelief.

The war between Big Red and the students at St. Peter's was long, legendary, and often led by me. She especially despised me for my stubborn resilience, and she'd exploded in frustration over my abject refusal to be blindly led out of temptation without my thorough examination of the temptation.

"DC, my mom talked to the vice principal at St. Cecelia yesterday when she turned in my admissions paperwork," Sheila said, coughing as she passed the smoldering butt my way. "So, you know what this means. Big Red will never let you into St. Cecelia's."

SAME NUN, DIFFERENT SCHOOL read the headline in the *Catholic Chronicle* of my mind. Determining the coast was clear, Sheila shoved the pack of matches into her maxi-dress pocket. I placed the crumpled Parliament pack into my A-cup bra, where there was still plenty of room, and we casually walked back toward the church basement.

"Forget Big Red not letting me into St. Cecilia's. I couldn't survive another day with her, let alone another four years."

"Like it wasn't enough to make everybody miserable in grade school, now she's going to ruin high school. But my parents say I have to go to St. Cecilia," Sheila said, opening the church door. "You're lucky your parents won't make you."

"You're right, I should be happy, but Big Red *is* ruining high school for me, because now I have to go to a different school."

THE SUMMER SWAM BY LIKE MARK SPITZ in a lap-pool. This was a year after he made his gold medal splash in the '72 Olympics, but it had not been a gold medal summer for me. Labor Day weekend signaled summer's end, with not much chance to improve it.

Greased up with iodine and baby oil, my sister Lori and I sunned our Twiggy selves on the garage roof. I was contemplating the sins I'd already committed and those I might commit. Number one: It was Sunday and I hadn't gone to church, still a venial sin according to Catholics in those days. Looking outside church doctrine, as I often did for greater spiritual truth or less guilt, I concluded that according to the Ten Commandments, I was sinning only if I didn't keep the day holy. Vowing to keep my thoughts pure, and pleased with finding this loophole, I flipped from my back to my stomach. The big goal of the day was to keep the tanning session even.

Mentally, I reviewed the rest of the commandments. According to Big Red, I was a stubborn, blasphemous, heathen child, but that was only her opinion. Up against the Ten Commandments, I thought I didn't look so bad. I felt pretty smug and relatively holy in my Toledo backyard.

I wish we had a pool like the Butlers, I thought, gazing past our small lawn over fenced yards—hoping for a glimpse of cool water. Coveting my neighbor's goods? Maybe that was just a venial sin, too.

Frying in 80-degree heat and baby oil, coveting didn't seem like that much of a sin. I got by with a fairly clear conscience but got guilt-stricken on commandment number seven. Okay, I stole that last summer, but I stole money from an ex-con who was scamming people out of money, and I did try to find some of those people to give it back. Only I didn't find them.

Does it still count?

I wondered.

When I admitted the sin to Father Boyer in the confessional, he told me to say three Our Fathers and six Hail Marys, and it was my idea to chip in twenty bucks to save a Pagan baby, which we named John Paul George Ringo. (Catholics are, after all, allowed to have four names.) While most of the commandments seemed pretty clear, I felt further clarification was necessary for number six, "honoring thy mother and thy father."

Lori, like me, had opted against Catholic high school. She was more opposed to the all-girl thing than the other Catholic constraints. She liked boys. Not that I didn't. The difference was that I had crushes on boys whom I worshipped from a distance, and Lori had real, not imaginary boyfriends. I was Jan to her Marsha.

Freshman year for Lori was student council, a new boyfriend, choir, and a host of new, popular girlfriends. I tried to tag along when she had friends over, but other than these few hours on the roof, she wanted nothing to do with me.

"DC, I'm going to a party later at Janet's. You need to call Sherry at Trina's and tell her to come home for dinner."

As usual, she was ordering me around.

Sherry, our little sister, had two more years at St. Peter's. Lucky for her it would be minus one mean nun.

"What time are mom and dad coming home from the hydroplane races?"

"I don't know. Around 9, I guess," Lori said, popping the Billy Jack soundtrack cassette into the portable player. "*Go ahead and hate your neighbor, go ahead and cheat a friend; do it in the name of heaven you can justify it in the end,*" lulled the lyrics.

I didn't have any plans for that afternoon or evening—or ever, for that matter, though I was hoping my first week at the public high school would change that.

I'd given up on my Catholic grade-school friends, at least for a while. I had only myself to blame for my lack of plans. No, make that my Mom. Having a cool Mom can backfire. At least it still could in the early '70s.

As a Saturday night ritual, a group of our friends would meet at the local movie theater. It didn't matter what was playing. Unless it was banned by the *Catholic Chronicle*, we were there. Parents took turns with drop-off and pick up. The girls would meet up with a group of boys from St. Peter's, pay no attention to the movie, and often get kicked out. Then we'd hang out in the parking lot, acting cool or coy, and smoking cigarettes. Other than the occasional hook-up or break-up of a new St. Peter's "couple," the routine varied little.

One Saturday late in June, my mom came to pick us up after *The Lion in Winter*. It was a historical period piece meaning: boring. We got kicked out, on purpose, early into the flick. We'd smoked a lot of cigarettes, and when we got into the car my mom told us we reeked of smoke. I told her that it was some other girls in the bathroom and the smell just got on our clothes. She didn't buy it.

"You know girls, smoking doesn't make you look cool, it makes you look hard and rough. I'm embarrassed for you when other people see you. DC, if you really feel you must smoke, I'd rather have you smoke at home than in public."

"You mean I can smoke at home?" I asked, shooting glances of delight at my friends in the car.

"Only if you promise not to do it in public."

Wow. Neat. My friends will really think I'm cool.

Little did I realize that her attempt at reverse psychology would backfire. It would do as much or more sociological harm than the physical damage the Surgeon General warned about.

I'm sure Mom didn't really want or expect me to smoke at home. She probably figured if she eliminated the danger of getting caught, and the bond of secrecy with my friends, this habit that was not yet a habit would lose its thrill. She could never have predicted the awful outcome.

All my friends, together since first grade, went home that very night and told their parents how cool my mom was, letting me smoke at home at the age of 13. This news, especially out of context from the rest of the conversation, resulted in action. The parents passed quick sentence. No one from St. Peter's was allowed to hang around me anymore.

The rest of my summer I spent sunning on the garage roof, baby-sitting and mowing the lawn for extra money. I also improved my unicycling skills and taught myself to juggle. If public high school didn't work out, I was preparing to run away to Clown School.

Ironically, I didn't smoke in front of my parents. Mom was right. Smoking openly at home took the pizzazz out of the deed. Besides, if he had seen me, my dad would have looked at me like I was a stupid kid trying to be grown up, which, of course, I was. I'd still sneak to the basement or the park, with a couple of neighborhood friends who hadn't been banned from me.

I routinely got cigarettes from Ron's, the neighborhood carryout. At these little mom & pop stores in the '60s and '70s—the precursor to chain convenience stores—every family ran a tab. Credit before the card. And it was convenient to charge snacks, Pepsi, and cigarettes for the entire family. I'd been charging Parliaments for my parents to our account since I was 7 and only recently for myself, which I justified as payment for making the trip to the store. Although Kools were cooler, it was easier to acquire the family brand.

Mom was sympathetic to my social exile and attempted to come to the rescue by calling some of my friends' moms to explain, but the damage was done. Their parents had had their doubts about me ever since I introduced the theory of evolution to sixth-grade religion class. I'd always thought that as you got older the world opened up and you got more freedom. I was wrong. Instead, my options seemed to be closing in. My friend world had imploded and I was confined by the smoldering remains.

I had a back-pocket strategy I was putting into place, which was to slowly infiltrate the "Chapel Veil and Bingo Set." I was openly repentant. A few times I volunteered at Sunday school and told my Catholic friends that I had quit smoking altogether. With such open penance, I was certain, it would only be a matter of time before the moms would soften.

"WHAT ARE YOU DOING?" LORI BLASTED AT ME, as I plucked my parents' extra set of car keys from the end table.

"What does it look like I'm doing?"

I thought that answering her question with a question of her intelligence made me appear clever in front of Lynn and

Julie, two neighbor girls who'd stopped by and talked me down off the garage roof. The sun-tanning was turning into a sun-burning, so they didn't need to persuade much.

Lynn and Julie had been in public school for eight years, and would be my classmates at Bowsher, the public high school. What they were recovering from, I didn't know. I knew only that it was time for my own self-imprisonment break, adolescent style. That's when I discovered the keys.

"You better not be thinking about taking the car," Lori scolded.

"What are you going to do about it?" I shot back.

Lori was a year older and had the bossy oldest child syndrome. Due to a family mutation however, I was a good five inches taller than she, my mom, and Sherry, who were all in the five-foot range. When I reached her height in sixth grade, I shoved her out the front door of our house after she pressed the hang-up button on the phone while I was talking to Sheila Hart. She was locked out, in her bra and underwear. She might have been thinking about the incident, since she didn't physically try to get the keys from me.

"C'mon Lynn, Julie, let's go for a little drive."

I practically strutted out of the door in defiance.

"Get back here! You've gotta watch Sherry. You're in big trouble!"

If Lynn hesitated at all, it was only momentarily as she sat by my side in the Stanfa family—no, make that my dad's—new Chevy Malibu.

Royal blue, thank you.

Lynn bit her bottom lip. "DC, do you know how to drive?"

"Sure, my dad lets me drive when we're on vacation."

I didn't mention that I had only been allowed to steer once on a quarter-mile stone driveway to a remote cabin.

Lynn was no innocent herself. She'd been caught a few times, ripping off items from Ron's carryout. She was also in the shadow of a more outgoing, confident sister, Lee, her

53

fraternal twin and my fellow Fair worker. Lynn was the more mischievous of the twins.

Luckily, or unluckily, the car was parked in the street. I doubt I'd have been able to back it out of the driveway. It was an automatic transmission, which was about as much as I understood. Not being a boy or a car buff, my knowledge was limited to simple facts. The car was big and it was blue.

Julie, quiet by nature, remained silent throughout the front-seat adjustment and the starting of the ignition. But once we were in Drive mode she asked, "Where are we going?"

Since I had not yet exceeded five mph, we had plenty of time to decide.

"Let's go to McDonalds," Lynn suggested.

"Cool," I answered, trying to send calming signals to my heart, which was beating faster than Mohammad Ali's fists.

I was having difficulty with the foot pedals, first confusing the accelerator with the brake and vice-versa. Finally, I kept one foot on each for a jerk-and-stop rhythm. Apparently the steering was the easy part, or so I thought for the moment.

"How 'bout I just take 'er around the block first, to get a feel for it?"

Hands shaking a bit, I tightened my grip on the wheel. As I came to a rolling stop at the end of Indianola and veered left onto Stengle, I spied Mr. Grabowski mowing his postage stamp of a front lawn. The lawns were tiny, like the houses that went with them: 800-square-foot crackerboxes with one teeny bathroom, assuring as much family closeness as one could stand.

As often accompanies the exhilaration of virgin experiences, time and space became distorted. The street narrowed, eerily. The lawn jockey came to life and swung his lantern in warning. The bowling trophies in the Grabowskis' front window loomed like skyscrapers. I shrunk low in my seat.

"Oh my God, what if he saw me?"

Somewhere in the momentary silence I thought I heard a unanimous, telepathic expletive.

"Oh shit!"

We never thought about neighbors being out on a sunny, holiday-weekend afternoon!

I navigated the next turn, left onto Roxberry, at what felt like full-throttle—about fifteen mph. Halfway around the block, I was beginning to think about possible consequences of my impulsive act. The Jamiesons were cleaning out their garage and Jimmy, age 5, was riding a Big Wheel in the driveway. Mrs. Jamieson paused from hosing down the garage floor to look our direction.

"She sees us!" screamed Julie.

"Duck!" yelled Lynn.

"Oh my God, she knows I'm not old enough to drive. She'll tell my parents!" my 13-year-old genius brain deduced out loud.

"Step on it!" Lynn shouted.

Unsure of my next move, I stayed steady, but low. So low I couldn't see out of the front windshield, which would explain how I missed seeing, and consequently hit, the parked car on my right, just as I rounded the corner from Roxberry to Copeland. It was more of a sideswipe than a direct hit, but I knew the battleship was sunk when Mrs. Dubinski ran through her front bushes in response to the metal-on-metal noise.

A feeling of unreality came over me. I detached myself from my body and wished I could distort time and space further, such as going back in time and leaving the car keys on the endtable. In my mental departure I easily relinquished control of the wheel to Lynn, who swerved us around the last corner from Copeland and back onto Indianola.

The getaway car sped away at thirteen mph and I felt another small jolt and heard another sickening crunch. I slammed on the brakes after seeing that we'd French-kissed the '69 Impala parked in front of the Butlers' house. I had regained control of the wheel but Lynn put her foot next to mine, which was on the brake, and forced it onto the accelerator.

"Let's get outta here!"

She echoed my thoughts exactly.

We were in the home stretch. I could see the safety of the little Stanfa bungalow about 250 feet away. Distracted by angry shouts from outside the car, I turned my head to see half a dozen eyewitnesses chasing us on foot.

"Get back here! Ya hit my car!" boomed Jack Butler.

In that brief distracting moment, the Malibu goosed the rear end of the Foltz's Ford pick-up.

Doesn't anybody park in their driveway anymore?

It was the first logical thought I'd had all day.

Once parked in almost the same spot from which we'd departed, Lynn and Julie vanished faster than Endora when Darren got home. I was alone: The little witch of the neighborhood, only I couldn't twitch my nose out of trouble. The villagers were gathering in the front yard, intent on a hanging—at least a verbal one. Lori met us on the front porch.

"Where are your parents?" demanded Mrs. Butler of Lori-in-charge.

I ran inside ahead of the pack and, in typical adolescent style, locked myself in my room.

The only part of my body that wasn't shaking was my eyeballs. They were tiny rafts, lost in churning, hydraulic, class-six whitewater rapid tears. Collapsing into a fetal position on my bed, I cried and prayed.

Please God, let me go to sleep and wake up to a different reality, where I'm cute and popular and David Cassidy is my boyfriend and where my parents don't bludgeon me with my lava lamp.

And then I was aware that I could not fall asleep, especially with the sound of the siren whining louder and louder. I knew without lifting my head from its trembling, coiled, knee-rest that the siren had stopped in front of our house.

"DC, you'd better get out here! The cops are here and I'm not talking to them! Come out or I'll get a bobby pin and pick the lock!"

I knew she wasn't bluffing. I also knew the closest I would get to David Cassidy would be the poster on my wall—which hopefully they'd let me take with me to prison.

COP #1 WAS FLIPPING THROUGH PAPERS on a clipboard. I tried to hide behind a wad of Kleenex I'd cupped around my dripping eyes and nose. I cowered, slowly shuffling my feet on the pea-green shag carpet toward our black vinyl couch.

"I called my mom and dad. They're on their way," Lori told him.

The cocky kids called them "pigs" in those days, holding most uniformed authorities responsible for Vietnam, the Kent State killings, and the infringement on their right to smoke pot in public. I was not feeling cocky at the moment and decided instead to call him "Sir."

I recognized this cop, though I couldn't recall his name—and barely remembered mine at the moment. He occasionally patrolled McDonald's to control teenage loitering as we lingered for hours watching cars cruise through orders of shakes and fries. As for me, I was shaking and I was definitely fried.

And so the interrogation began, although I wasn't listening. I was visualizing, instead, what life at reform school might be like. There was a kid in our neighborhood who'd tried to burn down his grandma's house. He was sent to a reform school in Indiana. I wondered if reform schools had jail cells or dorm rooms with bars on the windows. Out our front window, my view was unobstructed by bars. Jack Butler and Caroline Foltz were clearly telling Cop #2 the whole crash-bang story.

The last time cops had been to Indianola was the previous winter. Charlie Fogerty, an 18-year-old "burn-out" was caught peeking in our window. My dad tackled him in the snow and held him until the law arrived.

"Are you all right?" asked Cop #1. "Are you hurt?"

"Not yet. But she will be when our parents get home," Lori answered for me, reading my own thoughts.

"Was anyone in the car with you?"

"Yeah. Two girls," I heard myself saying.

"Where are they? Are they okay?"

"Judging from how fast they ran, I'd say they're all right."

He studied me. "Are you under the influence?"

Putting a wad of Kleenex on the end table, I looked up to meet his eyes, for the first time.

"What?"

"Have you been drinking alcohol or smoking marijuana?"

"No, she's just very stupid and obviously a terrible driver." Was Lori defending me or taking a shot at me? Probably both, which is what siblings do.

Then my parents burst through the front door. Cop #2 followed behind. The neighbors must have retreated home to inspect the damages.

"Gloria, Denny," Cop #1 addressed them in a serious tone of voice. "Your daughter Denise here apparently took your vehicle for a drive and hit a few of your neighbors' parked vehicles."

"Yes, Ken, when Lori called, she told us."

My dad's voice was calm, but he was looking at me as if I were a stranger.

My mom wasn't quite as calm as my dad.

"My God, what were you thinking? You couldn't have been thinking. You could have killed someone!"

I had a flash of little Jimmy Jamieson on his Big Wheel and faced the horrible awareness that my joyless ride could have been very tragic indeed. I began shaking and crying again. Whatever punishments I might suffer, I consoled myself, I deserved. At least it was only property damage. That I could live with.

The growing mound of Kleenex wasn't large enough to cover up my vinyl-couch-island refuge. As Cop #1 and Cop #2 reviewed the accident report with my parents, I avoided eye contact with everyone except the family dog. Sam, who must have felt my anguish, lay loyally at my feet.

When Cop #1 started talking with my parents about court proceedings, I listened intently.

"You'll have to accompany Denise for her appearance in juvenile court, not traffic court, since she's an under-aged, unlicensed driver. In addition to a fine and court costs, Denise will probably remain on probation until she is 16. It will then be up to a judge to decide if she can obtain a license at that time. She may have to wait until she is 18. It depends on how clean she can keep her record for the next three years."

Wow, at least he didn't mention juvenile hall or reform school, and at the moment, I have no desire to get behind the wheel of a car anytime soon.

I was relieved.

The cops and parents shook hands and my mom, ever polite, even thanked the officers. "See you at the reunion-planning committee meeting, Ken," she said as she walked them to the door.

I was planning on not having a reunion with the cops.

Ever.

"You stupid, little girl," said my dad, his devastating disappointment revealed in this one true statement. He looked at me as he spoke, again, as if he didn't recognize me.

If he would have just been angry or hit me or threatened me, it wouldn't have hurt so much.

My body sank deeper into the corner of the couch and my heart fell into the basement. The fact that what I had done would affect my parents was just beginning to dawn on me. The real epiphany was how terrible I felt about disappointing them. I no longer needed clarification on the "honor thy father and mother" thing.

Mom had come to some quick decisions. "Don't worry about being grounded," she said. "You won't have time to do anything other than chores and baby-sitting. You won't be

59

going anywhere until you pay for everything, all the damages to all the cars and fines and court costs. Everything!"

I nodded in agreement. Lori was already on the phone with her friend Janet, filling her in on the story. I felt like a bowling ball had been dropped on my stomach. I knew that the story would be all over Bowsher High by the first day of school. And what would everyone think? They'd think, like my dad, that I was a stupid, little girl trying to be a grown-up, which of course, I was.

And, I knew, that for the rest of my life, when I'd hear about someone rumored to have "been around the block," I'd be able to say, "You have no idea."

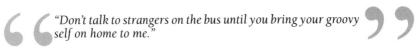

"Don't talk to strangers on the bus until you bring your groovy self on home to me."

—Nancy Sinatra singing to Elvis in the 1968 movie, *Speedway*

S T R A N G E R S
O N   T H E   B U S

My FRESHMAN YEAR AT E.L. BOWSHER High School was devoted to three things. First, I was still recovering from the brain spanking of Catholic school, which brought me to the second thing: Exploring the new freedom of public high school meant fewer boundaries and more choices. This brought me to the third thing: working my butt off to repay $750 in damages to my dad's and our neighbors' vehicles, which ironically limited my new freedom.

I babysat so much I was sure I'd never want children of my own. I also mowed grass and shoveled snow. Luckily, I was breezing through classes without ever taking a book home. Junior high in Catholic school had covered most of my freshman curriculum.

While I was quickly paying off my debt, I was missing a critical area of concentration for all teenagers' formative years: finding out where I fit in. The little free time I had was spent with my sisters hanging out and watching TV shows like "Don Kirshner's Rock Concert" and "The Sonny and Cher Show." Older sister Lori made it clear that I was not to hang around her or her popular friends while at school. My younger sister Sherry had two more years until high school.

I ate lunch in the cafeteria with my one friend from St. Peter's who opted, along with me, to escape Catholic high school. Her parents couldn't afford the tuition. But Connie had a steady boyfriend, a carry over from St. Peter's. He was in the all-boys Jesuit high school, and outside of school, she hung out with him.

Although my little drive around the block had cost me, in the short run, I tried to look at it from a long-term learning perspective. I had merely waded knee deep into the stupidity pool and gained invaluable insight into what might be lurking in the deep end. It was full of scary creatures named Consequences. Consequences are not predators. You usually fall victim to them by your own actions.

Submerged in the idea of making better choices, I consequently began looking for new friends my sophomore year, when my accident debt was finally paid.

I conducted auditions by sitting at different lunch tables in the school cafeteria. Apparently all the good friend parts had been filled. Individual drama groups emerged as a result of freshman year typecasting calls. They were called cliques. There were the Jocks, the Socials, the Geeks, and the Burnouts. I was a clique of one, a sophomore in search of an understudy role for the high school play that opened freshman year.

I WAS LISTENING INTENTLY TO TARA HENDERSON, as I choked down a chili-dog. She was babbling on about cheerleading.

"Jennifer Jewel really heffed up over the summer. I mean, she must have put on about ten pounds. She'll never make it to Varsity. She might even get kicked off the J.V. squad if she can't do the jumps."

So, even the cheerleaders don't always stick together, I thought. Tara acted like Jennifer's best friend when they were together.

"Anyway, we're gonna start on the homecoming float next Saturday. We're building it in Diane Gerkin's garage," said Betsy Lidel, a cheerleader who was also sophomore class VP.

I had no plans for Saturday—or any other day I could think of.

"What time?" I thought, out loud.

Several of their glances were curious, several disapproving. Two girls chose to continue to ignore me altogether.

"And you are…?" Tara grilled.

"Uh, DC Stanfa."

"Are you Lori's sister?" asked Betsy. Betsy's boyfriend, a gorgeous blue-eyed, black-haired varsity wide receiver sat next to her. He stroked her back as she spoke.

"Yeah," I answered.

I'd figured they already knew, which was the only reason they had allowed me to sit at the table in the first place.

"Haven't I seen you riding a unicycle to school?" Tara rolled her eyes a bit at the other girls.

"Uh, yeah, I ride it if the weather is decent." I didn't know why I should be embarrassed, but I was.

"That's kind of weird," Tara concluded for the group as they all went back to ignoring me.

And you wear a stupid little uniform, and, your big goal is to do the same thing in college, where guys stick their hands up your skirt and lift you into the air in front of a couple of thousand people. Who's weird?

SATURDAY NIGHT ARRIVED, AND I'D TURNED DOWN two baby-sitting jobs. I did not, however, go to the homecoming float party. Lori was at the junior class float gig and Sherry was spending

the night at a friend's. I was lying on my bed reading *Jonathan Livingston Seagull* and my mood ring was black. Mom and Dad were watching "All In the Family" in the living room. There was a tentative tap on the bedroom door, which was slightly ajar. My dad pushed it open farther and poked his head in.

I put the book down and turned on my side, facing the door, propping myself up on my left elbow. Although his eyes were full of concern, he wasn't going to ask me why I didn't have plans or suggest I call a friend to come over. We'd been through that before.

"*Cool Hand Luke* is coming on at nine," he said. "Why don't you watch it with us? Your mom is going to pop some corn and I'll hard-boil some eggs."

He was making a joke, a reference to his favorite Paul Newman movie and my own favorite scene, where he eats fifty eggs for the entertainment of his fellow prisoners.

My dad looked a little like Paul Newman, similar nose and cheekbone structure. But he had dark brown eyes and hair, like me. He didn't care that he was handsome and had no desire to be famous outside our family. Dad was spending more time at home the past couple years, after getting a D.U.I. and having my mom threatening divorce. The first dozen years of the marriage, he stayed out with the boys after work golfing or bowling or just drinking. Having just recently survived his own growing-up pains, he was empathetic to mine.

I knew he saw through my smile. He took my right hand.

"Things a little rough right now?" he asked.

It was a rhetorical question.

"You know, when it's too rough for everybody else, it's just about right for us Stanfas."

Never having been in the military, Dad did a pretty good Patton impression.

"Yeah, we're tough," I mocked, unconvincingly.

"You just don't know how tough you are," he said. He wasn't kidding anymore.

"I'll show you. Here, squeeze my hand. Squeeze it as hard as you possibly can."

I returned his grip with all my might, channeling my depression into the palm of his hand, hoping he might free me from it.

"Is that all you've got? Are you squeezing as hard as you possibly can?"

My face grimaced in concentration as I nodded.

"Okay, now. I want you to squeeze just a little bit harder. C'mon. You can do it."

I felt an added surge of energy as my grip tightened around his hand.

Where did that come from?

"When you're sure you're trying as hard as you can, don't give up. Try even harder," Dad said.

This bit of wisdom was historically imparted to boys. Dad's mom, my Grandma Stanfa, raised three boys by herself and worked in a factory to support them. So Dad knew women had to be tough sometimes too.

IN THE WEEKS AND MONTHS FOLLOWING MY get-a-better-grip lesson from Dad, I began a psychological study of the leftovers and misfits who didn't belong in the clique groupings. There were several in each of my classes. I made a point to get to know them each a little better. There were a few painfully shy types that I couldn't draw out. There were also a couple that were so confident in themselves that they were ambivalent to or above the whole high school fitting-in process. I admired them greatly.

I finally found common ground with three girls: Janice Meyer, Robin Lewis, and Molly Mingey. They, like me, had siblings a year older who were more popular than they were.

Janice's sister dated a football player. Robin's brother was in the social clique of the class of '76. All of us girls, except Molly, were middle children.

Along with similarities, there were obvious differences. Janice Meyer had hills, make that mountains, the size of the Rockies. My chest was as flat as northwest Ohio. There was a rumor that boys climbed in her bedroom window and reached new heights. She was an unlikely friend, since my sexuality had not yet surfaced. My hormones seemed to be dormant, lurking in some glandular underground cavern.

Robin and Molly were friends since freshman year. Robin was a classic blonde beauty, but broke stereotype with her intelligence. Molly was a flower child, from a wealthy family, youngest of four. Her parents were as old as my grandparents, and they traveled extensively. Molly's trademark was her huge mane of auburn hair. She looked like she belonged on a Woodstock poster.

By early spring, the four of us were hanging out at McDonald's together and attending house parties we'd heard about, even though we weren't actually invited. Here, cliques actually intermingled. Jocks and Socials and Burnouts, oh my! The three middle children and a baby clique provided me with a social foundation. Finally, I had plans.

Sometimes, when Molly's parents were out of town, the four of us would spend the entire weekend at her house. She had the best record collection of anyone I knew, and her older brother and sisters had frequent parties. We blended in by drinking and smoking like everyone else. We even got in on a couple of spin-the-bottle games.

I SOON FOUND ANOTHER COMMON DENOMINATOR between my new friends: We all bored easily. By early summer, we even tired of hanging out at Molly's pool. Janice had the solution. "I'm going to visit my aunt next month. She lives on a ranch in Colorado. Why don't you guys see if you can go too?"

Wow, I'd been to Michigan and even Canada on family vacations. But Colorado!

Luckily, I had developed some persuasive ability. The truth was that my parents were so relieved that I'd stopped moping around and had finally acquired some friends, it only took a phone call from my mom to Janice's for them to approve the proposed venture. Molly and Robin were given green lights as well.

The parents all agreed a plane ride might be safer. While Molly and Robin's parents could afford to ante up for the pricey tickets, $275, Janice and I could barely swing the $85 round-trip bus fare to Steamboat Springs. Being an-all-for-one group, Molly and Robin decided the bus ride would be more of an adventure. They wouldn't be wrong.

"We're stopping already," Molly observed.

The Greyhound had barely approached the speed limit before we stopped and loaded more passengers in Bowling Green, twenty miles south of Toledo. The scenery through Indiana and Illinois was disappointing. Cornfields and barns led to more cornfields and barns as darkness approached. We were pumped up and chatty for the first six hours, then mellowed out into morning. We were awake all night because of stops, starts, and transfers. We changed buses three times by Des Moines, and were eventually delayed enough to miss an important connection in Omaha. The next bus going west departed in four hours.

"This is freaking me out," Robin announced, as we chewed on sandwiches we'd gotten from a bus station vending machine.

I thought she was referring to the sandwich, until she elbow-pointed toward a man seated cross-legged on a nearby bench. He appeared, from his facial features, to be a white man, but he was so dirty it was difficult to tell for sure. He was shoeless, and his dreadlocked head was bent over a foot. He was picking something out of his toes.

"Gag," gagged Janice.

"Which reminds me, we have to stop sitting in the back of the bus. The smell of the bathroom is making me sick," said Molly.

"Which reminds me," I said, "Thank God they kicked that drunk guy off in Dubuque. I thought he was going to puke on us all."

"Which drunk guy, DC? There were so many," Robin made a sad, but funny point.

"I need a bath," Molly said.

"It's not exactly the glamorous, cross-country trip Mumsy had planned for us," I added in my best Mrs.-Drysdale-from-"The-Beverly-Hillbillies" voice.

Janice, who had been chain-smoking since we left Toledo, blew a big smoke ring.

GREYHOUND'S MOTTO WAS "LEAVE THE DRIVING TO US." And we did, for what seemed like an eternity. There was the occasional charming town and the not-so-charming bus depot we passed through. Night was falling for the second time on the trip. We had been on the road twenty-nine hours by the time we reached Cheyenne.

After Omaha, we'd tried to spread out instead of sitting together, attempting to get some sleep. We were also taking advantage of the luxury of the newest bus we'd been on. Molly was across the aisle from me. We were in the back, in the smoking section. She was draped over two seats and dozing from exhaustion and Dramamine. Nobody had slept more than a total of three hours. We didn't have to get off to change buses in Cheyenne, but a couple dozen passengers boarded our luxury bus.

A small-faced woman sat down next to me. I nodded and smiled in the dim light. I should have kept dozing. Sometimes courtesy doesn't pay off. She instantly began to chatter.

"I'm going to Denver to visit my ex-husband and pick up a car," she informed me. "I haven't been able to drive for years because I couldn't fit behind the steering wheel."

I opened my eyes wider for a better look. She wasn't more that five and a half feet tall, my own height, with a medium build. She seemed pleased by my blank stare.

"I used to weigh 425 pounds. The doctors said my obesity would kill me before I turn 50. So I had my jaw wired shut. I lost 280 pounds in the last eighteen months!"

She beamed like a little girl describing a new puppy. But she'd lost the equivalent of several dogs, let's say, greyhounds. Apparently Chatterbox had a lot to say after they'd unwired her jaw, and I was lucky enough to be in the audience. As she and the bus rambled on into the night, I'd occasionally nod, and then nod off.

Where's a doctor when you need one to do a quick re-wire?

"I can't wait to see the look on my ex's face. He's not gonna recognize me."

After one hour or ten, I looked across the aisle at Molly, hoping for a rescue. A man with a large afro had wedged his way into the window seat next to her sometime after the Cheyenne stop. Molly's head was bobbing side to side as the bus rounded curves in the winding road. Amidst the hairiness of her own mane and the huge afro next to her, I noticed a hand, which wasn't Molly's, on her knee. I reached across Chatterbox and smacked Molly's shoulder, since the offending hand was out of my reach. Afro man immediately recoiled as I shot him a hard glance. He repositioned himself toward the window, pretending to look intently for something in the darkness.

"Are we there yet?" Molly asked sleepily.

"I wish," I said. "C'mon, we're going to the bathroom. Grab your purse."

I excused myself from Chatterbox and pulled Molly up from her seat. Instead of walking toward the back of the bus, I pushed Molly forward into an open seat behind the driver. "Hey, buddy, we need a bodyguard back there."

And some duct tape, I thought.

WE REACHED DENVER IN THE MIDDLE of the night, and our last bus transfer proved to be the most memorable yet. The bus transporting us to Steamboat Springs was on another bus line, a Greyhound partner. The depot for that bus line was located in a nearby hotel. We grabbed our heavy, standard-issue, parent-borrowed luggage and limped out into the night. Samsonites did not have wheels in the 1970s. As we walked and moaned in the direction pointed out by a Greyhound employee, we caught our first glimpse of downtown Denver, which was an old man urinating on the side of a building.

A small crowd of flamboyantly overdressed women in stiletto heels paced and smoked as we passed the corner of the first city block.

"You bitches better get outta here. This ain't no neighborhood for runaways," one of the ladies warned us. "Besides, the mens that come around here don't like real girls."

Curiosity turned me around for a second look. One of the not-so-real girls had pulled up her skirt and was waving something at us from the area of her crotch. I was certain it wasn't a gun. It was a different sort of concealed weapon, exposing a genuine gender.

"Run!" I screamed, and we did.

As we approached the corner of the second block, two police officers casually walked toward us.

"Where are we goin' at two in the mornin'?" The clever cop attempted a bad rhyme, and succeeded.

"Trailways Station," Robin answered nervously

We were all out of breath, but lit cigarettes anyway. We finally had bodyguards.

"Girls, there's no way you should be out here, any time of day or night. Don't you know this is the Hill District?" he said, deciding to play smart cop/dumb cop.

"We're from Toledo," Janice explained.

"Is that in Canada?" asked the dumb one.

"No, Ohio," I said. "You're thinking of Toronto."

I tried not to sound condescending.

The cops told us it was another five blocks to our destination. They hailed us a cab. As the cabbie loaded our luggage into the trunk, Molly whispered in my ear, "His fly's unzipped."

"It could be by accident," I said.

Unconvinced, she whispered, "We'll all squeeze into the back."

IT WAS EARLY MORNING, AND IN THE LAST COUPLE of hours since daybreak, the scenery was breathtaking. The mountains were palaces in the sky, and we were part of the kingdom. The bus was our caterpillar and we were impatient teenagers in the cocoon of life, waiting to emerge into the beauty and power around us.

Thirty-nine hours after our departure, and six hours behind schedule, we arrived in Steamboat Springs. Needless to say, it was no surprise that no one was there to pick us up, unless you counted two strangers in cowboy hats and boots who looked like they might want to tie us up. Janice called her aunt from a pay phone.

"My Uncle Doug is coming to get us. But he won't be here for an hour."

We walked out into Steamboat's downtown streets while we

71

waited. It looked both rustic and updated with historic, renovated landmarks. It looked like the old west had met a new paintbrush.

Janice's uncle arrived in an old Ford pick-up.

He hugged Janice, then gaped open-mouthed at the rest of us and our luggage.

"You all going to Summer Breeze?"

There was an emphasis on "all" and the look of surprise on his face turned to worry when we nodded in unison.

Molly could barely keep the cigarette lit as she passed it to me in the back of the open truck-bed. Robin hunkered down behind one of the suitcases to block the wind, while Janice rode up front with her uncle and the dog.

WE STOPPED IN FRONT OF A HUGE A-FRAME with a brick foundation. Several different colors adorned the front entrance, as though the painters had used leftovers from an assortment of cans. Janice said that it was a trappers' lodge when her aunt and uncle bought it, but now they rented rooms year-round. Trappers were not their only guests, according to Janice, there were also artists and musicians, too. The Bohemian lure of artists and musicians was more appealing to all of us than smelly men who trapped animals.

We talked about meeting guys.

"Maybe Cat Stevens will be staying there," Molly joked.

The lodge was named after her aunt and uncle's daughter, "Summer Breeze." Very Seals and Crofts.

Janice's Aunt Donna was hanging clothes on a line by the side of the house. There was even a little girl riding a rusty tricycle on the rocky lawn.

Summer Breeze rode the tricycle toward us, and Aunt Donna practically bolted over, but there was no hug.

"What the hell is going on?" Aunt Donna complained loudly,

throwing her hands on her hips. "You said you might bring a friend. You did not say three. What were you thinking?"

Janice could not hide her embarrassment. The rest of us exchanged looks of bewilderment.

"Well, I'm sorry to disappoint you, but you can't stay," said Aunt Donna.

Janice looked at Uncle Doug, who shrugged his shoulders.

Either these people have a wicked sense of humor, or we're going to take turns killing Janice.

JANICE AND HER AUNT REMAINED OUTSIDE to discuss the situation, while the rest of us went into the lodge. Uncle Doug poured sun tea and Summer pretended to sweep the kitchen floor with a feather duster. As Doug poured tea into glasses, the sound of cracking ice was deafening.

"We can stay," Janice announced as she bounced into the kitchen.

Aunt Donna followed her in. She was not as cheerful.

"O.K. girls, you have to understand. Money has been pretty tight since we bought this place. We rent space here. That is how we make our living. So if you stay here, that's space we can't rent. Plus there are food expenses to consider. What I'm saying is, you can stay, but you'll have to earn your keep."

The looks on our faces were like patients in a dentist's lobby. Molly, who didn't know the meaning of the word *work*, looked like she'd been drilled without Novocaine.

"Doug and I will put together a list of work that needs to be done. You'll be expected to work at least three hours a day," said the wicked hippie step-aunt.

Our room was the attic, which was also the Pelt Storage Room. A queen-sized mattress sat on the floor and a mirror was propped up against a wall. Otherwise, the room was just a fury of furry pelts on racks, nailed to walls, and hanging from rafters. There was a slightly pungent odor, but at least it didn't gag us like the bus bathrooms. In addition to the inside stairway, a wooden stairway led up to the garage-roof level, providing outdoor access. We decided the roof would also serve as our tanning and observation deck.

The temperature had dropped from 80 degrees to 56 degrees by dusk. Wrapped in blankets and fur pelts, we talked and smoked on the deck. Everyone was too exhausted to argue or point blame at Janice.

"Check out the stars!" Molly gasped, and we all tilted our heads for the spectacular show.

We were in the heart of the Rocky Mountains with two weeks of freedom and untold possibilities ahead of us. What was there to argue about?

THE ATTIC RETAINED THE HEAT OF THE DAY, keeping us warm, and the four of us slept sideways across the mattress, our feet hanging off the end. By mid-morning, we were baked awake as the sun sizzled through the large non-shaded windows.

Motivated by my bladder, I rolled off the mattress and headed to the bathroom where, in privacy I washed my face with the face cleaner prescribed by my dermatologist. After patting dry just like the doctor ordered, I inspected my skin for any sign of progress.

The face that launched a thousand zits.

Such clever words to hide my pain, and I could not even laugh at them. I hated what I saw in the mirror. Why me? Why was I the only one! How could God be so cruel? It wasn't fair that none of the other girls had acne. Janice complained now and then of an occasional (and to me imaginary) zit. Molly and Robin had perfect complexions, and boyfriends AND ex-boyfriends (they'd recently dumped) back in Toledo.

Coincidence? I think not.

I turned from the mirror and hastily rubbed on some medicated cover-up. It might be better if I just didn't look. Keeping my head turned from the mirror, I brushed my hair and headed out to join the others.

God, what I would give for a boyfriend. Better yet, a boyfriend I could dump someday. THAT would pump up my self-esteem.

Adorned in bathing suits, we moseyed down to the kitchen. A Tupperware bowl filled with some kind of mixed grains and nuts sat on the counter, along with a note.

'Help yourself to homemade cereal. Fruit and juice are in the fridge. We'll be back by noon.'

"Yuk," Molly said at the sight of the cereal. "How about a ham and cheese omelet?"

An hour later we were sunbathing on the deck.

"My Aunt Donna is crazy," Janice said. "Like, I'm sure she didn't know I was bringing you guys."

"Oh my God, look over there! In the creek!" Molly practically screamed.

Three longhaired figures were splashing around, knee-deep in the water, and even at that distance, about a football field and a half, we could see they were naked. A voice called from somewhere near the garage. It was Uncle Doug.

Is it noon already?

"You girls ready to get to work?"

We threw T-shirts and cut-offs on over our bathing suits, and I put on my simulated-leather-grain hiking boots. Everyone grabbed at least one bandanna. Bandannas were big that year. We wore them around our heads, around our necks, and draped them from back pockets. We scrambled down the garage stairs and were met by Uncle Doug and four shovels.

"Girls, we're going to get you some exercise, mountain style. We're digging a drainage ditch." Before his first two sentences registered, he spoke two more. "Janice, your aunt would like you to give Summer art lessons, so you go on back to the kitchen."

Janice's facial expression mixed great relief and a minor apology as she turned to walk away.

It was Robin's turn to crack the ice.

"Where do you want us to bury the bodies, boss?"

She smirked and grabbed a shovel from Uncle Doug.

MY SHOULDERS WERE ON FIRE AND MY BACK was threatening to go on strike as Uncle Doug passed a plastic water jug to Molly. He'd worked side-by-side with us, supervising the depth and direction of the ditch and helping us improve our digging techniques.

"Break time," he announced, walking toward the lodge.

After we guzzled, we splashed water from the jug on our faces, and in the shade of a small stand of trees, we collapsed on our butts.

"At least we're getting a tan," I said with a positive lilt in my voice.

"Yeah, poor, poor Janice doesn't know what she's missing," Robin added.

I loved her sarcasm; it reminded me of my family.

Molly's humor was more self-deprecating. She knew she was spoiled and pampered and was admittedly lazy because of it. Molly made us laugh at her dramatic suffering of anything that took effort, which was why it was amazing that she appeared to be doing all right, despite the labors of work camp. I'd heard her complain more about menstrual cramps than our hard-labor sentence.

But smoking her cigarette in the shade, Kool-Hand Molly was secretly plotting an escape. When Uncle Doug called quitting time, we limped and moaned our way back. Instead of going into the lodge with Uncle Doug, we detoured to the creek. It was frigid on my shoeless feet, but I splashed the iciness over my body.

THE SECOND EVENING, OUR DECK PARTY was a little livelier than the night before, as Janice had stolen whiskey from a stash in the kitchen. We drank it straight up from a Tupperware container. We also found a pair of binoculars in the bathroom.

"These two guys, college students staying here, asked if we wanted to go into the sauna with them tonight. That's the little building near the creek," Janice confided as she handed the binoculars to Robin.

"So you've been picking up boys while we're breaking our backs in the field," I said in a hick Strother Martin voice.

"It's too dark to see faces, but there is definite smoke and nakedness coming out of the sauna," Robin reported smugly.

Molly and I fought over the field glasses. I won. There was a small chimney spewing smoke from the side of the building and several figures moving in the dark toward the creek. We strained, listening for voices.

"Let's go get naked and sweat with a bunch of strangers," Molly said, making progress in the sarcasm portion of the trip.

We were ready for Operation China-Dig and had a strategic field position on day two. We figured it was best to get it all done before the sun rose too high. Molly went through the motions, but there was little earth moved by her shovel. Robin and I also slacked off, partly due to muscle soreness, partly due to mental soreness. We were also aware that the clock, not ditch-depth, was our measurement. Someday, we'd make great government workers.

By noon, we'd eaten lunch and showered. Aunt Donna had told us we were restricted to two showers per week. We planned to break this rule whenever they were out of the house, however. We hit the road in our jean cutoffs and embroidered T-shirts. Janice stuck a thumb out, and the second passing vehicle, a Jeep, picked us up.

The driver was a sandy-blond guy, cute in a dimpled kind of way. His passenger looked Native-American and had darker, longer hair that flew back as the topless Jeep bolted toward town. These boys appeared to be 18 or 19 and were coincidentally shirtless. It was a tight squeeze. Molly sat on Robin's lap, déjà vu the Denver cab ride. The guy in the passenger seat tried to persuade Janice to sit on his lap.

Free from work camp, we couldn't contain ourselves, and we jammed to the Rolling Stones on air instruments. We were animated and wired for sound. We were Disney on a mountain parade, set on a mission to buy Coors beer and get goofy.

OUR SHIRTLESS COMPANIONS INTRODUCED themselves. Kirk was the blond, and Bryce was the American Indian who led us through the trackless wastes of the IGA. We flash-backed our bus journey story to them while we threw snackable dry goods into a shopping cart. They were amazed and amused. The Denver transvestite episode had us all laughing tears.

"What in the hell did you think would happen on such a long bus trip?" Bryce asked.

"We had no idea we'd have so many stops and transfers," Robin said.

"Yeah, we though it would be, like, one continuous ride with the same perverts we boarded with in Toledo," I said, hoping they appreciated my sarcasm and respected our innocence.

Our Jeep transporters insisted on taking our groceries and us back to the ranch. They said they didn't have much else to do, explaining they were ski instructors, bored by the off-season. They also wanted to take us out later.

As we unloaded at Summer Breeze Lodge, Kirk said, "We'll pick you up at eight."

It was a welcome rescue from the garage roof/deck party.

Our snacks were safe in the attic and four six-packs of Coors were hidden in a rock dam in the creek to keep them cold. The boys appeared on schedule, and Aunt Donna and Uncle Doug de-briefed them on a reasonable curfew for us: midnight.

The dirt mountain road was barely wide enough for the Jeep as we navigated the climb. I appreciated the darkness, knowing if I could see the steep drop over the edge, I would have a heart attack.

"When you said you wanted to take us out, you really meant OUT, didn't you?" Molly was waxing sarcastic again.

"Well, we knew you were too young to get into bars. So prepare for a real Colorado experience."

As Kirk spoke, we hit a rut in the road and the Jeep jolted. The headlights went out.

"Oh, shit!" I screamed.

We were probably inches from careening off the mountainside.

"A little electrical interruption. It happens sometimes when we hit mountain pot-holes," Bryce said calmly.

The headlights went on again after Kirk jiggled the dashboard buttons.

We repeated the drill several times, hitting bumps, headlights going out briefly, and flickering on again. Stopping at a ledge, Kirk announced he had to get out to pee. The girls and I jumped out of the vehicle with the same thoughts, since we'd been drinking beer from their cooler the whole ride. The stars and the moonlight helped us navigate to separate bushes.

Squatting next to Janice, I said, "There's a new mountain river flowing," proud of my pun.

I heard Robin and Molly talking amidst the flowing rivers.

"Do you think we can trust these guys?" Molly asked.

"Well, it's either that or walk back," Robin answered.

As we emerged from nature's bathroom, Kirk was waiting.

"C'mon, let's sit down over here," he said as he reached into his over-sized army jacket and produced a six-pack.

Bryce was back at the Jeep checking on the electrical problem, so the rest of us spread out on the ground to take in the star show, which was even more spectacular at this elevation than we could ever have imagined. A beer buzz combined with a Rocky Mountain high elicited "Oh my Gods!" from all of us as we counted shooting stars.

A loud, startling rustle in the bushes tested our scream reflexes, which were working fine. The only non-screamer, Kirk, calmly assured us.

"It's probably just a mountain lion."

We found no comfort in that.

"Let's get out of here!" Janice screamed.

"Hey, don't worry, I'll protect you," Kirk said.

Molly, Robin, and I huddled around him on the ground. Bryce stepped out of the bushes into our view.

"We're not going anywhere. The Jeep battery is dead," he said.

"You had better not be screwing with us," Janice said poking her finger into Bryce's shoulder. "My Uncle Doug has a rack full of guns," she finished half-heartedly.

My heart was thumping hard against my rib cage.

Will these guys hurt us?

I looked at Molly and Robin in a weak attempt to read their thoughts. The chill in the air didn't compare to the one crawling down my spine.

What should we do?

Molly must have read my mind.

"You guys are assholes and I'm walking back," she said, quickly standing up.

Her spine was stronger than I imagined.

"Hey, we're sorry," Bryce said.

"Yeah, we were just having a little fun," said Kirk.

"There's nothing wrong with the Jeep," Bryce confessed. "I shut the lights off when we hit the bumps."

It was Kirk's turn to confess. "There isn't a mountain lion either.

That was just Bryce in the bushes. We sort of had this planned, just to scare you a little, but we're cool to go back anytime you want."

We were all dumbfounded, laughing, and scolding, but nervously relieved.

"Let's pick up all the beer cans," Bryce instructed as he began to gather up the empties.

What's this all about? We just toss our empties out the car windows when we're cruising in Toledo.

Environmental awareness had not yet hit the Midwest.

Janice sat on Bryce's lap on the ride back, which led to making out. Maybe it was the Coors or the mountain air, but I secretly wished I were in the kissing seat, instead of her.

DAY THREE OF WORK CAMP AT SUMMER BREEZE was largely unsupervised, as Uncle Doug came by only occasionally to check our progress.

"We didn't accomplish much yesterday" he said. "Let's put our backs into this today."

From a distance, we observed Janice outside the lodge teaching her niece tie-dying.

"Let's tie her up to die," Robin sneered, when Uncle Doug departed.

"This is bullshit!" Kool-Hand Molly proclaimed. "I'm calling my parents and checking us in to a real hotel. I'm not a maid or a maintenance man!" She angrily threw down her shovel and took off toward the house.

"Beats digging our way out of here," Robin said, slamming her shovel into the muddy ditch.

We followed behind Molly.

Janice glanced up from a bucket of dyed garments as we burst through the front kitchen entrance. Aunt Donna sat cross-stitching on the couch in the adjoining great-room.

"Don't worry, I'm calling collect," Molly shouted, as she dialed the phone. Janice walked in as Molly began a conversation with the other end of the phone line.

"What's going on?" Janice wondered out loud.

"I don't think this working vacation is working out," I said.

"Guys, I'm sorry. You know I'd be helping you, but these stupid big boobs get in my way. I have back problems, you know." Janice touched her mountains in a sheepish explanation.

"I think you have a much bigger problem than your boobs. I think you are a pathological liar," Robin said.

It was exactly what Molly and I were thinking too.

"Who's watching Summer?" Aunt Donna called from the other room.

That was Janice's opportunity to retreat outside, avoiding further confrontation.

OVER TUNA AND EGG SALAD SANDWICHES, Molly filled us in on the escape plan.

"My mom said that a hotel won't allow a minor to check in without an adult. She said if I'm ready to come home, just leave. I told her what a nightmare the bus ride was. So she said she'd get me a plane ticket. She's checking the flight schedules and everything."

Although we were a bit deflated by Molly's plan to leave, we made our afternoon hike to the legendary hot springs, heading out in the direction Uncle Doug had previously told us would lead to the springs. Hiking without hitching was pretty tiresome, and the beauty of our surrounding was lost, because we were afraid we were lost.

"I can't believe no cars have gone by," Janice said, panting.

"How long have we been walking?" Molly checked her watch.

"An hour and a half." I answered. "How stupid were we not to bring water?"

"There are plenty of fresh mountain streams, DC," Janice, the mountain expert, said.

Another half-hour went by before we found one. I was the first to scoop my hands into the coldness and slurp some down. I promptly threw up. The icy refreshment had shocked my over-heated system.

"Uh, how was it DC, pretty good?"

Robin and her sarcasm.

I would have laughed but I was afraid I might puke again.

"Look, a sign," Janice screamed. "Only half a mile to the hot springs."

About fifteen naked people, mostly adults, were floating and soaking when we made the spring scene. We did a quick huddle and decided to stick together and bolt if anything weird happened. We shyly entered nature's pool. Being the only hot-springers in bathing suits, we were an oddity. The naked people stared curiously at us and we tried not to return their gazes. Instead we clung to the side of a rock, bodies turned facing away from the pool.

"Girls, don't you know the lime in the springs will fade those pretty bathing suits?" a male voice from behind us boomed.

We slowly turned to see a thickly bearded, hairy-bodied Grizzly Adams stand-in, standing waist deep in the water.

"Thanks for the warning," Robin said.

He climbed up on the edge of the pool on a rock nearby. His back to us showed his hairiness was not just one-sided. We stifled giggles at the sight. As he turned to face us, we were horror-struck. None of us were experts on male genitalia, with the possible exception of Janice, yet we knew there was something seriously wrong. His testicles were the size of softballs. We practically swam to an open bank area and headed for our clothing pile.

"Elephantiasis of the nuts," Robin diagnosed.

We shot her quizzing looks.

"What? We have a medical encyclopedia at home," she added, as we threw shorts and T-shirts over still-wet suits.

"Nudity is overrated," I proclaimed.

We caught a ride with a middle-aged couple leaving the springs.

MOLLY'S MOM CALLED THAT NIGHT TO GIVE HER the flight arrangements. She'd be leaving in two days, Saturday morning, a full week ahead of our planned stay.

"Robin, my mom called your mom and she'll buy you a ticket to fly back with me, if you want to."

I knew what Robin's decision would be. It was the same choice I would have made if I thought my parents could afford the ticket. If I told them about the bus journey they might buy me a plane ticket for safety's sake, yet I didn't want to admit the whole trip was a mistake and end up paying for it, in more ways than one. I thought I might be baby-sitting and listening to parental lectures the rest of my high school life. Janice and I decided to reschedule our bus ride home to leave on Monday.

Friday morning, Aunt Donna told us to go exercise the horses instead of digging the ditch. She must have softened after Molly's cry for help. We took turns riding the horses, took a sauna, and then recovered our stash of Coors from the creek for our last night together on the deck.

We survived the bus ride, the ditch digging, and Janice's lies. But, for a brief time we lived in the majesty of the mountains, with stars so close you could hear their whispers.

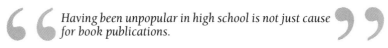

Having been unpopular in high school is not just cause for book publications.

—Fran Lebowitz

QUESTION MARKS IN THE SAND

M Y FASCINATION WITH THE BEACH BEGAN with a fascination—no, make that an obsession—with beach movies. Land-locked in mid-America, I had vacationed on the shores of the Great Lakes and smaller inland lakes since childhood. But the lure of the ocean was mystical and magical.

The ocean first beckoned to me from our new 1969 Zenith with rabbit-ear antennas, our first color television. I was 10 years old. I watched, mesmerized, as a bunch of teenagers frolicked during spring break along the beaches of Fort Lauderdale, Florida, in the 1959 (coincidentally, the year I was born) epic, *Where the Boys Are*. The song reverberated in my mind as Connie Francis crooned during the opening credits. Not only did the beauty and calmness of the sea await me, the hope of this perfect, romantic dream scorched its permanent panoramic-color image on my pre-pubescent soul.

I watched all the Frankie and Annette California beach movies. They *were* cute and comical, but the plot lines were as far-fetched as the girls' bust lines. But those movies lacked the depth of passion that ignited on the screen between Delo-res Hart and George Hamilton in *Where the Boys Are* as he sauntered across the beach to her and, with dreamy-eyes, drew question marks in the sand.

"'Til he holds me, I'll wait impatiently," was the lyric mantra that guided my beach-movie-branded soul through the malfor-mative years of high school in Toledo, Ohio. Seven cold winters after my first television glimpse of Fort Lauderdale, I was still waiting impatiently for "two arms to hold me tenderly."

It should be where the boys aren't, I thought, as I shuffled my platform-soled, laced-up boots across the linoleum-lined hallway of E.L. Bowsher High School and exited a back hallway door.

Along with about half of the senior class, I skipped out on yet another pep rally and headed for the railroad tracks. The other half, I knew from the repetitiveness of the drill, would stand in assembly at the rally until the Rebel flag unfurled and the band broke into "Dixie," our school song. The black kids threw fists of protest in the air, and the socials, the geeks, and teachers watched in amusement as the cheerleaders jumped and flailed in vain, trying to revive the dead school spirit.

Forced busing had certainly heightened our awareness of racial insensitivity, but all reason and rhetoric were lost at Bow-sher High when the symbol of the enslaved south flew high on the flagpole. While the administration failed to make the connection, many of the Rebels rebelled against the establish-ment, running marijuana and other substances up the prover-bial flagpole to see how high they flew. It was a microcosm of American culture in 1977. The grand spirit of my sister's class, the seniors of 1976, had exploded with brilliant red, white, and blue fireworks in the sky, which rained down their smolder-ing debris onto my apathetic senior class of 1977. We snuffed out the charred remains, like the cigarette butts on the railroad track up on Bowsher High School hill.

I shoved my hands in the pockets of my pea coat after a drag on the cigarette I shared with Amy Haas. It was cold, about

16 degrees, and the wind whipped across the open, elevated railroad tracks. A few dozen students were huddled in groups, smoking something. The rest of the pep rally skippers were in their parked cars or headed to McDonald's.

"God DC, you are so lucky, getting to go to Florida. There is no way my mom would let me," Amy said, through chattering teeth.

"Yeah, well, I've saved up a lot of money and missed out on a lot of parties from working at the Cinema. I've pushed a ton of popcorn and Good & Plentys, so I think I deserve it."

"Who all's going?" Amy asked.

"Christi and Lana and Gina," I answered.

"I know Christi and Lana from Human Relations class," said Amy. "Christi has kind of gotten around, hasn't she?" Amy's tone was more curious than accusing.

"Amy, just because she dyes her hair blonde and has a great body, people talk, you know? Really, she's great. I just don't believe those stupid rumors."

Amy got my cue and changed the subject, sort of.

"That other girl, Gina, are you talking about Gina Pancero, the homecoming queen who graduated last year?"

"Yeah, she's a good friend of my sister's. I work with her at the Cinema, and we're pretty good friends, too. Let's get the hell back inside where it's warm."

We lowered our chins into our coat collars for protection and began the short hike back to the school building. My nose began to thaw as we entered the building. Mrs. Baymiller, the truant officer, was escorting two girls who looked like freshmen out of the bathroom.

"Must have caught 'em smoking. Can you imagine?" I said smugly.

We both laughed. The previous year, Mrs. Baymiller caught Amy smoking in the bathroom. I'd just flushed mine, but my claim that Baymiller was crazy and her eyesight was shot did not go over very well with the vice principal. We both got three-day suspensions. I didn't get in too much trouble at home though, since the way I told the story made it sound like I was merely sticking up for a friend.

A stream of bodies flowed out of the gym as the band played "Dixie. "

Amy sighed. "Well, get a tan for me."

"A tan and a man. That's the plan." I said, winking.

TRUTHFULLY, I HAD A LOT MORE CONFIDENCE in my tan plan than in my man plan. My tan plan was pretty good: baby-oil and iodine on an immobilized body. But throughout my high school years, boys were more distant than the sun. I couldn't just re-position a lounge chair to increase my exposure.

My dating history was short. I'd had exactly one date. It was during my junior year with a guy who was sort of a burnout. Though I'd experimented to a fair degree with the illegal weed, I wasn't a burnout. I wasn't in any clique at all, which was part of the problem. I had friends, but I was more of a freelancer; I had friends from every group. My sister had been in the social clique class of '76, who were the coolest. I didn't think most of the socials in my class were cool, and apparently vice-versa.

My date, Pat, had picked me up in his green Rambler and we went to party in the woods with some of his burnout friends. He kissed me a few times, but it was gross. There wasn't anything about this guy that I even liked, except that he was the first guy who ever asked me out.

It wasn't like I was a dog. I was five-foot-six and a hundred and ten pounds, brown hair and eyes, according to my real driver's license. My fake ID made me five-foot-ten and blonde/blue, 140 pounds and 23 instead of 17. (Obviously, this was before photo licenses.)

The fake ID was my license to get beyond high school and

hang out at college bars with my sister and her friends. It was also crucial to the success of my first Spring Break in Florida.

I BLENDED IN WITH THE SHUFFLE OF STUDENTS heading back to class after the pep rally. The hallway was lined with lockers, and couples leaning against the lockers making out.

Like that's what lockers are for.

But I could endure it, because I knew the future. I could see that behind their jock and cheerleader facades, they were not challenged to develop beyond their high school image. *Like child-stars, their futures will remain focused on their pasts. They'll remain stuck in the barcaloungers of their dim suburban homes, re-living their glory days, getting fat and collecting unemployment, unequipped to move forward in a world without the rule of prom queens.*

It didn't tax my imagination greatly to envision this; I was only glad I did not see myself there, too.

I may have harbored just a bit of anger over being one of the lucky teenagers developing character instead of a social life, due to what I believed was the dual handicaps of an underdeveloped chest and overactive oil glands. But, all in all, I seemed to be actively developing my imagination.

As I sat in biology class, the formaldehyde fumes from the fetal pigs forced a mental escape that greatly taxed my imagination. I pictured my biology partner, Dean Wolfe, and I walking dreamy-eyed on the beach, hand in hand.

Dean bends down to pick up a conch shell to put up to my ear. I hear the ocean in stereo. He puts down the shell and cups his hands around the back of my head and passionately kisses me.

That's how it's going to be next week in Florida, I thought, even though I knew Dean would be staying in Toledo, with his girlfriend.

"Where are you, Denise Stanfa? You can't possibly be here,"

boomed Mr. Ebersole. "I've instructed you three times to pick up your knife and begin cutting."

I was always getting in trouble for not paying attention. Teachers called it daydreaming. I called it visualization. I knew that some day the positive energy would come back to me. It was better than the reality of a dead fetal pig you were required to dissect in order to pass biology.

"Mr. Ebersole, I don't feel well. The fumes are making me sick."

I left the classroom before he had the chance to tell me whether or not I had permission to leave.

THE AIRPORT WAS CROWDED AND STIFLINGLY HOT. I loved every minute of it. I wasn't daydreaming. I really was in Florida. Gina's cousin from Fort Lauderdale picked us up in a 1950s taxi that had been painted over.

"Great car," I said, as we loaded in the luggage.

"It's my brother's," explained Gina's cousin, Marie. "We're pretty sure somebody stole it and drove it down from New York. He bought it at an auction."

Marie was my age and Italian looking like Gina. More cute than beautiful and a little tomboyish.

"Oh my God! Palm trees!" I exclaimed, as we drove out of the terminal onto the feeder road to the Interstate.

"Just so you know, we hate tourists down here. The traffic gets all screwed up because they don't know how to drive when it's not snowing. I think snowbirds are basically slow and stupid, except you guys, of course."

Marie glanced at Christi, Lana, and me in her rearview mirror for our reaction. Then she blasted off onto I-95.

A warm wind whirled through the open window. Hair and cigarette ashes flew everywhere. In the midst of it all, I thought

I smelled orange blossoms, but since I didn't know what they smelled like, I wasn't sure.

Marie slammed the taxi into a tow-away zone at our hotel on A1A, across from the ocean in Lauderdale-by-the-Sea. We were miles away, not exactly walking distance, from the action on the strip. It was a nice, little two-bedroom-and-a-kitchen bungalow for $350 a week, which we could afford if we ate free buffets at happy hour and capitalized on dollar drink specials, which were strategic to our budget plan.

"I'll pick you up at eight," Marie told us. She had to get back to school. She was studying to be a dental hygienist.

I emerged from the condo bedroom in my two-piece bathing suit, wishing I were invisible. Gina, Christi, and Lana looked like Charlie's Angels. In comparison, with my skinny, flat-chested frame, I probably looked more like Charlie, who was never actually seen either.

As we headed toward the pool, Christi laughed at me and said with truth and no detected malice, "DC, you're the poster girl for the itty-bitty-titty committee."

Christi's thoughtless comment further deflated (pun intended) my self-image.

"I wish I were that skinny. You look cute," Gina said.

Lana, as usual, had no opinion or comment. Instead, she scoped the pool area for empty lounge chairs. Despite my prior rigorous defense of Christi's reputation, I momentarily decided Christi was a slut after all, and Gina was definitely my best friend.

THE FIRST NIGHT IN MAGIC LAND BEGAN WITH A SLOW drive down A1A, bumper to bumper, at about two miles per hour.

"Look at those guys," said Christi. "Are they hunks or what?"

I wasn't sure which group of guys she was talking about, as hundreds of people lined both the beachside and hotel side of the strip.

"Let's launch some tourist torpedoes," Marie menaced, as she reached into her purse and grabbed a tampon, which she quickly unwrapped while steering the car with her knees.

She tossed it into the El Dorado convertible next to us. The driver, an elderly man, turned in confusion to see what had landed in his back seat. Marie wove the car/taxi in front of his, looking for new targets. The rest of us were in hysterics.

My sister Lori and four other Toledo friends were staying at the Bahama Hotel, a primo location on the strip. When we arrived there at 8:30, a couple of dozen people, including my sister, were still poolside, clad in bathing suits, along with a couple dozen other people. Two guys with Bucknell University Hockey jerseys were playing cards under the light of a citronella candle.

"Hey Sis, we've got cheese and crackers and maybe some ham left in the cooler," Lori said. "I think somebody's going for pizza, but we have plenty of cold Stroh's, and that's all that matters!"

SUE, ONE OF LORI'S FRIENDS, INFORMED US that no one was up to going anywhere outside the hotel. "It'sh been a pretty wild day. We don't want anyone to rishk shlipping in the shower. Sho, we're gonna hang out here. Thersha's a toga party later on the shecond floor," she said in her best Drunkenese.

I was a little disappointed that we wouldn't be hitting one of the many hot spots I'd heard about, like the Candy Store, or better yet, the Elbow Room, which gained fame in 1959 as a result of my favorite flick, *Where the Boys Are*. It was still thriving almost twenty years later.

"The guys who invited us said it's a Nectar of the Gods

Party, whatever that is, and we're supposed to dress up for it like a Roman orgy." Lori laughed.

"The guys shaid they were kidding about the orgy part," Sue slurred.

By 10, I was catching up on the alcohol intake I'd apparently missed earlier in the day. My buzz was buzzing harder due to lack of solid food intake. In Lori's room, we stripped the bed sheets and pillowcases and attempted a toga-making workshop for drunks. If there are ten girls, two beds, a sofa-bed, and five cases of beer, how many sheets does each girl get? I figured the answer was three sheets to the wind.

Lori and her friends, as rightful guests of the Bahama, got the top sheets and two of the fitted sheets. Marie fashioned a diaper from two pillowcases, which she wore over her jeans.

Boring Lana whined, "I don't want to dress up."

Christi copied the tied-together pillowcase idea for a halter-type top, with nothing underneath. Gina took down the flowered cloth shower curtain and wore it as a cape.

"There's our little homecoming queen," Lori said.

Gina mocked a windshield-wiping wave to the crowd. She never took herself too seriously.

Pretty rare for a homecoming queen.

I had one pillowcase and a fitted sheet to work with, but the fitted sheet had a weird stain on it the size and shape of Brazil.

"This is disgusting," I said, in my best Roseanne Roseanna Danna voice.

"Oh, my God! DC, that sounded just like her!" Sue screamed.

As everyone was now watching, I went into a full-blown impression, repeating some of the Saturday Night Live sketch material I remembered.

It was unanimously decided that I would stay in character for the toga party, and everyone assisted me with wardrobe and make-up. We went with heavy lipstick and eyebrow pencil, and they teased my thick, wavy hair so hard, it bit. Topping it off, I wore a slinky half-slip, high-heels, and a pink tube top.

Standing in front of the mirror, I was no longer myself. I was the entertainer. I didn't care what anyone thought, as long as they thought I was funny. The laughter in the room provided my reward.

"DC, if I'm ever asked what's the funniest thing I've ever seen, I'll have to say it's you in a tube top," Christi said.

"That's Roseanne Roseanna Danna," I replied, "and you've got a gross little ball of sweat drip, drip, dripping down your nose, Dr. Joyce Brothers."

The party was packed. From the flag draped on the wall I detected our hosts were clearly Canadian. The partygoers were draped in sheets, towels, and bedspreads. It was more like a really bad ad for a white sale than Roman orgy. The party could have been the inspiration for the Animal House toga party. The beds in the room were up-ended and against the wall to make more standing room, and the Nectar of the Gods turned out to be a plastic garbage can filled with every liquor legally sold, including grain alcohol mixed with Kool-Aid and fruit. Of all the girls at the party, our group got the most attention, largely due to Marie and me. She'd just walk up to people and say,

"Did you see who's here? Elvis and Roseanne Roseanna Danna."

Then she'd grab me and I'd say to them, "Sorry, Elvis went out for jelly donuts. My great grandma Roseanna Danna likes jelly donuts but she doesn't have any teeth. So here she is a, gumming away, you know and that jelly, itsa drip, drip, dripping all down the side of her face and her tongue, itsa big, like a St. Bernard and she's a lick, lick, licking. It's disgusting."

After we'd worked the room for an hour, about half of us went down to the sidewalk in front of the hotel to make spectacles of ourselves to the people cruising the strip by foot and car. Since my material was already getting stale, I needed a new audience.

I WOKE UP FEELING MUCH BETTER THAN I should have. The fuzziness from the last few hours of the previous night cleared quickly. I was pretty sure that some guy Marie knew drove us home in her car. I was positive that we pulled over, not once, but twice for someone to puke and was 99% certain it wasn't me. Then I remembered the spins when I hit the bed. I had definitely passed out instead of puking.

Good for me.

We were all awake, albeit wounded, and were on the beach before noon. Five Italian boys from New Jersey immediately converged upon us. I couldn't be sure they were all Italian, but there were two Joeys, a Carmine, and an Anthony, which in New Jerseese is pronounced with a silent *h*, Antony. One Joey was really cute, the other not-so. The one guy's name I didn't catch, the quiet one looked a bit like Sonny Bono, but half his age and three quarters of his height.

"You girls want a squirrelly whirly?" asked the cute Joey, opening up a cooler.

"What's a squirrelly whirly?" Lana actually asked a question. *Way to turn on the personality, Lana.* Constantly armed with my Stanfa family sarcasm I opted to use a silencer this time.

"It's beer mixed with Chianti wine," the not-so-cute Joey said, handing a plastic cup to Gina first.

"Hey, uh, I'll be back in a while," I said. I threw on my aviator-style prescription sunglasses and went for a walk. I really didn't think I could stomach a squirrely-whirly and figured I'd be stuck with the other not-so-cute Joey or son of Sonny Bono. Besides, the ocean was beckoning. The water rolled over my toes and little crushed shells massaged the bottom of my feet as I walked in, my senses overwhelmed. My eyes followed the crisp blueness of the expansive Atlantic to its horizon. The sun was almost too bright, as if that were possible for me, the sun worshipper.

The coolness of the water enveloped me as I proceeded into its depth—about thigh high. I was finally connected to one of the greatest forces on earth, and despite the hangover, I'd never felt better in my life. I was thinking about diving in, but remembered my sunglasses.

"Watch out for the jellyfish," said a deep voice from above me. After I stepped around the slimy, little creature on the shore, I looked up.

"It might still be alive. They really sting," said the tall, gorgeous creature.

His hair was like Robert Redford's in *Butch Cassidy*, the same color and breezy style, not too short, but not too long. With teeth made for smiling, he was smiling at me.

"Where did you grow those legs?"

Self-consciously, looking down at my lower extremities, I realized that this was an actual compliment from a really cute guy. My usual wit was temporarily paralyzed.

"Uh, Ohio...Toledo," I answered.

"Small world, I'm from Ohio, too. Lima," said the dream guy with eyes the color of the ocean.

"Yeah, I've heard Lima stands for Lost In Mid-America."

He tossed his head back slightly as he laughed. "I've never heard that before, but I escaped a few years ago to go to college in Maryland." He paused for a second. "What's your name?"

"DC. Well, it's really Denise," I nervously tried to explain the nickname, "but everybody except the police calls me DC."

"You're in trouble with the law?" He whispered in a mock, secretive tone.

"No. But there are some laws I have trouble with."

"Let me guess—legal drinking age?"

Not wanting to blow my cover as a high school student posing as a college student, I said, "No, the law of gravity, actually. I'd like to go wherever I want and not have to pay airfare."

He laughed again. "And I have some real issues with Murphy's Law. Try to break it every chance I get."

Dream guy even had funny punch lines. More amazingly, he was still talking to me.

"What's your name?"

"Craig. You want to sit down?"

He motioned toward a blanket spread out in the sand.

There has to be a catch.

I was expecting him to pick up a camera, introduce me to his beautiful girlfriend, and ask me if I would take their picture.

We sat down. I looked around. No girlfriend in sight.

"Who are you here with?" I asked, taking extreme care to hold my stomach muscles taught as I reclined a bit.

"No one. I mean, I have friends here, but I'm staying by myself, here at the Villa Serena. How about you?"

Before I could answer, Gina approached, laughing.

"There you are! DC, you missed it! We were sitting there drinking squirrely-whirlies and a seagull flew over me and shit on my arm! It was so gross! I washed it off in the ocean, but I'm going back to the room to take a shower."

I laughed. "Too funny. Hey, Gina, this is Craig."

Craig nodded and they exchanged hellos.

His eyes did not follow her as she left, which surprised me. Guys typically fell all over Gina.

"So, what are you and your friends doing tonight?"

There it was.

Your friends. He wants to see Gina again.

"WHAT WAS THE QUESTION?" I looked at Craig numbly for a moment and then remembered.

"Oh yeah, we're going to some bar where the motto is 'Disco Sucks.' It's not on the strip, though. Gina's cousin who lives here is taking us."

"I know the place."

He was looking directly in my eyes as he spoke, very casually hooking a line onto my self-doubt and extracting it, like a painful tooth, from my psyche. His smile provided anesthesia.

"It's called Nards. They have a wild DJ. He burns disco records in the parking lot. Maybe we could meet there later."

His words hung like question marks in the sky.

"Uh, yeah." I stuttered my answer.

"First I'm supposed to meet some buddies at The Button for the wet T-shirt contest." Craig's gaze briefly broke from mine as he talked.

I'd get booed out of that one.

He must have read my mind.

"But I'm a leg man myself."

I felt an odd, warm sensation that had nothing to do with the sun. It was the same feeling I got when I daydreamed about being kissed and held and touched.

Could Craig possibly want to do those things with me? In real life?

WHILE THE GIRLS WERE GETTING READY TO GO OUT, I kept thinking about Craig and the powerful hour on the beach. Looking into the mirror, I was trying to see what he saw. After four years of dermatologist visits, my face was finally clearing up. I did have high cheekbones from my Italian father's side of the family. Unless I was distracted by my zits, I never disputed that I did have pretty eyes. The instructors at Barbizon Modeling School said I had an "exotic look," which is what I figured they told all the not-so pretty girls whose parents had paid them good money to help their daughters gain poise and confidence.

Barbizon was a modeling school. Never for a moment thinking I was model material, I looked at it like the finishing school it really was. I learned to walk without slumping my shoulders, as I typically did to hide the chest I didn't have, and they taught me how to use make-up to hide flaws and accent features. We even had a runway where we practiced modeling poses. Before long, I had a routine, a parody of modeling poses to entertain my friends. I was sometimes called upon at parties for the good laugh it provided.

Marie had a friend who was a waitress at Nards, so IDs were no problem, even though we all had fake ones except for Gina, who was 18 and at the time was legal. We also got a table near the dance floor. The music was rock and roll and some oldies, anything but disco. We danced, talking only when the DJ took breaks. Otherwise we could only shout above the music. This wasn't your standard spring break pick-up place, yet the sexual tension, if harnessed, could have launched a missile. I didn't mention anything to anyone about Craig. I doubted he'd actually show up.

The DJ announced a dance contest. It wasn't a couples' dance; it was a solo endeavor. The prize was a $50 bar tab and all participants got 'Disco Sucks' T-shirts.

"DC, I dare you," was all Marie had to say before I made my decision.

Fourteen people entered the contest, ten guys, and three other girls, besides me. The challenge was to not incorporate any disco moves into your dance, which wasn't as easy as it sounds, since Saturday Night Fever had recently swept the nation. The DJ was also the judge. I danced for twenty minutes straight. By throwing in some theatrics, like air guitar moves and leg-splitting jumps, I made it to the final three. The contest was down to me, a guy with a ponytail, and another girl.

The final song was "It's Only Rock-N-Roll" by the Rolling Stones.

"Okay audience, you get to decide this one," announced the DJ, turning up the volume so my ears rang.

Halfway into the song, I was sweating and giving it my all, imitating Mick and strutting across the floor. The male contestant was losing his steam. The girl, who must have conceded that I was the better dancer, lifted up her shirt. Her hooters got hoots and hollers. Then, a chant from the audience.

"No skin, no win. No skin, no win."

No fair.

I did a jump and run, then slid on my knees across the floor to my friends' table. Just as the song was about to end, I turned my back to my friends, bent over and shot them a partial moon.

The applause-o-meter from the audience was audibly higher for me than the boob-flasher. The guy got a smattering of claps and boos. I looked at my friends as I was officially proclaimed the winner. Craig was standing next to their table. My heart jumped through my throat, which made it impossible for me to talk as I returned to the table. He had on a wide-lapelled, polyester, Travolta-ish shirt, and Britannia blue jeans.

"Way to go, DC!" Gina slapped me on the butt.

Marie did a finger-in-the-mouth whistle. Christi signaled the waitress and ordered champagne. I grabbed somebody's beer off the table and took a generous swig. I still hadn't taken my eyes off Craig, whose smile was more of a smirk.

"Working up a sweat?" he asked.

I detected from my keen peripheral vision that my friends had their eyes glued to us as he spoke. I picked up a barely used bar napkin and mopped my face, as I sheepishly looked to the ground.

"When did you get here?" I asked, wondering if I should feel proud or embarrassed.

"Oh, let's see. I got here right before you turned into Mick Jagger. Nice end by the way, no pun intended. Does Mick do that?"

He was teasing me and I loved it.

Two bottles of champagne later, there were three conversations taking place at the same time and all of them involved Craig. I was admiring him and myself—in the Disco Sucks T-shirt I'd changed into in the bathroom.

"So, you're pretty tall. Do you play basketball?" Gina asked him.

"Yeah, for the University of Maryland."

"Where's the rest of the team?" Christi shot me a half-glance as she asked.

"I didn't come down here with the team. But my friends are still over at The Button checking out the banana-eating contest."

"Couldn't peel themselves away?" Marie beat me to the pun.

"Uh, I was in a pizza-eating contest once. I ate a twelve-inch pizza in ten minutes," I competitively interjected.

Craig laughed. "Different kind of contest, DC. How can I say this...it's not how many bananas the girl eats. It's HOW she eats the banana."

My friends laughed at his delicate attempt to explain. I was too naive to be surprised by my own naiveté.

"So, DC, want to go with me over to Big Daddy's?"

Craig's question was only aimed at me and not my friends. I felt grateful enough to bear his children.

"Sure."

I was anxious to get him away from my friends. Just in case. Having lost what I thought was a potential boyfriend to another "friend" sophomore year; I wasn't taking any chances. The girls said they'd meet me back at the hotel later.

As we were leaving, Marie asked Craig, "What are you doing hanging out at locals' bars, first here and now Big Daddy's?"

He smiled. "I just know some people."

CRAIG HELD MY HAND IN THE PARKING LOT AS WE walked toward his car. My palm was sweaty, but he didn't seem to mind. I tried to maintain my composure as he opened the passenger door of a fairly new white Corvette.

"I'd take the T-tops off, but it's a hassle to put them back on every time I park. I've already had the stereo stolen twice."

He's apologizing for a gorgeous car?

He held my hand again as we walked into Big Daddy's. We made our way through the front bar into a back room where people were shooting pool. He seemed to know just about everybody in the place.

"My grandparents live up the road in Pompano and I've been coming down to Florida for years," he explained.

We drank several beers and smoked cigarettes as he shot pool. I was surprised that he smoked, since he was a basketball player. When I asked him about it, he said,

"I only smoke when I drink. I don't do either during the season."

He ran the table for an hour until he got beat by a dwarf, who was barely big enough to reach the top of the pool table, but he didn't miss a shot.

Since we were headed for the hotel Craig took off the T-tops and the wind blew our hair back as Roger Daltrey and The Who blasted from the stereo,

"I'm free, I'm free, and I'm waiting for you to follow me." The lyrics amplified what my 17-year-old soul felt. I had broken free from the person I thought I was into the one I could become. It dawned on me in the darkness.

If I'm riding in this car with the coolest guy I've ever met, there's a real possibility I might just be too cool for high school and all the jerks that think THEY are cool.

We heard the laughter and music before we saw the partyers at the Villa Serena pool. We stood and watched the crazy Italians. Cute Joey and Carmine had fastened bras around their chests, but the ends of the garments didn't stretch the girth of their backs. They were dancing to the Bee Gees and singing in mock falsetto voices, "You Should Be Dancing."

Watching them reminded me that my legs were already feeling sore from my own performance earlier at Nards. I sat down in a lounge chair and looked at Craig for a cue or a clue as to what might happen next.

"I'm gonna go crash, I'm playing some hoops with a couple of buddies tomorrow, too early."

There was no lingering moment and no kiss. I didn't know what to think, so I chose to dream instead. I shut my eyes and blocked out the music and noise. I was back with Craig in his Corvette and I was free.

We're cruising through McDonald's with the T-tops off. It's summer, Craig is back from school and we're spending all our time together. I see envy in the eyes of girls and guys we pass.

I opened my eyes. I was on a lounge chair in Fort Lauderdale, Florida, and the possibilities were limitless. For the first time in my life, reality didn't kill the dream.

AFTER A BREAKFAST OF LEFTOVER SUB SANDWICHES, the girls and I settled into vegetative states on the beach.

"The sun is great. It tans you and sucks the alcohol right out of your body," Gina said, stretching back on the beach blanket.

"Making room for more," I added, drolly.

"So what's going on with you and Craig? Did you do IT? I mean, he's a fox!" Christi grilled me.

Gina countered the interrogation. "What about you and Joey, Christi? What time did you get home this morning?"

Lana, the anti-personality, was self-involved in her own drama, searching for tanning oil she was sure she had brought.

Before anyone answered anything, I elbow-nudged Gina, who nudged Christi even harder, when I saw Craig coming toward us.

"How's everyone feeling today?" Craig asked in a school-teacher tone.

"I need a nap," Christi rolled her eyes backward and reclined onto the blanket for effect.

"I have to go meet my grandparents for lunch, but I'm having a little party later. I stress 'little,' because it's a studio room. But we can see how many people we can pack into it."

"Thanks," Gina answered for all of us. "My cousin is picking us up for dinner. We're going to the Mai-Kai."

"Well, the party will probably go late. If I don't see you, it was nice meeting you. I have to take off tomorrow and get back to school, spring b-ball," Craig explained.

"Aw… that's too bad," Gina said.

But my heart shattered.

In my dreams, the Prince doesn't ride off into the sunset alone.

I BARELY WATCHED THE POLYNESIAN EXTRAVAGANZA at the Mai Kai. I was busy looking at my watch. I reached a compromise with the girls. We'd go to dinner, and then Marie would drop me off at the party. They were intent on going to Ohio State night at The Button. (We were pretending to attend Ohio State.)

After the Mai Kai, I stopped in our room first to put some more cover-up on a zit that was growing under my nose. Craig's room was only a short walk from ours, but it was almost 10 by the time I arrived. There were only eight people there and none of them looked like college students. They were his local friends. I recognized a few of them from Big Daddy's. They looked to be in their mid-20s. One girl—no, make that a woman—looked older than my 39-year-old mom. She was a bartender at Big Daddy's. I felt incredibly out of place. Craig was rolling a joint on the small kitchen table.

"Hi," he said. "Beer's in the fridge."

When the joint came my way, I almost passed because pot made my head feel like a lead balloon. *But it would make me blend in a little better,* I thought. Craig stood next to me, leaning against the kitchen counter.

"Hey, you should've seen this one at Nards last night! She won a wild dance contest," Craig announced to the room.

I smiled at Craig, thanking him for his endorsement.

"I think we should all dance," said a really drunk guy on the couch. His girlfriend's passed-out head rested on his shoulder.

Craig excused himself and went into the bathroom. There was a line for the end table where people were bending over and snorting something with rolled up dollar bills. I'd heard about cocaine before but had only seen people doing it in movies, not in real life.

This is a serious drug.

I wondered if Craig did it. Then came the wave of paranoia. *Maybe he's a dealer. Where did he get the Corvette? He said his father was a doctor, so they're probably rich.*

I looked at the kitchen table. The dwarf from last night was dancing on it, and the full sized-bartender woman was dancing on the floor, so they were about the same height.

A heavy feeling came upon me and I became ultra-sensitive to the pimple growing under my nose. It felt monstrous. I imagined it growing into a small, separate entity and dancing with the dwarf. I realized I was hallucinating. I wondered if there was more than pot in the joint.

I wasn't sure how much time had passed before I got up from the kitchen floor I'd been sucked into. I walked over to Craig, who was helping the passed-out girl's boyfriend carry her out to his car.

"I, uh, better go," I said.

He looked at me with glazed eyes and nodded.

A lizard zipped across my sandaled toes as I navigated the outdoor walkway. My heart pounded out the Morse code, which I had actually memorized in the fifth grade. S.O.S.—Save our ship. Save our sanity.

I pushed open our hotel door.

"Christi is in your bedroom with Joey." Gina looked through my dilated portholes and saw my sinking ship. "Are you okay?"

A tsunami tidal wave slammed me into the couch.

I awoke fully clothed. A beach towel was draped over me. The good news was, there was no hangover with pot. The bad news was, for me, it wasn't conducive to developing intimate relationships.

There was a light knock on the door. I arose, clutching a throw pillow for no apparent reason, and opened the door with my free hand.

"You forgot your jacket." Craig pushed the denim garment in my direction. "Here you are. I gotta go."

"I know."

I looked in his eyes for a sign of something I could hold onto. He just smiled. "It was fun."

"Yeah," I agreed.

He bent down and kissed my forehead, a kiss so dry it could have worn a raincoat, yet, I still felt oddly buoyant.

He was stuffing a duffel bag in the trunk of his 'Vette as I nervously approached him in the parking lot. "Here's my address and phone number," I said as I handed him the piece of paper. "Call if you're ever in Toledo." I tried to sound casual.

"I will," Craig said, with no detectable lack of sincerity.

As he pulled out onto A1A, I pictured him driving up into the clouds. A question mark clung to my cloud nine.

Why me? He could have spent time with any cute college girl he chose.

I imagined he was an angel sent down from heaven to save me from my pitiful life. But I didn't think the pot party was God's idea. Or maybe God wanted me to see the scary side of my imagination so I wouldn't venture there again.

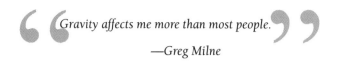

Gravity affects me more than most people.
—Greg Milne

GIDGET GOES TO COLLEGE

SEPTEMBER 5, 1977: "New Beginnings." That's what is printed on the front of this journal, a gift from Sue. Sue, one of Lori's friends, was in my art class my junior year and is now one of my best friends, too. She wrote on the inside of the cover, "May your future be worth writing about." I can only hope.

Summer wasn't too horrible. Three weeks of graduation parties, including mine, then swimming at the rock quarry when I wasn't working. I worked matinees and some midnight shows at the Cinemas plus about fifteen hours a week selling shoes, and I still have only $360 dollars in the bank to show for it. I really didn't blow that much this summer, I just get paid squat. Luckily, beer and bowling come pretty cheap, and for me, movies are free. What else worthwhile is there to spend money on in Toledo? That's why I've got to get the hell out. Robin and Amy are lucky, 'cause they get to go away to college and live in a dorm. Even if it is just twenty minutes from Toledo, Bowling Green is a really fun, party college, and I can't wait to go visit them.

I am stuck in this armpit town for at least three more months. I want to be a stewardess, but I can't even apply to the airlines until I turn 18. HURRY UP NOVEMBER! In the meantime, Mom and Dad convinced me to take a couple of classes at UT. Mom said, "You and your sisters are lucky I work there so you have a chance to go to college." Dad said, "I can't believe you'd pass up higher education." I know Dad wishes he'd gone to college, but Grandma worked in a factory and raised the kids herself. After high school Dad went to work in a textile factory to help pay the bills, then he met Mom and got married at 19. He worked his way up into the scheduling office from there.

I do not want to work in a factory, but I can't imagine four more years of trying to make friends and, along the way, figuring out who all the assholes are. College is probably just another cocoon of bullshit. Same as high school, only harder. UT is such a commuter school that Lori's been there a year and has only one new college friend. She still hangs around the high school friends, who I admit I like, including Sue. I try to get invited to go out with them whenever I can. She's been a nicer sister since Tim dumped her. God, she wasted three years on him.

So I've got a couple months to kill. Guess I might as well go to UT, but for one quarter only. I signed up for First Aid, which will help me when I'm a stewardess, and Psychology 101. (I'm still trying to figure people out, especially guys, and why I have only ever had one date and one almost-spring fling.) I LOVE YOU FORT LAUDERDALE! CRAIG, WHY DIDN'T YOU EVER CALL ME?? I'm also taking badminton just because I was good at it in high school gym class.

September 12, 1977
I started my job shelving books in the college library. I did it for three hours straight, and before going into a coma, I hid in a reading room until I woke up. A worse job might be

sorting and matching up socks in the eternal laundry of hell. (Trying not to be too negative.)

Got lost looking for First Aid class. Psychology homework was to read one chapter. I read six, just because I had nothing better to do. Then went to mom's office to complain about my job. "Just go back to the placement office," she said. She still had two hours before she could leave, and she was typing security reports. I checked the job postings at placement and applied for a couple, went back to the library, and got an abnormal psych book. Now I can prove I'm not crazy. I'm just suffering from post-traumatic stress disorder the same as everybody else. I cruised by the Student Union on the way back to the security department in search of fellow victims.

September 20, 1977

Hallelujah! I have the best job at the University! I work at Centennial Hall, for the phys ed department, checking student IDs and loaning out basketballs and rackets at the front desk. I also take turns with a guy making rounds of the building, to make sure the doors are locked on the upper-track level and spot check the weight room, basketball, and racquetball courts to make sure no one is injured. The most amazing thing is what I get to check out directly across the front desk: the Athletic Department training room. Every afternoon, all these football players walk in to get taped up before practice. Their bodies are right out of a magazine. I watched as one gorgeous guy took off his shirt and got a shoulder massage from one of the trainers, and I felt hot and sweaty and out of breath, even though I hadn't moved an inch. Glenn, my co-worker, caught me looking. Glenn says the guy is Jesse Carone, the starting quarterback last year, who hurt his shoulder in spring ball and is trying to recover.

Twenty feet and a million miles apart, I willed his eyes to mine, then cursed my will when he smiled at me.

I have to stop reading romance novels.

October 8, 1977

Can't believe the last few weeks. Little time to write. But, finally, I have something worth writing about. Barbizon modeling school sent my shot sheets from last year to a local agency and they called me! I was in shock. I only agreed to do the Barbizon thing because Mom said it would teach me poise and confidence (which I desperately needed). I met with Nancy, the owner of The Agency, (original name, not. But, hey, it's Toledo). She told me about a non-profit job to help me "gain experience and exposure." So Saturday I taped a PSA for the Keep America Beautiful campaign. I jogged across Swan Creek Park where another "actor" pretended to litter. I picked up the litter and tossed it in the garbage can. I'M GONNA BE ON TV! Nancy said my photo in jogging shorts and a T-shirt got me the job. I figure I was the only one in her book that didn't go for high glamour ('cause who would I be kidding?) Looking average has its advantages. Mom and Dad are thrilled, and Mom reminded me that a lot of models like Twiggy were also flat-chested. Oddly, I was not comforted.

I've started timing my building walk-throughs to coincide with the football team. They all sit on the floor in the hallway waiting to get into a room for a team meeting at precisely 4:15 each day before they go out to stadium practice. Every time I walk past them, a couple of guys whistle. Yesterday one guy said, "Hey sweet ass, you sure do have a sweet ass."

Then Jesse Carone stood up and started walking with me. I was beet red and nervous. He said, "If we knew your name, these guys might stop calling you sweet ass." I stuttered out my name and he pretended not to notice. HE IS SOOO NICE!

October 12, 1977

Invited to meet Jesse and some of the guys for happy hour at Charlie's Blind Pig.

Not hating life or Toledo today.

October 21, 1977

Classes are easy. I love my job. The biggest bitch right now is not having a car. I have to ride with Mom and Lori to and from campus every day in Mom's Pinto. The '65 Fairlane Grandpa gave us didn't make it through the summer. Lori has an 8 a.m. class, which we're never on time for, so she gets pissed. We all scream at each other and fight over the bathroom in the morning. Then at night, Lori and I have to wait for Mom when she has to work late. It sucks.

Work is not work at all. It is so fun. I talk to Jesse and his friends every day, before the team meeting. They've been teasing me about my commercial debut. The ad started running this week, mostly right after the 11 o'clock news. Got invited to a party at Jesse's this weekend. After my dismal high school experience, I'm due for some good luck in the love arena, even if I am micro-managing it (I read that somewhere). Lori begged to go to the party with me. Haven't said yes, although I'll probably let her. Want to make her suffer a little for all the times she's told me to "get lost." Called Sue. She couldn't believe my luck. She's definitely going! She said "DC, How did you manage this connection after only a few weeks in school?"

Exactly.

October 23, 1977

Went to the UT football game Saturday with Sue. We beat Eastern Michigan 21 to 10. It's so unbelievable to watch all these guys I know out there playing on the field. Jesse's still sidelined because of his shoulder though.

The party at Jesse's was INCREDIBLE! All night, Hank, Jesse's roommate, called me "Washington" instead of DC. I'm not sure I like the name, but I won't complain about the attention. There were way more guys than girls, which was fine by me. And most of the guys were football players, although I did meet two basketball players and a baseball player. Sue and Lori had a blast, too. Neil Houston asked Sue out; he's blond, a linebacker. Cute, but he has no neck, just big shoulders that support his head and ego. Hank and Jesse say he's O.K.

At one point, there were so many people that they opened the door in the hallway and the neighbors' door (also football players), so we had a two-apartment party. This REALLY BIG GUY, Fred, guzzled a pitcher of beer in, like, forty seconds. Then he took a bite of a glass ashtray, chewed it up, and swallowed it! Sue and I stayed late and helped clean up the apartment. I even hosed some puke off the back patio. Hank and Jesse hugged us goodbye like old friends. On the way to drop me off, Sue said, "We've hit the mother lode, Deece!"

I HAVE TO BUY A CAR! Applied for more hours, Saturday mornings, and "backstage hospitality" for concerts at Centennial. Elvis even played there last year, right before he died. Could be interesting.

November 15, 1977

Turned 18 yesterday. Mom and Dad gave me $100. Lori threw me a surprise party at Gator's Bar. There were like, fifty people, on a Monday night! We had to tell the owner it was my 21st, 'cause I've been going to Gator's for a couple of years. Everyone wanted to buy me shots. Lost track of how many I did. Got birthday kisses from Jesse, Hank, and a couple other guys. Think I asked for seconds. Rest of evening is pretty blurry. Had to be carried to the car. Did not puke. Mom says I inherited my iron gut from Dad. I also inherited his flat chest, which was not an even trade-off.

This morning I was a zombie when I turned in my psychology paper. I left half-way through class, and slept on a couch in the Student Union.

Nancy from The Agency called. She's booked me for a holiday bridal show. Good thing you can't see through the phone. REALLY LOOK LIKE A MODEL RIGHT NOW. I have to go for fittings Saturday, and otherwise it's "just a simple runway walk," she said. Mom and Dad paid for me to do a bunch of those at Barbizon. Never thought I'd get paid to do one. I'll get sixty bucks, ten for the fitting and fifty for the show. Nancy says I'm perfect "sample size" (five or seven) for the gowns.

December 13, 1977

Well, I'm staying in school at least one more quarter. I don't know what I want to major in (besides football players). Hank hooked me up with his advisor. I'm signing up for English Lit., Communication 101 (speech class), Racquetball, and Photojournalism. Mom says my new friends are a good influence on me, and Dad's always asking me about the "starters" and Coach Stobart. Mom met Hank when he came in to pay a parking ticket at the security department last week. She "took care of it." He promised not to tell anyone, 'cause if word gets out, everyone will be asking me if she'll "take care" of their tickets, too.

Did the Holiday Bridal Show. Mom came to watch. "It might be my only chance to see you in a wedding gown," she joked. At 18 and dateless, I didn't laugh. I was only nervous the first time on the runway. Didn't trip and that's all that matters. Everyone really just looks at the dress and the headpiece or veil anyway. I felt strange in the bridal gowns for some reason, not so strange in the bridesmaid dresses.

December 27, 1977

The holidays seem to bum me out worse every year—couples. Lori and Sherry have boyfriends over (as usual), and there's Mom and Dad and Grandma and Grandpa, and me and the dog. I DO have plans for New Year's (for a change) not a date, but a party.

As New Year's Eve's uncertainties linger amongst the crowd, we all remember why we're drinking (but don't recall out loud). We fill our empty glass of fear with shouts of the new and kiss goodbye forgotten dreams, as if they had come true. We hold onto the hands of time, a grasp we cannot flee, and laughter numbs the pain of change—as it always has for me.

Mrs. Seldon in creative lit senior year told us to turn pain into poetry.

There, I feel better.

January 2, 1978

Went to a great New Year's Eve party at Nick Sturgis's. Sturge and his roommate Robby live across the hall from Hank and Jesse. It wasn't a huge party, like Jesse and Hank's. A lot of people are still gone for Christmas break. Sue and "No-Neck-Neil" are still going out. They showed up for a little while. The tree was decorated with panties and bras, which they claim were left by their owners. Sturge is a tackle, and Robby is a tight end. I am learning a lot about football hanging around these guys. Hell, I'm learning a lot about guys hanging around these guys.

Jesse's girlfriend from Cleveland was at the party. Had no idea Jesse had a girlfriend. Hank says a lot of the guys have home town girlfriends, but while they're at school they just don't advertise it. Some of the guys screw around on the girlfriends and some don't. I've seen Jesse flirt, but not really be with anyone else. Carla, his girlfriend, is pretty nice. She's a stewardess. She says "flight attendant."

She told me about hassles that go with the job. Like, when you're new you can't pick your schedules and you have to fly horrible places where there's nothing to do. The airline seems to own you. Maybe I'm better off in college after all.

Sturge is the funniest guy I've ever met. He has memorized lines from a million movies and throws them into conversations. At midnight, as a joke, he threw me on the couch and started kissing all over me. I played it up by moaning and writhing around and everybody laughed. It's pretty obvious that I'm a sidekick or a mascot to these guys, nothing more. I'm Gidget without a surfboard. (Moondoggie, where are you?) But, I don't care. I finally belong.

Slept on Hank and Jesse's couch. Hank called my mom to tell her no one was sober enough to drive me home. He promised her he'd get me going to church again. Have no idea how that came up. But Hank and Jesse are Catholic and do go to Mass on campus sometimes. Woke up at 6 and couldn't get back to sleep. Had a strange desire to crawl in bed with Hank. I didn't.

January 19, 1978

I survived the blizzard of '78! The blizzard is barely over, but there are bumper stickers and T-shirts already printed. Other than driving in a whiteout Saturday morning on my way home from work, the blizzard was fun. The whole Midwest, including Toledo, shut down for three days. But after the first day, Lori and I got cabin fever and hitchhiked a plow truck to take us to Ermie's bar, which was open because Ermie was stranded there. She said she was sleeping on the pool table. She's a tough old broad. A bunch of people we went to high school with were there including Janet, Sue, Gina, Sandy, and Jenny. (They all live within a few blocks of Ermie's).

Then Sue and I hitched another truck ride to Hank and Jesse's. Since schools and businesses were closed, everybody in the apartment complex was partying. Played every drinking game we ever heard of, including Pass-Out. Then we started making up our own. Sturge made up a game called drink or spin. You had your choice to do a shot of Schnapps or spin the bottle and kiss the person it spun to. We ended up doing both, a shot then a spin. When Hank spun to me, the kiss was incredible (a little tongue action). But, then he did the same with Sue. She says she thinks he's a good kisser, too.

February 19, 1978

I'm a "helluva racquetball player," according to Hank and Neil. We played cutthroat today. The scores were pretty close, so unless they're cutting me some slack, maybe I am decent. But I got out of breath way before they did. I need to quit smoking and start jogging (for real). When we were done play-

115

ing, Neil patted me on the butt and blurted out, "You haven't met Buster yet, have you?" When I asked him, "Buster who?" he said Buster Hymen. Hank told him to shut up. My face turned red as a cherry (pun intended). How could he tell I'm still a virgin? Was I bending over THAT far?

March 11, 1978

Bought a car. It's not pretty, a 1972 shit-brown Dodge Duster. It'll get me around (not a Mustang, but for $400, what do I expect?) Haven't totally quit smoking. Cut down a bit. Jogged around the block twice without stopping. Didn't hit anything.

Not going to Florida for Spring Break. BIG BUMMER! Have to get wisdom teeth yanked instead. The oral surgeon says they're severely impacted. I am severely impacted by missing Ft. Lauderdale. Tons of people are going, including Sturge and Hank.

April 15 1978

Worked backstage for the Jackson Browne concert last night. Everybody in his band was really nice, just so normal. I guess I expected them to treat me like the hired help that I am and order me around. Jackson Browne is gorgeous!! I took extra towels and ice into his dressing room, and when he found out we had racquetball courts in the building, he asked me to show him where they were. He and a couple of guys in the band played racquetball for almost two hours after their show. My life is practically glamorous compared to high school. If I'm not a celebrity, at least I'm meeting them (okay, and cleaning up after them).

April 17, 1978

GOT ASKED OUT! Was doing my building walk-through, and Brad Highland just came up and started talking to me. He's a sophomore wide receiver and like a lot of the guys, has a nickname. They call him "Catch" because of a Hail Mary touchdown pass he caught freshman year to win against B.G.

Catch is quite a catch. He has smoky blue eyes and better lips than Al Pacino. He's not real tall, five foot ten and kind of soft-spoken, not cocky like some of the jocks. Not sure where we are going, he said "a movie or something." After my Cinemas job, I've seen enough movies to last me a lifetime.

April 18, 1978
Horrible news. Hank says he's pretty sure Catch has a girl-friend back home in Fostoria. Other than that, he says he's a pretty good guy. I'm keeping the date and will get the whole scoop myself.

Getting very tired of living at home. Would love to live on campus. Good thing I don't. I'd probably hang out in the jock dorm and flunk out from partying.

April 19, 1978
Been nervous all week about the BIG DATE. My face is zit-city. Using industrial amounts of Clearasil. Please God, enough with the humility lesson. May be exaggerating, but it really is a lot better than in high school. Okay, thank you, God, for that.

Prepared Dad for Catch's earring, explained that all the rookie players get either a Rocket tattoo or pierce an ear as a sign of camaraderie. Dad gave me the story about lemmings following each other off the cliff, but laughed. So I guess he's O.K. Mom actually got a program from a recent UT game to look at Catch's photo. Dad checked out his stats. Lori says she's seen him on campus and thinks he's cute. Told Sue about Catch's possible girlfriend. She said, "So what. He'll like you better and dump her." THAT is a friend.

April 22, 1978
I'M DEFINITELY IN LOVE! Catch took me to The

Ottawa Tavern to watch Loved By Millions, a great dance band. Except we didn't even dance. Catch was really sore from practice. So we talked instead. Catch told me he's been wanting to ask me out for months. But he was afraid to because of Hank and Sturge and the guys, since they watch out for me. He said one of the players asked Sturge if he was bangin' me and Sturge said "No, I'm bangin' your mother," and decked him.

"It's kind of a sister/brother thing with these guys," I told Catch.

We have this unbelievable connection, like an invisible string connects our eyeballs. It's like a staring contest with no loser. Catch is sweet and shy, in a small town way. Strong and vulnerable at the same time (great combination). He admitted getting intimidated by some of the bigger guys and thinks he should gain some weight, but it would affect his speed, which is more important in his position.

He asked me why I didn't have a boyfriend (as though it were my choice). I spilled my guts about my datelessness. He couldn't believe it. I asked him about THE GIRLFRIEND. He said they're broken up. She goes to junior college in Fostoria. I wasn't sure I believed him at first. But after making out in the car for over an hour, I'm convinced he wants to be with me. He also knows the other guys would kill him if he screwed me over.

April 24, 1978

Catch's roommate, Stan, is in my Biology class. He says Catch really likes me, and talks about me a lot. He and Catch went to high school together in Fostoria. Stan says Catch's ex-girlfriend is kind of psycho. He breaks up with her and then she stalks him until they get back together. When he broke up with her last fall, she just showed up at a dorm party and dumped a pitcher of beer on a girl he was talking to. The girl was at the party with another guy, not Catch. She and Catch got back together over the holidays and he broke it off again in January.

Catch called last night and invited me to a dorm party. Mom wants to know if we need to get me on "the pill." Guess she took one look at my face after the date and drew a quick conclusion. I told her I knew where Planned Parenthood is if I ever needed it. She seemed relieved. Glo's not ready to have grandkids before 40.

May 5, 1978

Several weeks of bliss, with the exception of Biology. I talk to Stan about Catch through entire lectures. Got a C on the mid-term (no surprise). Think Stan has a crush on me. Not my type (now that I have a type: Catch). We've all been hanging out at The Cavern, a little dive bar with a great jukebox and fifty cent drafts. Sturge and I have a couple of dance routines we do to the Animal House songs. We always end up doing the "gator" on the floor.

Lori and Sue went with us last night and can't wait to go again. Sue says she thinks Catch is in love with me, too, by the way he looks at me. Still don't need to be on the pill. Never seem to be alone with Catch. Stan is ALWAYS around at the dorm room.

May 26, 1978

Got an A on my Abnormal Psych term paper: "Post–Traumatic Stress Disorder as a Cause for Psychosis." To celebrate, Lori and I skipped afternoon classes and drank half the day away watching "Greeks on the Green," a fraternity/sorority thing. Lori and I called it Geeks on the Green, a lame game event.

Ran into Catch. Okay, we were drunk and we went to the dorm. Stan wasn't there. We had a couple more beers and Lori (thanks, Sis) left, to get a ride with Mom. Catch and I got hot and heavy. But didn't go TOO far. I had this vision of Catch's girlfriend first pounding in the door, then pounding in my head. It kind of killed the mood.

July 5, 1978

Bummer of a summer, so far. Catch is in Fostoria working construction with his uncle. He called once with an apology for not calling. Said he's too tired every day to drive to Toledo to see me and then drive back. I'm afraid he's back with psycho-girl. Hank and Jesse are in Cleveland. Sturge is still here, but he's taking a lot of classes so he can graduate on time next year, with the rest of the guys. As soon as he's done with finals we're driving to Ocean City for the weekend. Hank might go, too.

I'm on hiatus from dream job since there's not much traffic going through Centennial Hall during the summer, and I wanted something full time.

Joyce, my friend in the placement office, helped get me a job on the grounds crew. I'm the only chick on the crew, so I don't have to do heavy stuff. But I get plenty of shit jobs the guys don't want. My boss loves to give me weeding jobs. I've weeded every flowerbed on campus at least once. Tomorrow I have to go over to the University President's house and weed there. Hear his wife is an uptight priss and they go through help like Zsa Zsa through husbands. Guys on the crew are joking, asking what color dress I'll wear to weed.

August 12, 1978

Worked the Linda Ronstadt concert last night. Concert was great, but she's a little weird. She talked in baby talk to everybody and ran around playing tag and yelling, "You're it!" Guess you can act however you want when you're famous.

August 21, 1978

Ocean City was a blast. Hank couldn't go (think he's seeing someone in Cleveland, another back-home girlfriend in the making?). So it was just Sturge and me. Sturge says I'm so easy to talk to. I feel the same way about him. On the surface, he's this big, happy-go-lucky, funny guy. But he is really kind of lonely. He wants a girlfriend and says he wants to get married and have kids someday. Most guys just don't come out and tell you this stuff. He says he just hasn't met the right one. After the twelve-hour drive and a case of beer at the beach Friday night, I felt closer to Sturge than anyone, ever. We both decided we were perfect for each other and we should be more than friends.

We cuddled in bed the first night in Ocean City and even made out a little. But despite the alcohol, it seemed weird from the start and we just stopped after a couple minutes and looked at each other and laughed. Talk about kidding ourselves.

September 22, 1978
CATCH'S GIRLFRIEND ENROLLED AT UT!
Hank told me everybody at football practice gave him a hard time about it. They're calling Melanie "The Stalker." Catch swears they are still broken up and he couldn't keep her from coming to UT. He says he still wants to date me and asked me to go to the Marshall Tucker concert with him at B.G. in a couple weeks. In the meantime he says we should lay low because of Melanie.

Need to focus on school and try to forget about Catch and Stalker. Taking a news-editing class and going to write some articles for *The Collegian*. Pitched an idea for a feature to the editor and he said, "Go for it." Going to write about the General Hospital phenomenon. At 3 p.m. every day the Student Union gets packed with GH fans. Stan says it's the same way at the dorms, even the jock dorm. People even schedule their classes around it.

October 2, 1978
Bizzaro! Stalker Melanie is stalking me (I think). She is my new co-worker at Centennial. No warning from anyone on this. She just showed up, and my boss introduced us. She said she already knew who I was. She told me Stan says I'm really nice. She was suspiciously extra sappy-sweet to me and talked about Catch as if they were definitely together. She is absolutely

gorgeous. Blonde and flawless. No wonder Catch puts up with the stalking. She's got to know something about me and Catch. Think she might be plotting a freak accident, like a shove down the stairs. Told Sturge about it. He said I need to bulk up so I can take her if she tries to deck me.

He was joking, but it wouldn't hurt me to build up my pecs some. (And it might create an illusion of boobs). Sturge is going to meet me in the weight room tomorrow to show me how to use the Nautilus machines. Lori is more freaked out than I am about Melanie. She thinks I might really get murdered or something. I told her this isn't the movie *Carrie*. She says it's not *I Love Lucy*, either.

October 10, 1978
Went to the Marshall Tucker concert on Sunday with Stan instead of Catch. It was Catch's idea. Very bummed. He said it was probably no coincidence that Melanie is working with me, so she can keep an eye on both of us. He said it would be best not to piss off Melanie, even though he told her we were just friends. So, I've lost Catch (like I ever had him). Not going to get passed off to Stan. Melanie is still way too nice. Says she wants to go to lunch together sometime. Says she hasn't made many new friends since she's been at UT. Think her strategy is to kill me with kindness, instead of violence.

My General Hospital article made the front page of *The Collegian*.

October 25, 1978
The guys have been great, trying to help me get over Catch. Either Hank or Sturge tell me the plans for every upcoming weekend (unless there's an away game). Most away games I'm scheduled to work concerts anyway. Last night we went to Charlie's Blind Pig and got pretty toasted. Then we went to The *Rocky Horror Picture Show*. There were eight of us altogether. I was the only chick. I'd never been before, but the guys brought all this

stuff, such as squirt guns and newspapers and they didn't tell me why. Everybody in the audience was so into it, with props and costumes. Hank says it's like that every week. Couldn't hear the dialogue. But the songs were great. After the movie we went back to Hank and Jesse's. I slept on the couch (again). They made me go to church with them this morning, which wasn't too terrible. The campus chapel is not at all like St. Peter's. Mom and Dad were beside themselves with excitement about the church thing. They love these guys almost as much as I do.

Still wonder why these guys want to hang around me. They tell me I'm "one of the guys." It's more like I'm their little sister, though, which is interesting, 'cause Hank and Jesse come from all-boy families and Sturge is an only child. Still feel closest to Sturge. Think I've felt some chemistry with Hank since I met him. But he's never tried anything. He's had plenty of chances.

November 6, 1978

I am totally over Catch. Jesse's brother, Tony, was in town. He goes to school at Northwestern, in Illinois. He's every bit as good looking as Jesse, only a little taller and with a wickedly dry sense of humor. Friday night we hung out at the apartment. I showed them how to play Polish Euchre. Later that night, when I was coming out of the bathroom, Tony was standing outside the door and just grabbed me and started kissing me (nobody else saw).

Everybody eventually went to bed. Tony insisted I share the couch with him (although I could have walked across the hall to Sturge's couch). It didn't go much past making out, and I suppose the boys told him about my virginal status quo. Wished they'd stop protecting me so much. It felt great to fall asleep in his arms (that's a first). Called in sick to work Saturday morning (another first), then came home and slept most of the day.

Saturday night Jesse and Hank had a huge party. Tony stayed in arm's reach all night.

Sturge caught Tony and me making out in the hall and told us to get a room. Then he said, "Seriously, you can use my bedroom and I'll sleep on the couch." I was kind of surprised, but then it made sense, 'cause Sturge sometimes jokes with me about being a virgin.

"They've got a cure for that now," he says.

Eight days away from my 19th birthday and I'm still not cured. Think both Tony and I wanted to, but we both passed out soon after hitting Sturge's waterbed. Tony had to leave Sunday to get back to school. Says he'll call and will try to get back to Toledo soon. Probably just as well that nothing (almost) happened. Think I should be in love for real. I want a REAL boyfriend to cure me.

January 12, 1979

Another holiday season without a boyfriend. I hopped on a plane Christmas day to Ft. Lauderdale. Mom and Dad were flabbergasted. But I'm sick of Lori and Sherry having boyfriends over for every occasion. I hoped to run into Craig. Didn't. But Marie invited me over for Christmas dinner with her family. The weather was fantastic and we partied four nights in a row. But now my tan is fading as fast as my good mood.

Definitely moving south once I graduate, if I don't freeze to death first. Got frostbite on my toes walking in knee-deep snow across campus. My suede boots got wet and froze. On a good note: Finally declared a major. Taking more communication and journalism classes, so public relations is a good choice (according to my school advisor).

January 20, 1979

Have hardly seen Sturge, Hank, or Jesse the last month. They've all buckled down to try to get their grade-point averages up for the last two quarters of school. (I've got another two years to work on mine.) Worst of all, Tony has not called.

Lori is heavily dating Scott, and Sue is dating Jim, the perpetual phys ed major (six years and still no degree) who will barely let her out of his sight.

If it weren't for working concerts, I wouldn't be doing much on weekends these days. Of course, Tony hasn't called, but Jesse says it's because he's doing sports broadcasts for Northwestern's campus radio station. Very busy. Very likely.

February 12, 1979
Thinking about starting an anti-Valentine's day campaign. "Massacre the Day, better yet, just forget it." Only Valentine I ever got was in sixth grade, Tommy Haupriecht. Wonder what he's doing now? Ran into Jesse at U-Hall. He said Sturge and Hank are setting up job interviews, even though graduation is months away. I asked him how Tony is doing. He said "really busy" which is code for "he's not going to call."

I remember a cheesy poster in Sister Susan's sixth-grade class: "When life gives you lemons, make lemonade." I think I prefer to juggle them for amusement. Could use a little amusement right now.

March 18, 1979
Sturge hasn't called me for a month. I've left him a couple of messages and he hasn't called back. I miss talking to him (and the other guys). I'm not going to Florida for spring break. No one to go with. Sherry invited me to go with her on their senior trip. But her friends seem so young. It's hard to believe she's almost 18.

April 2, 1979
Well, Sue's getting married in September to the perpetual phys ed major who hates all her friends. Says she wants me in the wedding, but Jim doesn't. Says once they get married Jim WILL HAVE TO BE NICER TO HER FRIENDS. Not sure she actually believes it. I don't.

Had lunch with Melanie. She's trying to think of one of

125

Catch's friends to fix me up with. How ironic. Even more ironic, I do like her and don't see any more psychotic behavior in her than I do in most of my friends (past and present). We're all just survivors of post-traumatic stress disorder, which is my new justification.

April 27, 1979

It's two months until the beginning of summer. For the first time in my life, I don't care. It's less than two months until I say goodbye to the best friends and best two years of my entire life.

"Goodbye to the boys of winter who rescued me from the cold, who warmed me with their spirit and whose friendship gave me hope." I do get melodramatic. It's not like I'll never see these guys again. It's just that things are changing. I'm usually in favor of change.

May 5, 1979

Was in Charlie's Blind Pig, and ran into Sturge. He was with Betsy Lidel, a bitchy cheerleader from high school. He barely talked to me until she went into the bathroom. He apologized for falling off the face of the earth. Then he said. "Betsy says she and your sister Lori never got along in high school and, well, she also doesn't get us being friends. She says the only guy friends she's had are boyfriends."

I was in shock and he could tell. He tried to cheer me up. "Hey, we'll all get together and party soon. She'll love you like we all do."

May 9, 1979

Hank called and invited me to their Last Gasp for Freedom Party (sort of a pre-graduation party). It's like a M*A*S*H, military theme. Supposed to come in full camouflage. Good plan. Maybe I can hide from the truth, too.

My friend Joyce, in the UT placement office, called me

about this great summer job. It's working with Owens-Illinois (glass company) promoting "the good taste of bottled beer." I have an interview set for Monday. Sounds a helluva lot better than whacking weeds.

May 12, 1979

Sherry reminded me that she starts at UT next year. I know little sis and I haven't been very close the last couple of years. We've kind of been living in different worlds (I was wrong about college. It IS vastly different from high school). Guess I've always treated her like the baby of the family. Invited her to go the M*A*S*H party at Hank's with me tonight. Doing another bridal show next week. Think I'll invite Sue, so I can model the bridesmaid dresses that I won't be wearing in her wedding.

May 13, 1979

Hank really hit it off with Sherry. But Hank loves everybody and so does Sherry, with the exception of Betsy Lidel. Predictably dressed like nurse, "Hot Lips" hung around Hawkeye Sturge's neck like a stethoscope all night. Jesse and Carla announced their engagement. Another one bites the dust.

Everyone stayed almost all night. It was like nobody wanted to leave (especially me) because we know life will never be the same again after graduation. Wish I were graduating, too. It's going to be very strange without the guys. Cried when we left. Sherry tried to make me feel better, said we'll check out the new crop of football players together next year.

I'll be sure to screen them for back-home girlfriends.

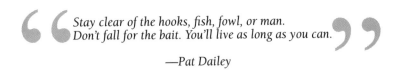

> *Stay clear of the hooks, fish, fowl, or man.*
> *Don't fall for the bait. You'll live as long as you can.*
>
> —Pat Dailey

P U T - I N - B A Y

AKE ERIE'S SOUTH BASS ISLAND LIES OFF the north coast of Ohio, a few miles from the peninsula of Cedar Point, home of the famous amusement park of the same name. The Island's small town, Put-In-Bay, has become famous for its own form of amusement, which is mostly poured from bottles and cans.

There's no debate that increased ferry service in the 1970s changed the island. Anyone with five bucks for a ferry ticket could visit a unique row of bars, including the longest bar in the world. Add the dynamic of underage drinking, which at the time was treated about as seriously as Yogi Bear stealing picnic baskets. *Bears will be bears and teenagers will drink.* Put-In-Bay went from a fishing retreat to Woodstock—without the bad acid—quicker than Country Joe and the Fish could say give me an "F." Oh yeah, there reportedly was a lot of that "F" stuff going on amidst all the drinking, too. Imagine that. The lure of the island was enhanced in the late '70s (and still is) by a folk singer-gone-bar-raunchy by the name of Pat Dailey, the Jimmy Buffet of the Great Lakes.

My best friend from college, Nick Sturgis, "Sturge," alleged that Put-In-Bay invented the cure for virginity. He called it Put-Out-Bay. It was early summer 1979, and I was approaching 20 with my virginity intact. I was brooding over a different loss—friendship. Sturge had recently begun dating a girl who didn't know me well enough to hate me, but she did anyway. She told Sturge she didn't understand how he could have a best friend who happened to be a girl. She was clearly Yoko, and I was now a solo act. Sue, my other ex-best friend, was marrying a guy who wanted her to be his prisoner of love, with no visitors, as he decidedly hated all her friends. As a result, I was stuck re-acquainting myself with the family dog, Sam, and Gilligan reruns.

Luckily, I have a survival instinct that often accompanies my darker moods. Unlike Gilligan, my idea was to escape *to* an island, rather than *from* one. This time the plan was easy: tag-along with my sister and her boyfriend to Put-In-Bay. My summer job prohibited anything more exotic, since I had no time off except weekends.

I couldn't complain much about the "time on." I figured it was the best summer job available in Toledo. "Field Promotional Representative for Owens-Illinois, Inc., Glass Container Division" is what my card read. I was responsible for promoting the good taste of beer in bottles. I was passionate about my work and proved it to bar owners, beer distributors, route drivers, and store managers every day. With hard work and truth in advertising, I decided I could be successful in increasing bottle sales vs. can sales by summer's end. Being on the "beer crew" saved me from being on the "grounds crew" at the University of Toledo, my summer job the previous year. Promoting beer drinking beats whacking weeds all day long.

LORI AND SCOTT FILLED ME IN ON PUT-IN-BAY traditions and etiquette as we stood in line for the oldest bar at the bay, The Roundhouse Bar, built in 1873. As the name would indicate, the building is round. The bar was (and still is) famous for buckets of beer—not bottles. The bar was wall to wall. With feet flailing in attempted dance moves, gallons of beer splashed over the bucket sides and slopped onto the floor. Mix the beer with the squishing of hundreds of feet on cigarette butts and dirt, and you end up with a finely ground, black lacquer-like substance that covered the entire floor of the bar.

"There it is, DC," Lori said, pointing to the floor, "the bar-slop I was telling you about."

Lori had a theory that it was this bar-slop that put a spell on people. Concentrated liquid doses of full moon and Mardi Gras seeping up through sandaled feet. A powerful aphrodisiac and a helluva paint thinner.

"If you fall down in it, you'll never get the stains out of your clothes," said Scott.

"Or off your soul," Lori added.

After we finished our first bucket of beer, Scott and Lori insisted I put the bucket on my head.

"All Put-In-Bay virgins must wear a bucket on their heads at The Roundhouse."

The tradition referred to first-time visitors, of course, not sexually intact ones. I put the bucket on my head for, unfortunately, I qualified in both senses.

A green-eyed, freckle-faced, lanky, grown-up Will Robinson-"Lost-in-Space" look-alike stepped into my small space in the bar.

"There's something about a girl with a bucket on her head. Makes me crazy," he said, with a wink and a smile. "Wanna dance?"

I removed the bucket and fluffed my Farrah hair self-consciously as we twisted across the floor, bar-slop oozing over my Docksiders.

Great, now I'm going to have bucket hair.

We mirrored each other's dance moves and were forced closer together as the crowd moved to the music. As often accompanies virgin experiences, time and space became distorted. Our eyes embraced in a tango while our bodies barely touched. Halfway into "Soul Man," I was pretty sure I'd met my soulmate. At least for the night.

Swishing our way through bodies and bar-slop back to Lori and Scott, our dancing slowed and our eyes didn't miss a beat.

"Here, we got a table," Scott said.

"There was a couple sitting here making out and Scott gave them ten dollars to leave," Lori said.

"It won't buy 'em a room, but they can get a six-pack and go make out in the park," Scott pointed out, with sound logic.

As I listened to them talk, I watched Will Robinson. His green shirt reflected the green in his eyes. While I was betting myself he was Irish, "Brian Callahan" introduced himself.

We did likewise.

"Did you know you have a hole in your shirt?" Lori asked Brian.

Sure enough, there was a small hole on the left-breast side, which I hadn't noticed before. He smiled.

"Yeah, I know. It's an Izod shirt. Izod makes nice shirts, but the stupid alligators are so, well, predictably preppy. I just cut them out of the shirts."

Scott, Lori, and I all exchanged looks of approval.

"Brian, trust me when I say this, you and DC are definitely cut from the same cloth," Lori said.

The Stanfa family humor, while generally sarcastic, occasionally works in a good pun.

We eventually left the bar for a quieter retreat at another bar, The Boat House. Unlike the fitting name of the Round

House, this bar is not shaped like a boat, nor does it resemble a house. Our conversation there revealed that Brian was 25, lived in Cleveland, and was a lawyer. He and his friends were renting a cottage for the weekend on the island. The non-verbal exchanges between Brian and me revealed a lot more. Legs touching under the table, his hand on my knee, my hand on his, fingers stroking fingers.

When Lori announced, "It's almost midnight. If we're going to catch the last ferry we need to get going soon," my boat, I mean heart, sunk.

Brian threw me a lifesaver.

"How about staying with us? There's always room on the floor."

Lori, being an oldest child, spoke for the group. "Thanks, but we really need to get back."

For what? So she and Scott can get cozy at his house, where she's already spending enough time?

In a whiny, middle-child attempt to have it my way, I begged, "Please?"

Since Scott had driven, and Toledo was an hour drive from the ferry dock on the mainland, I explained I would have no choice but to go with them.

"Stay and I'll drive you back tomorrow." Brian's eyes glowed at me like neon signs in the bar, charged with currents of unrequited lust and hope.

I was plugged in.

Lori's casual shrug told me she trusted Brian with her little sis.

But Scott, sometimes too logical, persisted, "Brian, you live in Cleveland. That's an hour east of here, and Toledo is an hour west. That's two hours out of your way."

His quick calculation relieved any doubt that he was sober enough to drive. But I was ready to give him ten dollars to get a six-pack and go make out somewhere with Lori.

"No problem," Brian said.

Lori was unusually supportive.

"Tell you what, Deece. Have him drop you off at Scott's in the morning. I'll call mom and tell her you're staying with us tonight."

AFTER LORI AND SCOTT LEFT, BRIAN AND I walked across the street to the park and made out on top of and then underneath a playground slide. As we paused to catch our breath, Brian said, "You know, you look like That Girl."

"What girl?"

"You know, that old TV show, "That Girl," Marlo Thomas."

"How many beers have you had?" I laughed, but made sure I left out the part about him looking like Will Robinson, just in case he wouldn't take it as a compliment.

On the way to the cottage, I expressed my disappointment in not seeing Pat Dailey.

"It's twenty minutes until closing time at The Beer Barrel, but let's go poke our heads in anyway," he suggested.

The longhaired, bearded man in jeans, T-shirt, and black leather vest had the crowd on their feet, laughing and singing along to every song. The lyrics were filled with sexual double meanings, as if the sexual energy on the island needed any more fuel. And we had our own fuel, lightly groping each other as we groped our way in the dark to the cottage.

His friends were already there, seven of them: two couples, and three "uncoupled" guys. They were sitting around the kitchen table playing liar's poker. Brian introduced me and pulled a few dollar bills from his wallet.

"We're in," he said.

We switched to blackjack for even higher stakes. I opted to watch, not wanting to lose the little bit of money I had left. Sensing my reason, Brian offered me a twenty, which I politely refused. Brian's friends were older than me, like him, and had "careers." The card games continued until four in the morning, when the beer was gone. The other two couples got the two bedrooms. Two guys shared a sofa-bed, and one grabbed the couch. Brian took cushions off the sofa-bed couch and made a cozy bed for us in the corner of the living room.

"This will be more comfortable than the sofa-bed I slept on it last night. It killed my back."

His big arms wrapped around me and we began heavy breathing exercises. After just a few horizontal minutes, our synchronized sizzling was doused by satanic sounds coming from the bathroom. Someone was quite devotedly praying to the porcelain god of he-who-has-drank-way-too-much.

Our passionate moods shattered—and still fully clothed— Brian and I faded off. Slow, rhythmic breathing gave way to synchronized sleeping, in this case, a non-competitive event.

ON THE FERRY THE NEXT MORNING, completely sober, I was as wanton as a wench in a romance novel. Brian kept his arm around me and kissed my ear as the large vessel lurched forward—of course, I'm referring to THE BOAT.

I was thinking about what happened the night before but looking into Brian's eyes I knew we were both thinking about what didn't happen and wondering if, and when, it would. The power of unrequited lust was microwaveable: Left alone on high, in three minutes, corn would be poppin'.

"You know, we could get a room in Port Clinton," he whispered.

"I know, but I have to get back."

"Probably the best thing would be to at least take you out to dinner first." He looked at me with a combination of sincerity and just a tad of sarcasm.

134

"And you'll respect me in the morning?" I winked as I threw this old standard line at him.

"It's morning, and I respect you now." He pulled me closer and hugged me tight.

When we reached Brian's car, a large blue Buick sedan, I noticed government license plates.

"What gives? I thought you were a lawyer."

"I am, I work for the government."

"Doing what?"

"I can't tell you." Although he wasn't smiling, I figured he was kidding.

"If you told me, you'd have to kill me, right?"

"No, seriously, DC, I can't even tell you which branch of the government I work for."

He *wasn't* kidding.

"Uh, O.K." I said, quite taken aback. "But it is OUR government, right? Daddy wouldn't want me cavorting with a foreign agent."

Brian's eyes were focused on the road, but he swung his right arm around my shoulders and pulled me toward him. "Just know I'm here to serve and protect you," he said.

When he kissed me goodbye, I held back, only because I had not brushed my teeth—as I hadn't anticipated staying at The Bay with someone I just met. Yet as he drove away I felt a twinge of sadness; I was afraid I might not see him again.

Life quickly turned blissful again as Brian called every day that week and drove to Toledo the following weekend. Scott and Lori offered to let us stay with them. By the time Brian came to pick me up Friday night, I already considered him my full-fledged boyfriend. I had never felt this sure about someone.

Mom and Dad had high hopes, too. He wasn't just a college kid. He was a lawyer and worked in some secretive area in the government. Brian arrived, still dressed in his suit. On this Mystery Date, I picked the dreamboat instead of the dud.

"Sorry, but I didn't have a chance to change."

"You can change over at Scott's. We're going to pick him up before we go to the restaurant."

Mom offered Brian a beer and as we sat together on the couch, petting Sam, we talked about our favorite movies. Everybody smiled when Brian said his favorite movie was *Butch Cassidy and The Sundance Kid*. Paul Newman was a Stanfa Family favorite. I couldn't have Xeroxed a better picture of the first meeting of parents and boyfriend.

When Brian excused himself to go to the restroom, Dad looked at Mom with wide eyes. "Did you see that, Gloria? He has government-issue shoes and wristwatch."

"He has such a nice smile. I'd have to guess CIA over FBI, wouldn't you, Denny?"

Dad shook his head. "Secret Service," he said, turning up his bottom lip and giving us the two-finger peace sign in a Nixonish impression.

By the second week in the forest of love, I was falling so hard my heart was shouting "Timber!" warnings. My brain comprehended and processed the warning into action. I made an appointment at Planned Parenthood. It was time to go on the pill. Time to prevent certain consequences from the imminent cure for virginity. Brian and I had come very close to doing It, but I couldn't go through with It, because I was sure I'd get pregnant the first time. He wanted to use a rubber but I told him, "That's how my sister Lori was conceived. My mom said they can break."

Brian and I talked on the phone at least an hour every night, and he came to Toledo for the weekend again. Friday was a double date with Lori and Scott. The potent margaritas at Loma Linda's were an unnecessary aphrodisiac, like Spanish fly on prom night. We were already the sappy, eye-gazing, handholding couple I despised in high school.

On the night I was cured, I wanted to call my friend Sturge and tell him, but I was afraid his girlfriend would be there. Instead, I had an imaginary conversation with him. I proudly announced the occasion, and he congratulated me as if I'd just won a racquetball tournament.

"How was it?" he'd say.

And I'd say, "From all the hype it gets, I'd have to say it's sort of overrated."

"Not with me it isn't," Sturge would say. "It's an X-rated experience. I get rave reviews."

And I would laugh like I always do when I talk to Sturge.

I regretted not being able to have that conversation, and I resented Sturge's girlfriend for taking him out of my life. However, the next day, Lori gave me that I-know-you-did-it look. I asked her if she'd heard us, and she said, "Hell no, the air-conditioner in Scott's room is louder than a jet taking off."

When I admitted that, from what I had built it up to be, the actual experience was somewhat anticlimactic, she just said, "Don't worry, it will get better."

As things continued to get better into the heat of July, I voted Brian and me "couple of the year." When he arrived one Friday with a bouquet of flowers, Mom and I exchanged he's-the-one glances. That night, on a solo date at the drive-in, not watching *Star Wars*, I told Brian, "I think I'm falling in love with you."

I was so sure what his answer would be, I wasn't even nervous saying the "L" word first.

"No matter how I feel about you, you have to understand that my job comes first." I didn't exactly feel rejected as he sweetly kissed my face and neck. But I felt a little like Luke Skywalker discovering who his father was.

Later, during the loud, star-splitting special effects, I thought I heard Brian say, "I love you, too. Will you marry me?"

It was actually Obi-Wan Kenobi and I just wasn't interested in him at all.

On the drive back to Scott's love shack and diner, Brian said, sort of matter-of-factly, "You know, whoever I marry will have to go through a whole security clearance routine."

I judged the statement as evidence he did have plans for us after all.

Lawyers just don't throw comments around without meaning something.

Of course, I really didn't know any other lawyers. I told him about my brush with the law, my little driving incident/accident when I was 13. He laughed and said, "Don't mention that you are a Mafia princess and you'll be just fine."

On Sunday we went swimming at the quarry with Scott and Lori. We joked about how bad the jukebox was as we lounged in the hot sun. There were only three decent songs on it, so people kept playing them over and over. The live version of "Free Bird" played so many times that when the lead singer screamed, "What song is it you want to hear," everybody at the quarry would scream, "Not Free Bird."

"I'm going to have some kick-ass tunes at my party next weekend," Brian said.

He was hosting a Christmas-in-July party in Cleveland. Whenever he talked about it, he became really excited and animated, like a kid on Christmas morning. According to Brian, it was an annual event, held the last Saturday in July, and it got bigger and better every year.

"I have to take Friday off because it takes me all day to decorate. I put up a tree on the deck and Christmas lights everywhere. Mistletoe and eggnog in 80 degrees. It's so cool."

I was looking forward to the party as much as Brian was. I couldn't wait to see where he lived, sleep in his bed, and eat his Christmas porridge. I mean, I was finally living the fairy tale, wasn't I?

Thursday evening before the party, Brian called to give me directions. A few minutes into the call, before he'd gotten me past "take the turnpike east toward Cleveland," the call was interrupted.

"Emergency phone call for Brian Callahan," said a nasal operator.

Without hesitating, Brian said, "DC, I'll call you right back."

He did not call right back. By midnight, I was in a full-blown panic. My entire family tried to calm me down. I couldn't call Brian back because he had never given me a phone number. He always called me. He called me every night. I called Information. Since his number was unlisted, they couldn't give it to me. I tried to explain to the operator about the emergency. She said she was sorry, but she couldn't help.

By Friday night, my devastation was lamentable and I took to my bed. Even Sue, my friend imprisoned by her own love choice, paid her respects and attended the visitation. It was a tragedy, and there was no understanding it. Everyone agreed.

No phone calls came. I was in a daze for a month. Mom got a sympathetic female cop at the UT campus security department where she worked to run Brian's license plate number on the "leads" computer. Nothing. I thought I had memorized it correctly. But what did I expect, trying to illegally track a government vehicle?

No answers, no closure, not even a clue. I tried to convince myself that this was simply "the job coming first," and that he was temporarily on an underground assignment. He'd eventually call to explain. But as autumn closed in, I had other thoughts. Maybe the call was from an ex-girlfriend, or a wife he'd failed to mention. Maybe he was cutting me out of his life because I was too predictable, like the Izod alligator.

By November, Lori was still trying to be supportive, yet was tired of my whining. She and Scott were going to fix me up on a blind date with one of his friends. Lori reminded me that nothing lasts forever. She said to take the relationship for what it was—a summer love.

"DC, the magic of the bar slop just wore off."

I tried to find some comfort in that.

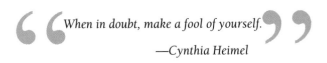

When in doubt, make a fool of yourself.
—Cynthia Heimel

N O   M O R E
F I S H Y   P A R T S

O KAY, YOU CAUGHT ME. I don't know what I was thinking, trying to sneak that by such a smart person as
you, someone with the foresight to purchase this
book. You, who have traveled with me so trustingly, halfway
through the journey of my pages. Along with your incredible
sense of humor, your terrific discernment may have you wondering occasionally throughout this journey, "Did that really
happen? Is this all true?"

Let me assure you, it all really happened and to the best of
my memory is true, except for that last part. Please forgive me
for my perjury, but I did not lose my virginity to Brian Callahan. Don't give up on me now. I won't try to trick you again. At
least let me explain. While the story is ALMOST completely
true, I held back one detail—a technicality. Brian was not my
"first." He was my second cure.

I met Brian, exactly as I said, on South Bass Island and fell
in love for the first time. He also disappeared as mysteriously
as I told you. The trip to Put-In-Bay was really two years later
than I claimed. My first cure was in 1979, as reported—but

by somebody else. Part of me has, and will always be, in denial of this fact. Who hasn't looked back upon a milestone event, which was so disappointing, that they wanted to scream, "I demand a do-over!"

Such is my sad, anti-climactic case. My mind and memory conspired, and re-conjured the story in reverse gynecological and chronological order. Time to put things right with my readers and my conscience.

"It almost didn't count," might seem like a thin membrane of an excuse for distorting such an important fact. The best argument for my defense is that losing my virginity gave me more frustration than relief, hardly a cure. It just "removed the cause, but not the symptoms,"(lyrics from a Rocky Horror Picture Show song).

The summer after my sophomore year, my best friends, the football players, had graduated to off-campus pursuits, like getting married and starting careers. Danny Mazurski was not a football player, or a jock, per se, although we met while I was working at the gym as a building supervisor. If I supervised well, and the building did as it was told, it would still be standing after my shift.

Danny was taking a Saturday racquetball class. He was not handsome, nor particularly charming or witty. He did have a nice smile. Nothing else about him is very memorable, which is what makes this chapter so difficult. Most of my stories aren't about mundane people or average situations. But here comes Danny-the-dud, my destiny. To say that we met during an extreme lull in my life would be an understatement. He helped me out of the gutter and onto the curb, not cloud nine.

It was definitely not love at first sight, a concept I remain skeptical about. However, I've learned not to underestimate the power of desperation and timing. We went out somewhere and did something, maybe even twice.

About a month into our dating we went to a Mazurski family wedding.

It was very Polish, lots of kielbasa and cabbage and beer.

Danny tried to teach me how to dance a proper Polish polka. His mother looked at me with disappointment when it became obvious I wasn't getting it right. That should have flicked the light switch to illuminate the future. My last name didn't end in a ski, and it was all downhill from there.

Apparently, we had some unexplained chemistry between us. Trying to explain hormones never stopped them from taking their toll. Hormones. They should demand immunity from the acts they trigger.

Sorry, your honor, I was really hormonal.

You all nod in sympathy. Been there, done that.

In my case It probably happened because all the hot and heavy almosts ganged up, hormones in hostage overpowering the prison guards of Catholic guilt, short-circuiting any alarms that Danny might not be "the guy." We actually planned to do It after another family wedding (my cousin's).

We rented a room at the Holiday Inn and left the reception before they threw the bouquet. The act itself probably lasted four minutes, if you include foreplay. I thought it was similar to a gynecological exam, with the difference being the instrument used. A little pain, no pleasure—and glad when it's over.

What a waste of a hotel room, I thought, when Danny said it was time to go. I felt as if we were throwing away leftover pizza. It didn't seem right. No cuddling. He didn't want to keep me out all night. While respectful to my parents, he was oblivious to a whole lot more.

A week later we found a remote area of a Metro Park, placed a blanket down beside some bushes, and gave It another go. It was over again, almost before It began.

This time I couldn't blame It completely on Danny. On this hot, steamy August night, at the edge of deep woods and stagnant ponds, our naked, sweaty bodies were bait. And the mosquitoes bit. We were completely swarmed by them. Swatting, swearing, and pulling up pants, we ran back to the car.

I later counted eighty-six mosquito bites as I emptied a

bottle of calamine lotion on them. They are the clearest detail of Danny-dating that I can recall. Funny, looking back. Yet neither of us laughed at the time. I don't remember Danny making me laugh much—which adds to the mystery of why he became my Buster Hymen choice. Of course, I thought I would marry him.

My naiveté at 19, almost 20, came naturally, a result of Catholic upbringing and parents who allowed, that while you may not be a virgin when you marry, you will marry the person you lose it to. I convinced myself that I was dreaming if I thought I'd end up with a gorgeous football player and that Danny was the best I could do (pun intended). And, despite such disastrous beginnings, I was sure the sex would improve. How could it get any worse? I talked myself into believing it. Post-coital guilt may not be a shotgun, but it is a persuasive marriage coercion device, in its own right.

It was an average thought in a world where I expected little, and was willing to settle for even less. So I was devastated when Danny stopped calling after the love-in-the-park incident. When I called him, he broke up with me with the same emotion he exhibited after sex. Time to get out of here, basically. Yet this time he was apparently unconcerned about what my parents might think. I really never got an explanation. Why? Maybe he thought I was a lousy lay.

I recovered from the blow with the help of my sisters, who provided a quick rescue. The most potent anti-venom for snake-in-the-grass bites, and getting dumped, is a trip to the beach. Labor day weekend: twelve hours in a Dodge Duster, Lori and Sherry making me laugh at myself, and what life would have been like down the road as Mrs. Danny Mazurski. Separate bedrooms, my hair tied back in a babushka, sweeping the floor of a house that smells of mothballs and cabbage.

Instead: Asateague Island. Wild horses. A tent. The ocean. The bars and the boardwalk of Ocean City. Cute lifeguards. Family. Peace. And Hope. Always Hope.

ONE OF MY BIGGEST FEARS IN LIFE IS THAT God has a wicked sense of humor and that He will link Danny and me, together in the afterlife, for eternity. I picture everyone paired up with whomever they first had sex with, just because they were the first—and for no other reason. God, the Creator, combining heaven and hell. Grand Producer of the saddest, funniest, longest running reality show ever.

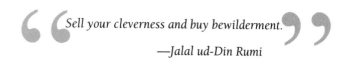

Sell your cleverness and buy bewilderment.
—Jalal ud-Din Rumi

NUTHIN'
BUT A
CARDBOARD
BOX

I SELL CORRUGATED BOXES FOR A LIVING; an odd occupation for a woman, considering all the jokes. "My wife can't wrestle but you oughta see her box" is one of the favorites. But, as they said in Dallas, which was my newest home, "that's the God's honest truth."

How I got from Toledo to Texas is, well, I talked my way there. I don't mean panhandling or hitchhiking. Although that's what I *would* have done, if necessary, to get out of Toledo. But, with the guidance of good parents and other angel allies, I not only didn't drop out of school or end up in prison like some of my grade school nuns had predicted, I went to college and graduated with a degree in public relations, and a double major in partying.

When the college fun was over, I looked around me and understood I was still in Tooleedoo (as we locals fondly call it). So during a job interview at Owens-Illinois when I was asked if I'd be willing to relocate, I stomped my foot and crossed my arms, looked the personnel director in the eye, and said, "I *demand* to relocate."

He laughed, presuming I was kidding.

Ironically, when I was finished with my training at the tech-center and corporate marketing in Toledo, the personnel director called me in his office and said, "Good news, there's a sales territory that opened up here. You don't have to move."

"You have to be kidding me. I told you I'VE GOT TO MOVE!" I practically shouted. "Please, get me out of Toledo!"

I found out through the grapevine that a territory in Texas was also open. However, the company was reluctant to send me there for several reasons: I was a rookie, a Yankee, and a female. Truth is, it was a risk, especially for industrial/packaging sales in the early '80s, the Good-Old-Boy network (G.O.B.'s) still being the driving force of commerce in the south. I had a pretty good inkling that I could be persuasive once I successfully talked my way out of the proverbial paper bag, and into selling boxes in Dallas.

The PR/journalism degree wasn't exactly going to be put to good use in the box job, but the money was a lot better. I could have earned $11,000 a year working at a community paper or $18,000 with the sales gig. I was as excited about the money as I was about the move. *Look out Good-Old-Boys, here comes a Bad-New-Girl!*

THE HARDEST PART OF ANY MOVE IS SAYING GOODBYE, unless you are moving yourself and have to get a sofa bed up to the third floor during an ice storm. I remember the look in my parents' eyes just before getting on the plane. It was truly painful.

"Let's pretend I'm just going on a long vacation."

"Right. And you can come home any time," Mom said.

The thing is I only got home a few times a year. Although I did still feel like I was on vacation after living in Dallas almost six years. I lived in Toledo for the first twenty-one years of my life, and if anyone asks, I grew up in Dallas. And I wasn't planning on moving back anytime soon, at least, I said, until I'd ridden all the rides. As they say, that's the God's honest truth.

Speaking of God, I finally got around to reading His book. Not exactly a laugh a minute but awesome stuff nonetheless. I never saw a Bible in Catholic school because the Church felt it should be screened first, then interpreted and packaged (Catholicized) into religion books. I guess every religion likes to think it can think through the Bible for us and then act as spin doctors, ministers, and priests: editors for God.

Texans say that God favored them, but from my experience, I'd have to ask which god. In the five years I lived there, I witnessed the ritualistic pagan worship of different icons and idols; maybe even participated a little myself. The most visible, at least in Texas, were the bad TV evangelists—I'm not being redundant; I *do* believe there are one or two good TV preachers—the money worshipers, and football.

Bad TV evangelists, who seemed to grow better in Texas dirt, had several things in common. Usually black devil eyes, slicked back pompadours, Eddie Haskell grins, and the "come forward and be saveda" accent. They seemed to excel at speaking in tongues and asking for money and scaring little old ladies into sending them their social security money by claiming their "ministry cannot continue without it." Terrified of being left without their leadership, the trusting little old ladies did as the evangelists said.

Another famous god that Texas didn't necessarily have the market cornered on was good old-fashioned money. There are three types of money people. First, is the group that I belong to, the ones that don't have much and need more to buy something other than garage sale furniture.

Then there are the people that have it, the twenty percent
of the population that has eighty percent of the money. There
are two categories of money-havers. Old Money People and
New Money People. Old Money People were born into it, so
they treat it like expensive inherited furniture: they respect it,
but are comfortable enough with it to say, "It's no big deal,
after all, it's just a couch."

Old Money People generally lived in places like Ft. Worth,
stayed home and barbecued brisket instead of going out some-
place *trés chic*, and the men still wore cowboy boots with their
business suits.

In Dallas, Old Money People had better sense than to hang
around the New Money People, who'd been imported from
other states to mess with Texas for awhile, then leave. They'd
take a ride on the high-tech roulette wheel while driving BMWs
on their way to Neiman Marcus, or to the private clubs, or to
score some coke. They wore their money like a bad toupee.
OK, I am being redundant: There are no *good* toupees.

The way they spent their money could be coincidentally
just as ugly, except New Money People didn't see it that way.
They thought they were the beautiful people because the other
nouveaux riches, also into self-worship, validated their beliefs.

There's a big god Texas likes to think they *do* have the market cornered on: FOOTBALL. SMU, Texas Tech, University
of Texas, "Hook 'em horns," and on and on.

You may wonder what interest a girl from Toledo, Ohio,
had in Texas football. Two words: Dallas Cowboys. It's no coincidence that I lived in Dallas, nor was it the luck of the draw
that I lived in an apartment complex inhabited by all the Dallas Cowboy rookies. I already explained how I got to Dallas.
I have to thank an in-the-know woman at an apartment locat-
ing service for the rest.

The apartment complex where I lived was in Addison,
north of downtown. Located in a high rent district, I felt safe,
but it was one more reason I couldn't afford store-bought fur-

niture. The complex had a workout room, racquetball courts, a clubhouse with a bar, and hot and cold running backs.

My affinity for jocks developed in college so I don't think I was being *entirely* superficial. Some women prefer men with liquid assets; I happen to appreciate solid buttocks. *Carpe Gluteus Maximus.*

One of my favorite things about football was the uniform. Make that the pants. They made me pant, begging for an open-palmed pat. If I could be coach for a day, the quarterback could just relax. I'd have made all the passes.

Unfortunately, the football player fantasy remained unfulfilled, except for a cute wide-receiver in college whom I dated but failed to get into the end zone with.

In reality, Dallas Cowboys dated Dallas Cowboy Cheerleader-types, super-models, or were married to the super-wife, super-mom type. I was just a girl from Toledo who sold boxes, so technically I could never be in anything but the dream zone. On the other hand, at least I had enough imagination to get myself there, where I could lie out by the pool in February and go out to fun bars any night of the week.

I didn't go out *every* night. It was tempting, but going out to clubs gets very expensive, and I *did* have other things to consider, such as getting up for work in the mornings. I was on what I called the break-even system physical fitness program. I either played racquetball or ran almost every day. This allowed me to feel less guilt over drinking and smoking (I still smoked, although only when I was drinking). Poison in, poison out.

WHEN I FIRST MOVED TO DALLAS it was pretty rough, not knowing anyone. I remember Dad telling me throughout my life, "When it gets too rough for everybody else, it's just about right for us Stanfas." I knew I had to tough it out even though

I felt truly alone for the first time in my life. The situation was similar to when I felt friendless in high school, but in high school I still lived with my family and had their shoulders to cry on. I credit my mom for giving me some of the best advice of my life, which served me particularly well, especially after the move to big "D."

"Go entertain yourself," she'd say when I moped around and complained I was bored. She meant that friends and activities don't just show up, you have to make some effort. I learned how to entertain myself at an early age, and later on I learned how to entertain others, which helped me make friends.

I started entertaining myself in Dallas by hanging out at the clubhouse and playing racquetball. I also talked to the bartender and apartment manager about helping with parties. I quickly became the unofficial social director and put together theme parties. My favorite theme was the "tacky" party. I got the idea when I started a tacky collection, beginning with a velvet Elvis painting and Joan Crawford paper dolls.

Other people at the complex donated decorations, including a picture of dogs playing cards. Everybody wore polyester and mismatched thrift store clothes. A lime-green leisure suit won first prize. We served tacky food, Spam and Cheez-Whiz, and played Barry Manilow and Captain and Tennille tapes.

In the process of entertaining myself and others, I made friends and dated a couple of the guys at the apartment complex. It was weird when you dated the neighbor and people saw him coming out of your apartment the next morning, and then a month later, he was dating another girl at the complex, and ditto. It was like a recycling program. When you got kicked to the curb, someone else was waiting.

I made eight really good friends, which was like having sisters without a sorority. They were all transplants, and like me, starting their careers.

My best friend, Jamie, was born and raised in Alabama, and taught me a lot about southern living, including the culture, the men, and the humor in it all. She told me that there were two girls for every man in Dallas, but, she said, "They're worth scrapping for." The guys were incredibly good-looking. It was as if there was some corporate casting call that went out for all the best looking guys from all over the country.

Jamie was fun and easy-going, except when it came to stupid people. She could not tolerate stupidity and called it when she saw it, even in me. For example, she thought my fantasy for football players was completely moronic.

"What is so great about the game of football?"

"I get excited by the raw emotion in it, and in the players."

"My 3-year-old nephew has more raw emotion *and* a higher I.Q. Do you want to date him?"

I was stumped.

Overall, though, I knew Jamie thought I was pretty smart. We were both readers and connected on a more intellectual level than a lot of my other friends. One of my peeves is smart women who dumb down to be more attractive to men. It irritated me even more when it worked.

There were enough totally dumb chicks in Dallas without adding the fake bimbos into the competition. According to Jamie, there were enough bimbos in Dallas that if you laid them end-to-end they'd cover the entire outer beltway. She suggested we do just that, and leave them there through rush hour.

"That'll thin out some big hair," she said.

It was bad enough that I had to deal with the competition in my job. The angle I'd chosen in both business and the dating scene was to just be myself—a shameless opportunist. My timing in getting into the box business was actually good. Buyers were getting smarter and seeing through the glad-handing G.O.B.'s. I've figured out that my straight-forwardness is appreciated, which earned the trust of a buyer. With the first sale I made, the buyer asked me, "Do you want to know why I'm giving you this order?"

"Sure."

"Because you are too green to play the game."

I chose to take it as a compliment rather than a comment on my naiveté.

The straightforward approach also worked on the social scene. I learned pretty quickly not to wait around to get asked to dance at clubs, or to get asked out. I bought men drinks, and on a few brazen occasions slipped business cards to a man while his date was in the ladies' room. It was a game, and I was *in*. I would have been even more naïve if I'd stayed in Toledo, and certainly more virginal, in more ways than the obvious.

The first time I slept with a guy I met there (I'd fallen head-over-heels in love and mistakenly thought he was my boyfriend), he said he'd "rather not get caught up in some deep emotional stuff." Basically, he was just interested in sex.

Whether you put out, or put yourself out there, you will still suffer the inevitable rejection. Sometimes the guy is straightforward, which I appreciate, and says he wants to date around: "No commitment, babe," a golden standard. Sometimes, if they're spineless, they say: "I'll call you." Smart girl that I am, I stopped believing it after the first hundred times or so.

Men weren't the only commitment phobics in Dallas. I admit that I was torn between wanting a long-term, meaningful relationship and the thought of what I might be missing out on, namely the next hunk that flirted with me at the red light. By the time the light turned green in Dallas, heads had already turned in the other direction. To bastardize some old song lyrics: " I found love on a two-way street and lust on the Dallas Parkway."

Impromptu auditions from corporate-casting could take place anywhere, anytime. Therefore, I never left the apartment without make-up and an alibi.

During my Dallas days I had as much human rejection as a baboon heart, but I finally got my big wish and dated a guy whom *I* dumped! He was a tall, fiery redhead I met on the racquetball court. He didn't live in the apartments, but his sister did. He wasn't a total hunk, but he did have a helluva kill shot. His name was Porter, which I thought odd but interesting and made me wonder what sort of baggage he was carrying around.

Porter and I dated for a couple of months until he got flat-out odd and I decided to unload him. I didn't agonize over how to break it off; I just told him the standard truth. It felt good to look into his almost baby blue eyes when he seemed like he was getting serious on me and repeat what I had so often heard: "No commitment, babe."

Later, he actually argued with me that it was his idea to break up. That really ticked me off. He was not going to take my first dumping away from me.

Call me superficial for liking "hunky" men, but we all have our weaknesses. I wished I could be attracted to character before looks. Unfortunately, my hormones wouldn't allow me to re-program them that way. I experimented by going out with guys who weren't that physically attractive to me but had other qualities or attributes. A virtuous but futile attempt on my part to look beyond the look. Take the millionaire I went out with; wasn't that a noble attempt for me to get outside the cardboard box of my type?

HIS NAME WAS ANTONIO, HEIR TO THE THRONE of Castanelli Tile Company, of Italy. I was introduced to him by some business acquaintances during a hotel happy hour.

Antonio was not unattractive, but a good ten to fifteen years older than me, something of a turn-off in itself, since my dad is also Italian and only twenty years older than me. He was not suave and forceful like a lot of successful businessmen. Instead, he was a bit shy and uncertain, and he spoke English with a very heavy, albeit redeemingly sexy Italian accent.

His friend explained to me that Antonio traveled the states

for months at a time and was lonely, and looking for someone to date.

Well, he could pay someone, like a prostitute.

According to his friend, Antonio had an interest in meeting a "nice girl," and he had picked me from across the room as someone whom he would like to meet.

I gave Antonio my phone number and he called twice a day for the next three days, asking me out. I already had plans for most of the week. By the fourth day, he told me he would "take me anywhere in the world that I wanted to go."

I was starting to get interested. When I told him I didn't have a passport, he suggested Newport Beach, California. He said it was beautiful and that he did some business there. Hard for me to refuse a trip to the beach. So I didn't. I did, however, make it clear to Antonio that I was a good Catholic girl and that I must have my own hotel room.

He honored the request for separate rooms. Although I'd not been physically attracted to him on our first meeting, I wasn't ruling out the possibility of a growing attraction. On the other hand, I thought I had better play it safe.

The weather was gorgeous, the restaurants he took me to were incredible, and he was hyper-attentive to me the entire weekend. I fell into the glamorous idea of being a millionaire's wife, or even mistress. On the other hand, neither my heart nor my body gave into the thought.

I did kiss him goodnight the first night and—with his hands he tried talking me into going back to his room with him.

Crazy Italians, always talking with their hands.

Despite the promise of an excellent return on my investment, there was—sadly—no growing attraction to Antonio, and by the second night, as his tongue searched my mouth for the New World, the Niña, the Pinta, and the Santa María couldn't have sailed me away fast enough.

I could muster no lust, but felt guilty enough about the money he'd spent on me to fake my way through a make-out session. To quote an Eagles tune, "Every form of refuge has its price." Then when he got really pushy, I told him I was still a virgin. I was back in my hotel room, alone with my lie, by 10:30. I called my sister Lori on the phone and, because I was bored, told her all the not-so-embellished details. She only had one comment: "He *believed* you when you told him you're a virgin?"

On Sunday Antonio and I went to the beach early, since our plane was leaving mid-afternoon.

Maybe because Antonio did believe I was a virgin, he treated me more gently. He smiled at me, talked sweetly, held my hand, and kept his tongue to himself. Meanwhile, I fought to keep my own tongue from hanging out of my mouth as I watched some gorgeous half-naked hunks (presumably poor beach bums) playing volleyball.

Although I learned there is no such thing as a free trip to the beach, I let Antonio continue to court me—from a distance. He called me a few times a week while he traveled, making his million dollar tile deals. During a call close to my birthday he asked for my address, and said with his thick accent, "I want to buy you a car for your birthday." I told him that he really shouldn't, even though I truly wondered if I'd put out for a Volvo.

My birthday surprise arrived on time—thanks to the trusty postal workers. It was a card. Sometimes you hear what you want to hear. Other times, karma—or carma—plays its little tricks.

SECURE IN WHAT TURNED ME OFF AND WHAT turned me on when it came to men, I tried not to over-analyze. Sometimes my legs moved faster than my head, and I was off and running to what turned me on before I knew much more about a guy than how sexy his biceps looked in a golf shirt. Admittedly not the wisest way to decide whom to date, but you had to start somewhere.

Still, in an attempt to go beyond type, I kept my eyes open

for something different and my calendar open enough for an occasional adventure.

My sales territory extended south from Dallas to Waco, and west to El Paso. Since there wasn't a lot between Dallas and El Paso, and it was over 500 miles out there, I flew out for a day or two a month. Once, I was caught off-guard in the El Paso airport parking lot by an artsy-looking, shoulder-length hair dude wearing Wayfarer shades and an earring. He was also carrying a briefcase. He had a unique charisma about him. I immediately noticed a dimpled, Kirk Douglas chin, and rippled muscles in his forearms. He asked me where the Hertz Row C was. I pointed in the general direction.

"Are you dropping off or picking up?" he asked.

"Dropping off."

"Too bad. I'm picking up."

"Are you talking about a car, or is that a line?" I said, flirting with my eyes.

He laughed. "Really, I was hoping you might show me around El Paso. It's my first time here."

Now that's a straight-forward, shamelessly opportunistic approach.

I liked it very much.

We shook hands.

"Hi, I'm Troy."

"I'm DC, but I'm heading back to Dallas. Maybe we'll run into each other again."

As I was turning in my car rental papers, the revolving thoughts in my head reminded me I was headed back to an empty apartment with no plans, on a Friday night.

Chalk up my impulse to guts, or to desperation and timing, but I revolved my way back out the airport door to see Troy, now with his car curbside, struggling to get a footlocker in the trunk. He looked pleasantly surprised to see me.

"Still want me to show you around El Paso?"

He answered by opening the passenger door for me.

I felt a twinge of panic.

I know nothing about this guy.

"Hey, do you mind if I see, some, like credentials first?"

Troy laughed and reached for his wallet. He produced a military I.D. The shocked look on my face made Troy laugh even harder.

"You don't look like you're military."

"Graduated from West Point and had a few months off, long enough to grow this," he said, as he flipped his hand through his hair. "I'm here for officer's training."

Troy looked a lot more like the photo on the I.D., and my type, after we checked him in to base and he got the standard G.I. crew cut. Luckily, he didn't start training until Monday. Because we had such a good time poking around El Paso, I missed the next fourteen flights to Dallas.

SEARCHING FOR LOVE AND SETTLING FOR LUST. Those were the days of my life in Dallas. Not too proud of that, but I learned a lot. It was enough to know I needed to learn a lot more before I really grew up. By the grace of God and other angel allies, I thought, I just might get there, despite the odds.

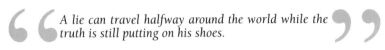

A lie can travel halfway around the world while the truth is still putting on his shoes.

—Mark Twain

PICTURE THIS

O SCAR AND FELIX CRACKED ME UP in the TV series, *The Odd Couple*, but I never wanted a roommate. I lived at home throughout college, sharing 850 square feet of space with two parents, two sisters, a dog, a cat, and one bathroom.

Several years into my post-college independence, having started my career selling cardboard boxes in the great state of Texas, I'd been spoiled by the spaciousness of Dallas, my apartment included.

Two friends and one aquaintance of my little sister Sherry came to visit after their college graduation. Sherry couldn't make the trip because she was starting a job at a Toledo area newspaper. It was fun to take them out—they were blown away with the lifestyle of the "Big D." But after a week of us all cramped into my one-bedroom apartment, I was more than ready for their departure. Sherry's two friends left, but the acquaintance stayed. She'd fallen in love with Dallas, and after several nights on the club scene, had more guys calling in one week than I'd dated all year.

Mandy, which was short for Amanda, was very cute: a

petite and perfectly proportioned strawberry blonde. She'd also perfected a naïve kind of Marilyn Monroe sexuality. Mandy told me her dream was to be a Dallas Cowboy cheerleader. So she picked up some lunch and dinner shifts at a Dallas seafood restaurant and took up residence on my sofa bed.

For the first month or so, it was actually kind of fun. When Mandy didn't have a date, we'd go out to the clubs. Country bars were in; discos were all but dead. We preferred early-'80s dance music, anyway. As Madonna-wannabees, in off-the-shoulder layers of spandex and lace, we moonwalked to Michael and bounced to Cindy Lauper, "cause girls just wanna have fun." We also frequented La Bare, an upscale male dance club, so often that they knew us by name.

Three months into our roomie experience, Mandy's dream was shattered; she broke her ankle at the Dallas Cowboy cheer-leader tryouts. Otherwise, I really think she'd have made it. She was irresistibly appealing. Just ask the boyfriend I'd been exclu-sively dating for about six weeks. His name was Chris, and he was the golf pro at a course near our apartment complex. I met him as a result of a golf lesson that was a gift from my boss.

Looks-wise, Chris was a bit out of my league. He was *GQ*esque, with Polo shirts and matching cologne. He was a nine on the ten scale. I was about a seven, give or take a half point for make-up or lack thereof.

From an intellectual level, he wasn't much of a challenge. He'd recently taken a self-improvement course and was writing his personal mission statement. He said he was trying to move beyond dating bimbos. I took that as a compliment. Chris, the golf pro, could hit 'em hard, long, and straight and he was gorgeous. With any thought, I should have predicted the out-come. But since I hadn't yet written my own personal mission statement, I was just winging it.

One afternoon, I returned home from a business trip. A good friend and neighbor seemed surprised to see me hauling luggage toward my apartment.

"You've been gone? When did things get so serious between you and Chris that you gave him a key?" Jamie asked.

"What are you talking about? He doesn't have a key." I was obviously confused.

"Well, his car has been here the past couple of nights. I'm sure, 'cause it's that silver Beemer with the vanity plate, BEEMEE, and I saw him coming out of your apartment this morning."

"That bitch!" I said, as my vocal chords tightened and I held back tears.

I'd been letting Mandy live there rent free until she got on her feet. Now she was in a walking cast and couldn't waitress for another month. I was about to yank the welcome mat out from under her and didn't care if she fell on her perky, little cheerleader butt.

My emotions weren't directed at Chris right away. I figured he was just being true to his gender, operating under the code of counter-intelligence in combat against the possibility of a committed relationship. But with Mandy, it was an incredible betrayal.

It wasn't as if I sat around and waited for disappointments. On the contrary, I had enough people and diversions built into my life to keep me going. I'd also been attending a quasi-new-age church. At Unity, they taught affirming the positive aspects of life and not giving energy to the negative ones. They also taught forgiveness as the key to healing.

On my spiritual journey, there was some definite work to be done in the forgiveness arena. But I did believe there were lessons to be learned from all experiences. This lesson was so remedial that I couldn't believe I was just learning it. The athlete and the cheerleader. *Duh.* Along with my anger, I had a sick yet gratifying fantasy about confronting them.

Mandy arrived back at the apartment soon after I got home but not before I made a few calls to some friends.

"Look! They removed the walking cast. I just have to wear this air cast now," she beamed.

Perfect. Air cast, air-head.

"Yeah, it will make it a lot easier for you to get around. And from what I hear, you've really been getting around."

Her little smile turned crooked and I knew she thought I was kidding until I flung this: "So did you and Chris use my bed or the sofa-bed? I'm really too exhausted to launder sheets."

"DC, you can't be serious! Where did you get the idea? I mean, I would never do anything like that!"

Mandy was a decent actress, considering she hadn't taken theater.

"Give up the innocent act. You were seen out at Club Memphis together, and he spent the night here while I was gone."

"Well, I did run into him one night and, um, we talked a lot. But I knew you really like him and I was just trying to see if he felt the same about you, because I would hate to see you get hurt."

She really said that. I think she even believed it. That was probably the line he threw at her in the first place.

I imagined their conversation:

Why don't I drive you back to the apartment? It's too loud to talk in here and I really want to get your advice. You see, I'm worried that DC is getting hung up on me.

It was a very effective missionary positioning statement.

The phone rang. It was Chris. He sounded surprised to hear my voice.

"Uh, DC, when did you get home?"

"Only about eight hours after you left, shithead. I can still smell your Polo cologne."

Dead silence.

"It's for you," I said, handing the phone to Mandy.

I went into the bedroom and felt like crying, but I didn't because I was straining to hear what Mandy was whispering into the phone. They didn't chat long.

When she hung up, I shouted, "Pack up whatever's yours and be gone by midnight."

I changed into some running clothes and zipped out into the Texas evening heat for a long, cathartic run.

DISCOVERING THAT MY BOYFRIEND and my non-rent-paying roommate were sleeping together made me change the locks to my heart, for security purposes. It was also dead-bolted. Not one to remain self-imprisoned for long, I plotted a breakout.

Sure, August 1985 had been no day at the beach, but luckily I was planning one. Make that a long weekend. Suffering the possible withdrawal of no more Spring Break trips with high school and college friends, a group including my two sisters made a pact to continue "girls trips." Despite my move from Toledo to Dallas, and a couple of the girls' marriages—and divorces—we managed to keep the beach party happening at least once a year. Every year we traipsed farther up the Atlantic coast, from Florida to North Carolina's Outer Banks and finally Dewey Beach, Delaware.

Dewey Beach was the year's choice due to its non-family-friendly-definitely single-beach community. My friends and my sisters would make the twelve-hour drive from Toledo. I would fly to BWI and take a puddle-crasher the rest of the way. I would have ridden my unicycle if I had to.

I was aware that there was a revolving door to the lobby of my life. It revolved faster after I moved to Dallas. Quick entries, quick exits. Relationships didn't last more than three months. My theory was that Dallas had a unique form of gravity. Three months was the amount of time it took for two bodies to revolve around each other's orbits until the gravitational pull of commitment from one body exceeded that of the other. Then the slingshot effect took place. One body went careening out into the universe in search of more heavenly bodies.

I was in charge of entertainment for the Dewey Beach trip and was luckily still in control of my imagination, if not my libido. I'd developed entertaining activities for our group (informally called the Infidels) on previous trips. One year, we staged a unique in-the-bar scavenger hunt with points for after-bar party invitations, hotel room keys we never intended to use, and toilet paper, since we were always running out.

My friend Sue and I also designed themed T-shirts. The previous year, we had "Infidels World Beach Tour" on the front and a list of famous beaches of the world on the back. We told everyone we met that we quit our jobs for a year and had traveled to each one listed. Both our vacation and our egos were enhanced.

A few days before the Dewey Beach trip, while I was admiring the magazine photos, one of those pesky subscription cards fell out. I noticed the nice little black and white *GQ* logo and imagined a new fake career path—something a little more glamorous than my real job selling corrugated boxes.

I'd gone to New York over Memorial Day weekend with a couple of male friends who were bartenders at the Comedy Corner in Dallas. Richard borrowed some cards from the club owner and passed himself off as a booking agent and talent scout for comedic talent. We got "comped" into a few Comedy clubs in NYC and got into the Letterman show without having to wait in line for tickets.

That is how Muffin Hardgrove was invented. A quick trip to the quickie print shop and I was Vice President, Talent Division, *GQ* magazine—according to the business cards.

"Make sure Sue brings her camera equipment, tripod, everything. And have Sherry get a generic photo-release form from the newspaper," I told Lori over the phone.

Thursday night before Labor Day weekend, my sisters, girlfriends, and I converged at the Dewey, Delaware, beach house, mulling over high school and the cool guys who were now either fat or exiled from the state of Ohio. The ultimate dreamboat, Don Spencer, an ex-Bowsher High School quarterback, was either in rehab for coke or hiding out in Florida with his third D.U.I pending.

A couple of cases of Tuborg Gold beer made us feel superior to the entire high school experience. For one, we were drinking legally; two, it wasn't on the railroad tracks outside of school before a sock-hop; and three, it wasn't Pabst Blue Ribbon (the beer we once ripped off from our parents' fridges). A lot can change in eight years. Cool guys become losers while we drink purchased beer.

After Sue dished out details of her recent divorce from the perpetual phys-ed major, I capitalized on a conversational lull. As the spokesmodel for relationships, past, present, and imagined, I got down to business with the *GQ* scam.

"We're going to do what?" Janet asked, laughing. Apparently, my sisters, Lori and Sherry, and friend Sue, had not filled her in on the entertainment for the trip.

"C'mon. Muffin Hardgrove. It's, like, unbelievable," Janet said as she flipped the *GQ* card at me, dealer style, across the kitchen table.

I affected an aristocratic accent, sort-of Lovey Howell and Joan Crawford.

"Pardon me, but Muffin is my given name, and not uncommon in Newport. Furthermore, I am fully qualified for this job. I have a business degree from Vassar. I interned at Ford modeling agency and was managing talent editor at *GQ* until the promotion to V.P., which came about, coincidentally, last year when Daddy was elected to the Board of Directors."

"Okay, okay, you've got the part, sis."

Sherry was getting in on the act with her best New York accent.

Janet, the resident skeptic and real-life accounting manager, finally buckled. "All right, I'll play along for now, but on two conditions: One, I want to be the team physician, and two, there's a real story behind that fake name and you're spillin' it."

"Cool," I said, "I suppose we could have a physician on the team, you know, for heat exhaustion and jelly-fish stings. And yes, there is a story behind the name. Muffin was the nickname an old boyfriend had for his favorite appendage. He said it was because it was a morning-riser."

"Was it bigger than a bread box?"

Sue had beaten the others to the first punch line. Even cruder ones followed.

On the beach the next morning, we set up camp per our usual vacation ritual: lounge chairs and blankets and books and cooler, preparing to bake out the beer in our bodies to make room for more later. By noon I was bored and antsy. As scoutmaster, it was my job to get the fire started, so to speak.

"OK, Sue, set up the tripod. Lori, Sherry, Doctor Janet, let's start scoping for our first victims…I mean, models."

The girls agreed to use their real first names so as not to complicate things further. Sue initially wanted to be 'Babbette,' but gave in after a brief argument.

"What exactly are we looking for—big and stupid?"

Janet appeared to be balking.

"Holy Stone Age, Batgirl, I mean, Muffin. There's a Neanderthal at nine o'clock."

Sherry stood up and lowered her sunglasses for effect.

We laughed until we checked out the subject for ourselves. He was either the tallest or the tannest guy on the beach. He looked like he spent half of his time at the gym and the other half in front of a mirror (often horizontal and not alone).

"There's your answer, Janet," Sue said, as she finished positioning the camera on top of the tripod. "The perfect specimen."

I threw on a Yankees jersey for a cover-up and an NBC baseball cap I'd picked up on my New York trip and headed over. I was a method actress. The perfect specimen was popping a tape into a boom box as I approached.

"Hi, sorry to interrupt."

No, I thought, *a V.P. of GQ from New York would never imagine she was interrupting, let alone apologize.*

Confidence shaken, I didn't follow up with anything else. I

just offered him the bait...I mean, business card. He read the card, then me.

"What's this all about?"

He either had violet colored contact lenses or was the offspring of Liz Taylor. Difficult as it was, I just maintained eye contact.

"Are you currently signed with an agency?" I countered.

Answering a question with a question had been an effective sales technique of mine.

"Uh, no."

He was on the line. Time to reel him in.

"Good, because we're looking for new talent to sign. What's your name?"

"Jeff," He said, running his fingers through his short black mane.

"Go for it, dude," one of his friends said.

"OK, what do ya want me to do?"

"You see that camera over there?" I pointed. "Just follow me."

Sue was white-balancing the camera against a T-shirt.

"Jeff, meet Sue. She's our photographer for this project."

The rest of my entourage was uncharacteristically silent as they contemplated Jeff.

"Sherry is an editor at *GQ* and Lori over there is our, er, grip and legal advisor. Doctor Janet is here for safety."

Jeff nodded at each. Sherry grabbed a talent release form while Lori provided verbal disclaimer: "You understand that by signing this document, you are releasing the photos we take to us. There is no monetary guarantee. However, if you are chosen to appear in *GQ*, you'll be compensated at union scale. Please include your social security and phone numbers on the form."

I was as impressed as Jeff and my colleagues on the professional delivery. Even if she was still in law school, with poker-faced lying like that Lori was going to be a great attorney some day. Lori was pleased enough with herself to get into the cooler for a congratulatory beer, and Sue posed Jeff in a beach chair.

After a few shots, I grabbed the latest issue of *GQ* from my bag and planted it in Jeff's hands. Sue snapped a few more with him holding the magazine, then she got him into some interesting beef-cakey poses.

Jeff was such a good sport, I almost felt bad about scamming him until a blonde bronzed sun goddess with double D's stepped out of a centerfold and into the perimeter of our photo session. She was both giggly and jiggly.

"Oh my God! Like, my friends over there said you're with *GQ* magazine. I can't believe my boyfriend is gonna be in *GQ* magazine!"

Jeff's grin blocked out the sun as he winked at her.

"That's a wrap," Sue said.

I glanced at Sue and then proceeded to deflate Miss Double D.

"Honey, it's not a done deal. Look around you. There are a lot of very buff and attractive men here. We're going to be at Dewey all weekend and only a handful will make it into the magazine."

Janet was on her feet.

"I'm a doctor and I couldn't help noticing that nasty sunburn on your chest. You'd better run and get some sun block on that right now. Better yet, a T-shirt. You have a suspicious looking spot on your shoulder and, um, melanoma is nothing to mess with."

We all managed to contain our laughter until Jeff and Double D departed. We took a beer break and toasted each other to the success of our first shoot.

"This is a riot, DC. I mean, I think he would have done anything we asked," said Sue.

"Like come back to the beach house and recline on our casting couch?" I fantasized.

"I've got an idea," said Janet. "How about if we pick the best Jeff photo and market him as the poster boy for the cure for vaginal dryness."

We convulsed in laughter.

After we calmed down, Lori said, "Yeah, this is pretty damn funny. But what if someone calls our bluff? I mean, that phone number on the card, DC, I assume it's fake. They could call and find out."

"Well, actually, Lori, the phone number's real. But it's for the *GQ* regional distribution center. They'd just get a recording, and it *is* Labor Day weekend. So they couldn't even get through to talk to anyone."

"Pretty cagey," commented Sherry.

Lori was still attempting to be the voice of reason.

"Well, what if someone here knows someone from *GQ* and we get caught?"

Then Lori answered herself, as lawyers often do. She was leading the self-witness.

"It's not like you're impersonating a police officer, you're just saying you work for a company and you don't. I'm not sure how legal that is, but the company would have to prove damages."

"What damages? *GQ*'s circulation rate in a specific East Coast region should increase after this. It's good PR." Sue made an excellent point.

"Not completely off the hook, DC. They could get you for logo copyright infringement, you know...the card," said my sister Sherry, the journalist.

I was unfazed.

Sue and I decided to team up and walk the beach in search of prospects. After a couple more successful shoots, it became almost routine. It felt almost real. With every great-looking face and each pumped-up body, there was typically an ego or attitude that took the bait. Ensnare the mind and the body will follow you anywhere. By mid-afternoon, Sue and I were both heady with our own power. For fun, we started staging little tiffs where we expressed our artistic differences.

"No, no, no. Sue, that pose looks too contrived. He needs to be relaxed, he needs to look like he's having some fun."

I sauntered over to our latest model. His face was Rob

Lowe-like and his shoulders and biceps were chiseled granite soon to be putty in my hands. I briefly massaged the back of his neck and said, "Guy, (because that was his name) you're a little tense. I know this is your first professional shoot, but try not to think about that. Why don't you just pretend that we don't work for *GQ* and that we're just some girls you met on the beach that want to take your picture?"

I shot each of the girls a devilish glance and walked behind Sue as she took the next photo.

"You were so right, Muffin. He's looking more relaxed."

By the end of the day, Sue and I were sunburned. We'd been focused on the intensity of our work and neglected sunscreen. It was probably the only thing we had in common with Double D.

THAT NIGHT AT THE RUSTY RUDDER, one of the popular Dewey Beach bars, we were recognized by a few of our "models" and were quickly surrounded by them, in addition to some wannabe models. Apparently, word was traveling as fast as the speed of our lies.

"Wow," said Lori, as we accepted another free round of drinks. "These guys are ignoring their girlfriends and the hottest looking babes to hang around us."

"Yeah, this is like a dream come true. Except, of course, that if they knew our real story they'd never even be talking to us," I added for clarification.

Sue leaned over the table toward us and, out of earshot of the two studs standing next to her, whispered: "It's not like we're dogs or anything. These types typically have rocks for brains and want the super-models who don't have brains, because they've puked them out."

For a secretary, Sue was quite the philosopher. She had finally gotten her college degree after her divorce and was about to start a new marketing job. Janet was on her second marriage and twice as cynical. Her new husband was in full-blown mid-life crisis and had joined a garage band looking for rock and roll stardom.

"Hey, check out the bartender."

Sue did a subtle elbow-point toward your standard tall, dark, and handsome. Before we could discuss the matter, she was bar side, presumably ordering up something tall and cool.

ON OUR WALK TO THE BEACH SATURDAY MORNING, a couple of guys with surfboards yelled across the road to us.

"Hey, there's the *GQ* crew!"

We had officially reached celebrity status and with that, were under some self-inflicted pressure to keep our fans happy, which meant another day of Muffin Hardgrove Company molding models. After all, they were putty in our hands.

Caught up in fantasy, a mind can quickly rebel to reality, as mine did at that moment. The smell of bacon cooking at a nearby restaurant flashed me back to earlier in the week and images of workers singeing hair off hogs on the kill-floor of a meat packing plant. The smell had been nauseating. The meat packer was a customer, from my real job. It was a distant departure from the glamour of my *GQ* alter-ego. I mentally regrouped and gratefully re-conjured Muffin Hardgrove.

THE SATURDAY SHOOTS WENT MORE SMOOTHLY, therefore more quickly, which was good since we had lined up appointments with several guys from the night before at the Rusty Rudder.

Sue's favorite bartender, Brock, was first on the list at 11:30.

After his photo session, Brock joined our lounge chair entourage to observe Sue and me in action. Luckily, we didn't have to do much prospecting. We had attracted quite a crowd, picked a few, and had some others volunteer. I was responsible for the photo release forms since Sherry was already tiring of the scam and was deep into reading *The World According to Garp*. I also gave a very abbreviated disclaimer, as Lori was studying a law book on torts: tort, n. (<L. torquere, to twist) a wrongful act or damage for which a civil action can be taken.

His hair was a mixture of sand and gold. Was it natural sun bleaching or professionally highlighted? He was gorgeous in the chiseled-featured Hollywood sense. He approached as if he'd just been to Saratoga and his horse had naturally won, which was impossible because I recognized him from the Rusty Rudder. He had a small entourage of his own, two male friends and a Golden Retriever.

"Sorry I'm late. I tried on a lot of things but couldn't decide."

He pulled several swim trunks and shirts from a duffel bag for our approval. The choices ran from surfer shorts to Speedos.

Sue and I voiced our opinions. Brock voted for the surfer shorts. Lori and Sherry remained neutral.

"I think you should go for the grape-smugglers," said Janet.

The model and his friends looked confused.

"She's talking about the Speedo," I interpreted for them.

"How about if we do a couple of wardrobe changes?" offered Mr. Indecisive.

"How about you WEAR THE DOG?"

It was early, but Janet was already at the top of her game.

After an hour in front of the camera, Mr. Indecisive, AKA Dog-Boy, was opting for another wardrobe change. His love for his taste in clothing was only surpassed by his love to hear himself talk.

"I've got a great idea," he said. "How about if around five or six I come back, you know, with an 'out on the town' look?

Besides, I think that with the sun so high in the sky right now, I might have been squinting."

"Sorry, we're already behind schedule. Thanks anyway. OK, who's next?" Sue blew him off like a true professional.

A little while later I overheard Janet telling Brock about her med-school experience and him asking her very knowledgeable and specific medical questions. It turned out that Brock was in his last year of dental school. Janet, on the verge of getting caught, offered to go grab lunch for us.

Sue was obviously getting distracted with Brock, so I told her to take a break. I photographed our last appointment model myself. The crowd of observers had dispersed in the blazing sun. I shed my beach cover-up and stepped into the ocean, contemplating DC Stanfa and her quest for fun.

As I floated out to the buoy line, my mind simultaneously swam.

The difference between this entertainment and the previous years' is the depth and breadth of the scam. Not only is the entire concept more complicated with our roles, we have to stay in character all weekend to make this work. Or we are doomed to be victims of our own scam.

With the anxiety of these thoughts and the pressure to continue the scam, there was no way I could really relax. This wasn't how you are supposed to feel on a vacation. My entourage was already bailing. I longed to lay back in a lounge-chair as DC and swap real stories and memories with my sisters and friends, but we had created a monster beach party of hunks and Richard Gere wannabees begging us to "discover" them. A Zen conundrum came to mind.

Master, will I be punished for my lies?

No, grasshopper. You will be punished by your lies.

When I returned to the group, Sue and Brock were gone. Janet, acting as spokesman, addressed me in her usual reverent manner.

"Hey, Muffy, we've decided we're tired of this shit. Can we, like, wrap up the entire project? You know, put it in the can?"

"I'm sorry guys. I didn't realize how, like, intense this was gonna get." I dug my toes into the sand and stared down at my disappearing feet as I spoke. "I'll just say we're done working for the weekend and don't want to talk shop if people start coming around again. Why don't we go into Ocean City tomorrow? We can be anonymous there."

"Great idea," Sherry concluded.

Brock and Sue returned with frozen margaritas for everyone. Sue took me aside, a few feet away from our group. "DC, I, uh, kind of like this guy. I also feel bad about lying to him," she said, sheepishly.

"So if you trust him not to tell anybody else, just tell him the truth. Tell him we're just having a little fun."

"It's not that easy. I mean, he thinks he really might be in the magazine and, well, he has more than half a brain and there's some definite chemistry going on so I don't really want to risk pissing him off by letting him know we've been lying all along."

I sank into a beach chair. Through the squawking of seagulls overhead, the dark voice of reason, sounding freakishly like Alfred, Hitchcocked its way into my head.

The web of deceit is so tightly wound, I can no longer tell if I am the spider or the fly. I've become the victim of my own scam. In more ways than one, I am indistinguishable from my victims, celebrity seekers, greedy for attention.

I realized this truth between my lies. In the wise words of Dr. Johnny Fever of WKRP in Cincinnati, "There is one thing all successful scams have in common: the greed of the victims."

SATURDAY NIGHT WAS A NEAR REPEAT OF FRIDAY NIGHT. We, of course, went to the Rusty Rudder. We were surrounded by the wannabees and had a paltry bar bill, due to our model benefactors. Only this time our attitudes were different.

Janet was giving flippant advice to everyone who spoke to her. Sue kept an eye—and her mind—on Brock behind the bar. Dog-Boy had attached himself to my hip, working his way toward my groin.

"Muffin, whaddya say we get out of here and go for a walk on the beach?"

Through the fake lust and false promise in his eyes, I saw my reflection. Is this what I was looking for? Janet overheard Dog-Boy and answered for me.

"Listen, Muffin's really not supposed to screw the talent. That's your agent's job. But since you don't have one, just leave Muffin your number and sit by the phone. She'll call soon. Right, Muffy?"

"Yeah, I'll call you, hon. Really, I will."

In that brief moment, my sisters, Janet, Sue, and I all connected with amused, affirming glances. The lie felt so good to tell. No wonder guys tell it all the time.

ON SUNDAY, OUR GQ TALENT CREW PUT THE scam to rest. We escaped our celebrity status in Ocean City, Maryland, about twenty miles south of Dewey.

After Sue had guided us through *Glamour's* "Can you trust your man?" multiple-choice quiz, Janet spoke. "Let's have a toast," she proclaimed, lifting her beer in the air. "To the first day of our *real* vacation."

We clinked cans. Compulsive as I am about having the last word, I felt certain that I should say something.

"Here's to true friendship and the timely death of Muffin Hardgrove."

The Dewey Beach photos from Sue arrived the following week. My grin grew larger at every picture. There were no boring sunsets, just gorgeous models smiling at Muffin Hardgrove and company.

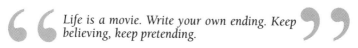

> *Life is a movie. Write your own ending. Keep believing, keep pretending.*
>
> —Kermit T. Frog
> (singing lyrics written
> by Randy Newman)

FLEETWOOD'S CHICAGO

I STOOD IN THE HOTEL LOBBY HOPING that Jack's plane was on time and wishing I'd worn more comfortable shoes. As usual, we only had a few days to spend together, and as for Chicago end-of-December weather and holiday delays at O'Hare, well, Murphy's Law usually rules. Except where Jack's Law overrides, as it was often known to during our on-going, long-distance let's-meet-for-a-fun-filled-weekend-somewhere relationship. Jack's Law was basically this: Never underestimate the power of a great attitude, and—when in Mexico—a $20 bill.

We'd met several years earlier at an apartment complex pool. In the mid-1980s, if you were single and in your mid-20s, you couldn't beat Dallas for launching a career or a good pick-up line. It wasn't just Debbie doing Dallas in those days.

The first time I saw him, Jack was wearing Rayban Way-farers like mine, and we were reading books at opposite ends of the pool. I was reading *Fear and Loathing in Las Vegas* by Hunter Thompson. He was reading some snoozer hardcover on real estate law. I waded through the shallow end and sat on the edge of the pool within striking distance.

At first glance he looked older, because his hair—although thick and gorgeous—was prematurely salt and pepper gray. As I got a closer look, I could see there were no wrinkles on his perfectly symmetrical face, and I guessed he was only in his mid-20s. His body was tan, with nicely defined muscles, but not muscle-bound. I launched the first line, although admittedly, not the best in my career.

Glancing at his book I said, sarcastically, "Looks like a sure cure for insomnia."

He lowered his Raybans and, with eyes the color of gravity, pulled me in.

"Are you referring to me or the book?" he said.

After we dated only a few weeks, Jack was transferred to Tulsa, Oklahoma, then Minnesota and finally California. In between other relationships and career demands, we somehow managed to keep whatever-it-was-we-had going for several years. As a matter of fact, we had incredible good fortune and fun amidst our crazy schedules.

Besides the gravity eyes, Jack was dynamic in every sense of the word, brilliant, worldly, spiritual, and funny. Most important, he made me feel like I was all of those things, too.

Getting together with Jack was a complicated cocktail, and something unusual always went into the mix. He wasn't easily pinned down and nearly impossible to dissect.

A Harvard MBA, financial wizard, and an executive with a major hotel chain, he was two parts Zen, one part James Bond, and equal parts of Larry, Curly, and Moe. It was a combination that opened the padlock on my heart.

He was more interested in hearing the life story of the janitor in his office building than meeting with the CEO at a Fortune 500 company. He was rarely serious, always self-effacing, and his comic Zen approach to life's journey taught me, through my travels with him, to never get attached to the outcome. I found out that unexpected detours to the destinations of life could provide the most interesting experiences.

Life with Jack proved that the funniest things do happen on the way to the Forum.

I checked my watch and sat down in a cushy, brightly upholstered chair with a good view of the hotel entryway. I thought of an almost-missed flight to New Orleans in October, and the past New Year's when we were going to have to sleep on the beach because of a hotel mix-up in Acapulco (saved by the $20 bill). Before Jack, holidays were lonely, even if I was with my family. My sisters always had boyfriends sharing the joy—and no matter what gifts I'd give or receive Santa never left me the one thing I'd been begging for, a date for New Year's Eve. Until Jack. *Two years in a row*, I thought, *if there isn't a blizzard.*

With Jack, the weirder things got, the more fun we had. Like dining at a four-star restaurant then ducking into a peep show in Austin and spending $10 in quarters to watch a video of a woman expressing her fondness for oblong fruits and vegetables.

There was also a balcony scene (not out of Romeo and Juliet) we performed on the tenth floor of a Waikiki hotel while a luau took place on the beach below. That same vacation, we went pool-hopping at nearby resorts, and got thrown out of one for behaving like goofy children. What a picture! Jack, the Harvard MBA, splashing around in the kiddie pool, sporting borrowed water-wings.

Adventures with Jack were like a Doctor Seuss cartoon, and while not always G rated, they were just as harmless. If he'd been a Seuss character, his name would have been Hector Connector. No matter where he went he made instantaneous connections with people. He could have a frazzled flight attendant laughing and giving us free drinks in no time. When I was with him, I felt more connected to myself, to him, to everyone and every experience we had. He was a cornerpiece in my puzzling life.

I glanced toward the revolving door of the Hyatt just in time to catch his sparkling blue-green eyes. The look on his face was like he'd tasted a new tequila-flavored jellybean and couldn't wait for me to take a bite. On perfect cue, he moved toward me and with a hug spoke these magic words into my ear.

"There's someone I'd like you to meet."

As Jack pulled away, I shifted my glance to the left to spy someone deeply tan with stark white teeth and slicked back silver hair standing beside him. He was about the same height as Jack—a little over six feet tall—and wore a bright red tie and a suit that had a gold metallic hue. If clothes could talk they would have said, "You have to be filthy rich to afford me." My initial take was that he was a celebrity whose name I couldn't register.

"Fleetwood, this is DC. DC, this is Fleetwood."

No celebrity with this name that I could recall. Nobody except Fleetwood Mac, a group that never had a member like this.

"Fleetwood and I met at the airport."

This man with the orthodontically perfect smile offered his hand to me and simultaneously bowed.

"He piscked me up," Fleetwood slurred, full of innuendo.

"We shared a cab," Jack corrected, as he searched my face for a reaction.

Slightly intrigued, yet unsure of the joke, I was still waiting for a punch line.

"You shee, Michael here was such a lambp to share the taxi with mee thadt I inshisted on shtopping for a fine bottle of scotch to shtare on the way."

Fleetwood held up a brown paper bag.

"Glen Livet. Love-it." he whispered pointing at the bottle-shaped bag, glowing with pride in his $2,000 suit.

On the way to the elevator, I had a twinge of regret that Jack and I wouldn't be alone to catch up on lost lust, but I was sure we would have fun for an hour or so with this Fleetwood character.

As the bellman delivered our bags to the penthouse, I engulfed myself in the vastness of the room and the view of the city.

"Got it for the price of a regular room," Jack gleamed. "Sometimes it pays to be in the hotel business."

The suite had a bar, a piano, a spiral staircase, and a bedroom on each of the two floors. With no attempt to unpack or settle in to our room, we nestled up to the bar. Fleetwood filled three glasses with ice and scotch. He held his glass high. "Leth have a toast," he said.

Toast: There it is, probably the best metaphor I could find for Fleetwood. He was toasted white bread, a bit overdone, and sure to be stale after a couple of days.

"To thish tall handsome man who reshcued me from the lonlineth of riding in a taxi by mythelf," he nodded to Jack.

Jack and I took our respective sips, Fleetwood his gulp.

"And to DC, my companion on the road to outrageous fun," Jack said with a wink.

We drank again. My turn for a toast is never a pass.

"To outrageous fun with Fleetwood," I said, winking back my approval to Jack on his choice addition to our Chicago adventure. *This will be interesting for a few hours, partying with this funny character.*

Jack slid his hand up and down my inner thigh. Our eyes connected with a rush of lust, but quickly disconnected so as not to be rude to our guest. I gave Jack my best we'll-get-to-that-later wink.

"I'm thupposed to be shtaying with some friends, but sinth we're getting along sho famushly, whadda ya say I show you MY Chicago?"

Our intro to Fleetwood's Chicago began three quarters of a bottle of scotch later, when we decided we'd better go eat.

Fleetwood was sitting next to me, legs crossed Indian style, on a huge Moroccan print pillow. Jack and I sat likewise around the two-feet-off-the-floor table. An aroma of pungent spices piqued my senses as Fleetwood talked. I studied his features closely, as an artist would his model.

"I'm jusht really a cowboy," he beamed.

Right. Perfectly manicured hands and soft, evenly tanned skin.

This was not the result of an electric beach. It was the kind of tan you get basking on a secluded patio in a coastal French villa.

"A cowboy and a dreamer," he continued, waving his hands in front of his face, a mystical gesture that causes people on acid to see trails of fingers, or so I've heard. Even the structure of his face screamed of lineage and old money. A lot of it. His facial expressions shouted, "I'm Peter Pan!"

I flash-backed to the movie *Arthur*. Yeah, that seemed right, a taller, older, gay version of Arthur. Cowboy, my ass. Fleetwood was a trust-fund kid, soon to retire from never having worked a day in his life.

He scooped a mouthful of a spicy Moroccan concoction from a decorative ceramic bowl with his right hand.

"Of courth, you know why in many cultures one muthst never eat with their left hand?"

Jack and I looked at each other with the understanding that we wouldn't actually answer so Fleetwood could continue his monologue of world travel for our entertainment.

The volume and flamboyance of his tirade increased proportionally with his intake of wine, the anti-sobriety vehicle by which Fleetwood swerved us past the concrete embankments of our minds: a forced detour to our imaginations.

"Anyway, thank God and Mr. Whipple for the comfortsh of Charmin and the flush toiletsh of the free world is all I can shay."

Fleetwood made a dramatic, yet brief, and futile attempt to locate his wallet when the check arrived. Jack subtly slid his credit card to the waiter.

We sauntered out into the Chicago wind-chill, past the newsstand and a street saxophonist.

"The night ish a peacock," Fleetwood said, gazing at the sky as his head bobbed upon his neck. "You can't appreshiate ish true beauty until it shpreads itsh wings."

Was that insightful prose off the top of his 100-proof head? I thought, as he led Jack and me through the doors of a speakeasy style bar called The Filling Station.

Inside, Fleetwood moved toward the bar like a wounded John Wayne. Jack must have made the same mental connection about the swaggering gait.

"See, he *is* a cowboy. Or a big cowgirl with a penchant for scotch," he whispered.

In the bar, it was reigning men. Hallelujah.

Despite our own intakes of alcohol, Jack and I became instantly aware that we were the only heterosexual humans on the premises, which of course, both delighted and despaired us.

Usually quite secure in his own sexuality, in *this* place Jack was in need of an anchor. He settled for a Molson and me, holding each of us with opposite hands, as if for balance.

Neither Fleetwood nor I were in need of additional beverages other than coffee, but we ordered black Russians.

"Ith not sho important if he'sh black or Russhin, just sho he's cute," Fleetwood told the bartender.

While sipping my drink, I made special note of two white American "actors," clad in open flannel shirts, revealing tight undershirts and pumped-up pectorals. I nudged Jack with my shoulder and raised an eyebrow in the direction of the television screen. Somewhere between the time these men of the "movie" had their shirts off and the end of the shower scene, Jack had headed for the exit door. He was expecting me to follow. Curiosity kept me tuned in but admittedly not turned on.

Jack and I were ready for this detour on the road to outrageous fun to straighten out a bit. I soon caught up with Jack.

"I'm ready to roll."

"Yeah. Where's Fleetwood?" I asked.

"Who cares?"

"We can't just leave him. I mean, his suitcase is in our suite."

Suffering equal parts of guilt and responsibility for our fleeting thoughts of Fleetwood abandonment, we found him staggering in our direction.

181

"Hey, uh, will you, uh, be OK if we leave you here?" Jack asked tentatively.

By this time, Fleetwood's eyes had rolled somewhere between his imagination and ours.

"Perahpth you could contact my freindth and they could come get me," he managed to say, as he teetered to and fro on his heels and toes.

What he didn't manage was to come up with an address, phone number, or anything other than the first names of his friends, Stephen and Garrett.

I awoke fuzzy-headed and hoping that Fleetwood would be gone, trying to remember if there was a bathroom on the second floor of the suite. I tickled Jack's ear.

"What time is it?" he yawned.

"Nine something."

Jack stroked my back, sending sensory signals elsewhere. And reminding me that Jack and I, due to the combination of alcohol, the exhaustion of the late hour, and the strain of parenting Fleetwood, had not consummated our weekend reunion. Sleep instead of sex, while a good idea at the time, now seemed like a consolation prize.

I turned toward Jack.

A nuzzle. A sweet closed-mouth, morning-breath kiss and those three special words.

"Have to pee," I said, jumping off the bed and throwing on a plush white Hilton robe from the closet.

"Wait, I want to see if *HE* is still here," Jack said.

We descended the stairs together like children on Christmas morning, unsure of what surprises awaited below. Santa Claus had not left the building. He was sitting, in fact, not quite straight up at the bar pouring the last of the scotch into a glass.

"Oh what a beautiful morning, oh what a beautiful day. La, la, la, la...feeling everything's going my way," he sang.

So that's what he sounds like without the slur.

It would be back soon, after the scotch hit his blood stream.

"Speaking of going your way, Fleetwood, did you ever find, er, uh, remember, your friend's phone number?" Jack was ready to return the present he'd brought me. Unfortunately, we didn't know to which store.

"I'm afraid I'm just no good with details," Fleetwood said, apologetically.

"How about some last names?" Jack inquired.

Fleetwood shrugged. His alcohol-induced amnesia had apparently continued.

"Next of kin?" I asked, half-amused, half-serious.

"Mums is in Bangkok and *she* usually checks in on *me*. Matter of fact, she'll be quite worried when she tries to reach me at Stephen and Garrett's."

He sighed and finished the last swallow of his amber waves of grain.

Jack and I barely spoke as we took, unfortunately, separate showers. By the time we were finished, Fleetwood was on the couch, sleeping off his liquid breakfast. Jack and I exited the building in the direction of a taxi. Although our good judgment told us not to leave Fleetwood alone in our hotel suite for long, our sanity required it. We needed to re-group, eat some solid breakfast, and shop, in that order.

The note we left said, "Went in search of your birth parents. If you find them first, write often. Love, DC and Jack."

"Hey, I'm sorry, DC," said Jack, with utmost sincerity.

I lifted a bite of eggs Benedict to my mouth and nodded in agreement.

"We'll just go back this afternoon and if he's still there, tell him he has to leave," he added.

"If we were going to ditch him, we had our chance last night. Any one of those Rock Hudsons would have kept him safe," I protested, knowing I really didn't believe it.

"I wanted to justify that last night, but you know he'd more likely stumble into John Wayne Gacy's den, and we'd never forgive ourselves."

He had a point. Plus we both really liked Fleetwood. He had this warmth about him—an authentic force of energy that didn't come in a bottle.

The sun was setting through our twenty-foot high windows, and Fleetwood was again at the bar with a drink in his hand and his ear to the phone. He was talking to someone. I put down my packages and Jack almost leaped over them to get to Fleetwood before he hung up.

"Is it James or, uh, Garrett?" he begged for confirmation.

"Just a minute, baby," Fleetwood said into the mouthpiece. Then, animated as ever, turned to us.

"It's my favorite Chicago Pooh Bear," he giggled, pointing to the phone.

"May I say hello?" I asked, thinking that whoever was on the other end of that line was our ticket to freedom from Fleetwood.

"Sure, Lisa," he said, handing me the phone. His amnesia was now affecting short-term memory as well.

"Hi, this is DC, uh, a new friend of Fleetwood's. Who's this?"

"An old friend of Fleetwood's, Rick."

"Hey, Rick, we were wondering if you could help us find where Fleetwood is supposed to be staying this weekend. He's a bit confused about things."

I'm sure I sounded desperate.

"Well, I'd come get him myself, only I'm in a playoff game tomorrow, you know, and I need a full night's sleep, and with Fleetwood, that can be difficult."

"Playoff?"

"Yeah, didn't he tell you? I play for the Bears."

I gulped back my disbelief and continued.

"How about Stephen or Garrett, do you know these guys?"

"Sure, hold on while I get their number."

Rick was more than a football hero. I flashed a relieved smile in Jack's direction as I inked the number on a bar napkin.

For me, Saturday night was a blur of room service and more scotch, as the day had apparently been for Fleetwood. While we'd been out, he made excellent use of the hotel hospitality. Who needs a mini bar when nice young men in monkey suits will deliver full size bottles of whatever you wish to torture your liver with? He even added solid foods of some substance to his liquid diet, as Jack ascertained from his $150 room service bill.

Two friends of mine, in Chicago visiting relatives, stopped in before dinner for a drink. I took Jamie and Eric aside and, with a weird combination of pride and angst, explained as best as I could how Fleetwood had become part of our furniture. Jamie and Eric then took the let's-have-a-look-at-this-alien-who's-landed-in-your-field approach.

"So where are you from, Fleetwood?" Jamie ventured after several glasses of Chardonnay and a lesson in Buddhist chants from Fleetwood.

"That is what I've been trying to tell you. I'm from everywhere! I'm a student of life at Universal U," Fleetwood said while he fastidiously arranged a vase, a wine bottle, and other items on the coffee table, as if he were planning on painting a still life.

"Is that near Universal Studios?" quipped Jack.

"The universe is my master and I am a mere professor of life in this fishy, wishy place we call the world."

"Up the academy," Eric saluted, then lifted his Corona in a toast.

My mind was aswim in a turbulent sea of scotch and wine. I passed on my chance to toast, a first for me.

Later, refueled on shrimp, pasta, and cognac, Fleetwood worked to earn his keep by continuing somewhat incoherent, yet entertaining tales of world travel, never to be published by Fodor's. He retrieved a small satchel from his suitcase and showed us photos of people, mostly barefoot children standing in front of shacks. "This is an Indian Village I adopted," Fleetwood said, with all the pride of a new father.

Wine. Scotch. Cognac. Keeping up with Fleetwood was not easy, nor was it an aphrodisiac. My eyelids played peek-a-boo with my eyeballs. I fought it, but I finally passed out on the couch before Jamie and Eric left. Jack not only held up the hospitality of saying goodbye for me, he helped me up to bed and put a waste-basket next to me, just in case.

NEW YEAR'S EVE MORNING WAS SIGNALED by the buzz in my ears, which turned out to be the phone. I picked up the receiver from the night table without opening my eyes.

"Hello?"

"Hello, yes, this is Garrett Garvin. We had a message on our machine to call this number. Is Fleetwood there?"

Clearing my foggy head and opening my eyes, I answered, "Yes!"

"We've been worried to death. Can we come get him?"

Jack's Law had endured, I thought. Though endearing and entertaining, it was way past time for Fleetwood to take his show back on the road. All I could think about was Jack, giving me a private New Year's Eve performance—without his "sidekick."

"Where are you? We'll bring him there," I said, trying to exert control over the final act of this comic drama.

"Tell you what, let's meet for brunch. Do you know OVER-EASY on Rush Street?"

"No, but we'll find it," I assured him.

"How does 11 work for you?"

I squinted at the digital alarm clock, which read 9:33 a.m.

"Perfect. We'll see you there."

Over a splendid buffet spread of omelets, croissants, and carved roast beef, Jack and I became acquainted with our Sunday saviors, the perfectly attired and groomed middle-aged Stephen and Garrett.

Fleetwood was immersed in flirtations and requests with the jazz quartet. He opted to order from the menu—steak tartare. Bloody Marys and raw meat, a carnivorous combination, fare for vampires and a fitting final repast with our creature of unknown comforts, Fleetwood.

"We can't thank you enough for taking Fleetwood under your wings," gushed Stephen.

"You see, his care was entrusted to us by his mother, who's on holiday in Bangkok. She wired us money in advance. Can we reimburse you anything for your troubles?" asked Garrett.

"No trouble," Jack said, graciously declining his offer.

"Who, exactly, is his mother?" I inquired.

"She is a client and a friend. We assist her in acquiring antiques and art to furnish her homes, here and abroad. But I'm afraid she insists on anonymity," Stephen explained.

"Suffice it to say that she and Fleetwood are amongst the most wealthy and celebrated families of this century," finished Garrett.

I leaned back in my chair, and as Jack's arm came around my shoulder, turned to him and smiled. Jack, not taking his gravity eyes off mine reached over and gently pinched my butt.

"God, I can't wait to get back to the hotel," I whispered in response.

Jack put his mouth ever-so-close to my ear, and in a voice the color of momentum, nudged another idea: "What do you have against the back seat of a cab?"

He sounded like Cary Grant.

"What do you WANT to have against the back seat of a cab?" I said, with raised eyebrows.

Another Zen moment of awareness.

Don't attach yourself to the outcome nor the destination. Enjoy the journey. Even if it is nothing more than a cab-ride.

Fleetwood made no attempt to search for his wallet, and Stephen unabashedly laid his credit card on the table when the check came. The joke was over and I was no longer attached to the punch line.

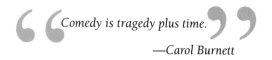

Comedy is tragedy plus time.
—Carol Burnett

B E A C H
T H E R A P Y

"YOU WANT SOMETHING, SEÑORITAS?" We shook our heads from side to side. "No, *gracias*," we answered in tandem.

"Almost free for you today," said the teenage boy, pulling a white sundress off the top of the pile, but not relieving the heaviness of the many garments he balanced on his left arm. His wide flirtatious grin flashed teeth to match the dress.

"Sorry, still can't afford it—all we have is *dinero para cervezas*," said Lori.

Lori, always the pragmatist of the family, was conserving our beer money. The boy shuffled away, sand sifting through torn leather sandals.

I marked my place in my book with a postcard I found in the desk drawer of our resort. "This is hysterical. This Hiaasen guy cracks me up."

"What is it?" asked Lori.

I showed her the cover. *Tourist Season.*

"What's it about?"

"Tourists getting murdered."

"Yeah, sounds real funny, but a little more dangerous and not near as fun as tourists getting hammered."

"What else is there to do in Puerto Vallarta?" I asked Lori.

"Is that a rhetorical question?"

VERBAL BEACH VOLLEYBALL, WHILE THE BEST non-stress exercise for what aches your soul and what pains your ass, can become tiresome. We ordered Bloody Marys for the nutritional value of the tomato juice and the medicinal value of the vodka—though my heart was more in need of healing than my head. Hangovers rarely make it past noon, heartaches tend to hang on a tad longer.

"Here's to drinking past Jack," I said, offering my glass to Lori's for a toast.

"To palm tree therapy and sandy cures," she answered.

"Feeling better already," I said, not aware I was lying.

"DC, maybe we should shop for a Jack replacement for you while we're here."

I frowned, unconvinced.

"Lori, the cure for getting dumped isn't always another man. Remember when I got food poisoning from eating Mako shark? Did I go out looking for more Mako shark?"

"Problem was, you ate it in Indianapolis. You should know better to eat shark that far inland."

"So, metaphorically speaking, are you saying that Jack, being a midwestern shark, was the poison and that something a little more coastal, here, might be the anti-venom?"

"No, I was just referring to your poor food choice. But, I like your antying-up with the metaphor."

"Thanks for being the caring older sister, but really, this vacation is all about R&R not S&M. And I would have to be a masochist to be looking for another relationship right now."

"You still haven't told me exactly what happened," said Lori.

"It was the 'I love you but I'm not IN LOVE with you' speech. You know, 'We're better off as friends.'"

"Ouch. And Jack is a smart guy. Harvard Boy couldn't come up with anything better than that?"

"Here's the funny part. He's probably right. I don't think he ever saw us as getting married, but I did. He was my best friend. We connected on so many levels, spiritually, emotionally…"

"How was the sex?" Lori interrupted.

"That wasn't a big focus of the relationship—I mean, it was deeper than that, but I'll admit that neither one of us was what I would call sexually vulnerable with each other. There may have been some passion, way back in the beginning."

"So maybe you'll stay friends?"

"I guess so, until he gets some jealous girlfriend that won't let us stay friends," I said.

"Like Sturge, in college," Lori summed up.

I shrugged. "I guess my life does have its patterns."

I SIPPED THE RED REMEDY AND SQUINTED into the sun. Lori adjusted her bathing suit top to prevent strap-line marks, an adroit move of a professional tanner.

The beach. A place where my spirit is renewed, my confidence reborn—where I become someone better than the person I see in the mirror. The ocean—where I see the true reflection of who I am.

Carl Jung's theory on the world of water and the relation of our bodies to water: where all life floated in suspension; where the soul of every living thing began; where I was invisibly this and that; where I experienced the other in myself, and the other in myself experienced me. In other words (my own) any day at the beach is better than even a good day selling boxes.

"I think I want a new career, not a new boyfriend," I told Lori.

"Me too, but recycling Coronas into sweat and pee doesn't pay as well as being a lawyer."

"But it's a much nobler profession, don't you think?"

SO THIS IS WHAT WE DID ALL DAY, exchanged inane insights and snippets of observations like a scrapbook of sarcasm: a tapestry of trite and true. It's this that helped most. It was this tapestry that had bandaged my wounds in the past—from my first senior-year-spring-break-savior, Craig (aka Dream Man), to Asateague Island and Ocean City with Lori and Sherry after losing my virginity (and then losing the boyfriend I lost it to). All the trips were bound by that same cloth, a veil to the past. *The veil that hides the face of the future was woven by the hands of mercy.* I remembered the quote but not the source. The veil that hid the face of the past was woven by the same merciful chick apparently—at the beach while she intermittently sipped cold adult beverages, read a good novel, and avoided bathing suit strap-lines. "Multi-basking," I called it.

What we did at night on a beach vacation was bask in the bar-light and partake in the local culture and cuisine. In Mexico, that meant drinking tequila poppers and dancing on table tops, but this was early in the evening and Lori (again the pragmatist) decided that we should try to pace ourselves, which meant eating a solid dinner. The fajitas arrived, sizzling. I tried to block out the memory, but even Mexico reminded me of him. I couldn't help re-conjuring Jack, momentarily reliving a moment with him on a balcony in Acapulco.

"A peso for your thoughts," Lori said, ushering me back to the Puerta Vallarta present.

"You look really tan in that coral color shirt," I said, quick to cover.

A 40-ish looking guy with salt and pepper hair (like Jack's) brushed past our table, then turned on his heels, as if standing guard for us. Lori and I exchanged glances.

"You look like you could use a bodyguard," he said.

He was sort of cute, in a Tom Brokaw-at-the-beach kind of way, so we let him stay and buy us drinks. After awhile, I thought the waiter was a Mexican Mel Gibson and I was sure I was drinking past Jack.

Margaritas on the rocks, cutting Cupid off at the knees.

"THE TWO GENTLEMEN DOWN THERE would like to buy you a drink," the waiter said, with a thick Spanish accent that reverberated in my hollow morning brain.

"It's not even 10:30," Lori said, checking her watch.

"*Si*, señoritas, but the bar is open."

It was no mystery *which* two gentlemen, since they were the only ones besides us in the outdoor café. All the other tourists finished breakfast long ago. Lori and I tried not to be too obvious but wanted to get a better look at our admirers, about fifty yards away.

"Just bring us a bottle of tequila," I joked, then quickly retracted the joke, as I knew the waiter would surely comply. "No, really, we can barely keep the orange juice down this morning, thanks," I said, pursing my lips and taking a slow sip to show the effort.

We offered a friendly wave and decided to check them out closer after breakfast.

Conversation revealed they were American, brothers from Atlanta: Simon and Sandor Karikas, Simon being the older one and Sandor (call me Sandy) the younger. We explained we were too H.O. to be drinking this early, but negotiated a rain check for later, poolside. Lori and I agreed that they were not unattractive and she pointed out that Sandy's body language spoke the universal language to me. Which I claimed I didn't notice.

Soon it was high noon, and the band played a mixture of American oldies that apparently had just been discovered in Mexico, and some annoying Charo-inspired La Cucaracha stuff. Sandy and Simon pulled a bucket of Coronas next to us, which we were cool with and proved by accepting beers from relative strangers (it's a brother pun). Simon was a lawyer, which we found ironic, because Lori was in her last year of law school, yet I read from her body that she was NOT interested in speaking the universal language with him.

Sandy was another story. His eyes were chocolate ice cream. Between his heat and the sun's rays, I was melting. They told funny stories about their "night before" and we told ours. If it was a contest, we won. Our story, about not having pesos for the cab driver and then me trying to cash a traveler's check when we got back to the resort, and the desk clerk telling me no, he wouldn't cash it because the signatures didn't match, and me telling him of course they didn't, I was at the bank and sober when I signed it the first time, and now I was drunk in Mexico, really had them laughing.

Competitive Sandy wanted to entertain us at a higher level. So he jumped on the stage during a band break. We thought he had a request. We were both right and wrong. He requested not just a song, but also to sing with the band. He started with a Julio Iglesias/Willie Nelson one-man, two-persona comic rendition of "To All The Girls I've Loved Before." He was really good. The sun-worshippers showed their appreciation with whistles and applause. Simon told us glibly that we hadn't seen anything yet. Of course, he was right, because Sandy went on to do Elvis, pelvis and all, singing "Ain't Nuthin But A Hound Dog."

Lori looked at me, nodded to the stage, and mouthed (making sure Simon couldn't see her), "DC, he's perfect for you."

I shrugged my shoulders and threw open palms up to the sky, as if to say *I know I told you this vacation was about R&R, and I'm not shopping for a Jack replacement, but what's a girl gonna do? He's Elvis, for God's sake.*

Four Coronas and a tequila shot later, and after a brief swim with Sandy, he talked me into getting on stage and playing maracas while he sang. I could no longer be responsible for my actions (that life pattern thing again), I told Lori later.

Where's that chick weaving that veil when you need her? The future seems all too clear right now.

A VACATION IS SOMETHING YOU TAKE AND don't have to give back. It was a good deal, especially with the value of the dollar in Mexico. Now, love is something you make, not take, which is also a pretty good deal, but first someone must make a move.

The sun was mid-sky, and Sandy and I were halfway submerged in the ocean, the waves pounding against us, pushing our bodies together, like we needed any help with that. Despite the cold water, I felt heat as Sandy kissed up and down my neck. His body was muscular but not muscle-bound. I wrapped my legs around his waist. Blood rushed to body parts I hadn't made full use of for a while. I thought *I know where this is going*, so I stopped.

I can't do this, I just met him. Okay, at least not now, in daylight, with people around.

Thank God for naps, another one of those things you take and don't have to give back. It was a gorgeous Puerta Vallarta night, and the Karikas brothers were taking the Stanfa sisters out after a post-sun siesta.

We were greeted like celebrities at Filipe's Restaurant, because this was where Sandy and Simon ate the night before, and it seemed they made the wait-staff very happy. Sandy didn't even attempt to hide the $20 bill he gave the maitre'd (another flashback to Jack, who in Acapulco taught me the power of $20). We were seated at the best table closest to the edge of the terrace, which considering we were halfway up a mountain, made me a little edgy. Sandy's hand on my leg calmed me a bit and worried me at the same time. Sandy and Simon told us about their family business, Karikas and Sons, which bought and sold commercial furniture. They had us in convulsions when they relayed the story of having to repo some hotel furniture and taking a naked couple by surprise.

After the Pouilly Fuisse was poured and despite the breeze, I felt the heat again, and Sandy's dark eyes like black-holes sucking me in. In danger of never escaping, I looked in another direction. Lori's raised eyebrows signaled me she was looking for a rescue. Obviously, Simon wasn't reading her sign that clearly read, "Keep your hands and feet inside the car at all times—or to yourself, anyway."

"You know, I'm in love with your sister," Sandy said to Lori.

That'll do it. Send a shock wave around the table to divert Simon's focus from Lori.

Of course I thought Sandy was kidding around, so I laughed.

"I am," he said. "I'm serious."

He pulled me in again with those eyes and put his arm around me, kissing me too deep and too long for anyone on the terrace not to notice. The guitar player, as if on cue, moved to our table and started strumming and singing in the most beautiful melodious voice, "Memories, " from *Cats.*

So this was what it is like to be swept away, and not just a broom sweep, more like an industrial grade vacuum. I am powerless to pull away.

If love is something you make and a vacation is something you take—if you do both at the same time, it is so good it feels illegal. That just might be that old, Catholic guilt.

Religious by-products not withstanding, by midnight back at the resort, Sandy wanted to make it legal and elope. Sure, we were all very drunk, so we thought the idea was hysterical. Lori decided we could perform our own ceremony, reminding us that Simon was an attorney, and so was she—almost. The ceremony took place in a courtyard. The bride carried a bouquet of freshly picked flowers and wore a half-slip on her head for a veil. This was not the veil that hid the face of anything. It just sort of covered my hair. Lori was my maid of honor and Simon was, well not the priest, minister, or rabbi. He just presided, and we made it up as we went along. Although I was giggling, I felt the wave of love knocking me down when I looked into Sandy's eyes. *We aren't just pretending, are we?* my eyes said back to him.

Simon had a wedding present for us: little black capsules. Spanish Fly, he explained. Talk about redundant and dangerous, like alcohol on prom night; we took it anyway. Lori and Simon went back to their respective hotel rooms.

We retreated to our honeymoon suite, which was actually a soft, flat rock at the ocean edge. As the tide ebbed, we drifted into a wine-and-sex-induced slumber. We didn't sleep long. I woke up in a cold sweat, heart racing. Sandy was already awake, and smoking. He handed me the cigarette.

"The Spanish Fly is kicking in," he said. "Some strong herbs in them. We're gonna be wired like this for hours."

So we talked until the sun came up. I'd never seen the sun rise at the beach, and it was unbelievable. Now I understood how the Tequila Sunrise got its name. Orange and red and delicious.

Sandy told me he wanted to get married for real, and although it was a little scary to even think about, I thought I wanted to, as well.

Am I in love or in love with the idea of being in love? (One of Mom's big CAUTIONS).

Of course, we wanted to have kids, but we wanted a couple of years to ourselves first, and I was almost 27, so it would be a long engagement (but not too long) and then a huge wedding. My family couldn't afford it, but Sandy's family sounded like they had quite a bit of money. Not that money had ever been that important to me, certainly not when it came to which men I was attracted to, but in this case it was just a bonus.

I LEFT HEAVEN ON THE BEACH AND ARRIVED at hell on the job. The new boss, Bill, couldn't make a decision to save his life. It was like trying to corner somebody in a round room. Then he made a comment during lunch in front of all the sales guys that totally embarrassed me (and I rarely got embarrassed).

"Hey, ya'll, watch DC eat that Jalapeño pepper, isn't that sexy?"

I could joke and kid around with the rest of these guys all day long, and there was never any tension like there was with Bill. He was just a pig. The guys thought so, too.

When I told Sandy about him, he wanted to come to Dallas and kick his ass. I said OK, knowing when he came to Dallas for the weekend, I wouldn't let him waste any energy kicking anybody's ass. I couldn't picture him being violent anyway.

He's just sweet and funny.

I could barely make it through my sales meeting on Friday, knowing I'd see Sandy in a few hours. As Bill told stupid golf stories, I fantasized about Sandy; replaying the honeymoon scene over and over in my head. I felt myself getting physically aroused, and a blush came to my face.

After I picked Sandy up from the airport, we went to dinner at my favorite place, On The Border, and sat out on the patio.

We talked about how much we missed each other all week, and re-capped some of the Puerto Vallarta vacation. I was wearing the large silver and amethyst ring Sandy bought me from a beach vendor the last day of the vacation. It was on my wedding-ring finger, until I got a diamond.

Sandy was stroking my upper thigh under the table and

telling me how beautiful I was. I couldn't believe the intensity of the passion: something that was missing with Jack. As far as connecting on deeper levels, I knew we would. But it would take time.

When we left the restaurant, I noticed an elderly couple, the woman pushing a walker, ambling their way toward the exit. Sandy walked in front of me, brushing right past her, not holding the door for any of us. I was stunned.

Hard to believe he didn't see them.

I held the door for the couple and then went out myself, spotting Sandy in the parking lot lighting a cigarette. *Jack would have walked the couple to their car*, I thought, *then offered to drive them home and buy them groceries.*

I brushed this episode off. The weekend went by way too fast to worry about something so minor. We spent much of the time in bed, making love and talking. I mentioned going to a friend's party—I really wanted my friends to meet Sandy—but he talked me into staying in. He didn't exactly twist my arm as much as he caused sudden involuntary muscle contractions in other parts of my body, which was really more persuasive anyway.

Sandy bought me a plane ticket to Atlanta for the next weekend, and told me that he would have to work a little while I was there, which was okay, because I could go for a jog and do some shopping while he worked.

His house was huge. The only house I'd been in that was bigger was my Aunt Mary and Uncle Paul's (a necessity with ten kids). Plus, the décor was incredible—Sandy had a professional decorator. An open-air patio room sat in the middle of the house with a hot-tub on a pedestal-style deck. We looked up at the starry sky and sipped champagne, and I heard Robin Leach's voice telling the pretend TV audience in my head about our rich and famous lifestyle. I asked Sandy if he'd ever been in love before, and he said there was a girl in college, but he wasn't ready to get married and she was, so she broke up with him and married somebody else. Then he told me about Melissa, his last girlfriend, who slashed his tires. I asked him what he did to deserve that kind of revenge. He just laughed.

I accompanyed Sandy to a furniture auction Saturday morning. As we were walking around surveying the goods, he unscrewed a couple of knobs off a large mirrored dresser and put them in one of the drawers, looking at me slyly. I knew what he was doing. He was lowering the value of the piece, so he could get it at a lower bid. I didn't let on that I was not impressed.

WE WENT TO DINNER WITH SIMON and his girlfriend Joanna. Who knew the entire time Simon was hitting on Lori in Mexico he had a live-in girlfriend? She drove a Mercedes and dressed like a model. She worked at the Estée Lauder counter at the Atlanta version of Needless Markups (what in Dallas we called Neimann's). Simon had his own law practice and was also involved in the family business. I was sure Simon bought her the Mercedes, which Sandy confirmed.

"And the boobs," he said.

I looked down at mine.

"You're just fine the way you are," he said.

But much later, as we watched an adult film in bed, he said, "If you do want a boob job, I'll pay for it."

I would look a lot better in a wedding dress, not to mention a bathing suit.

Sandy's eyes were still on the video while he made love to me, which made me feel a little like a surrogate.

On Sunday after brunch, on a whim, we went house-shopping. Sandy said we had to find a bigger place, with maid's quarters, and then told me he wanted me to be a full-time wife and mom.

"You won't need to work," he said.

I had never pictured myself to be a stay-at-home type, but that was growing up in Toledo and a different lifestyle altogether.

I'm not as crazy about the box business as I used to be and I wouldn't have to deal with Bill anymore. Maybe staying home isn't such a bad idea. What would it be like to have a maid and drive a Mercedes?

We did the back and forth of it, Dallas one weekend, Atlanta the next. Six weeks into it, I began to see a pattern: Sandy not wanting to meet or hang out with my friends. Us spending more time with his brother and their friends, including Joanna—whom I thought vapid and vain. Sandy was pushing for the boob job and wanted me to convert to Greek Orthodox although he never mentioned going to church. Recovering Catholic that I was, I couldn't see joining another religion. Although not opposed to organized religion—just religiously fueled violence—I'd become a big believer in unorganized peace.

Just when I was sitting on the fence over what to do about the relationship, I got knocked off with a big rock. Not a diamond ring, although we had been shopping. I was in Atlanta and it was Saturday night. Sandy had to go to Macon for a meeting. "The family business," Sandy explained. "Just the men, for a few hours. Simon, my dad, my uncle, and my cousin."

"Go for a jog and order a pizza," he said. "I'll be back by eleven."

I got my running shoes from my luggage in Sandy's bedroom. The phone rang and I let the answering machine click on. "Sandy, it's Melissa. Where are you? You're supposed to be here for dinner. My mom and dad have been here for an hour."

Whack! The sound of my butt hitting the floor. I picked myself up, and went to pick up the phone, but I heard her hang up before I could get there. *What in the hell?*

Think, I told myself as I ran down the sidewalk. I did some of my best thinking when I was running. Only now, my adrenaline was pumping so hard through my body, I couldn't think past the whooshing sound in my ears. I didn't run for long, but I ran faster than I ever had (without someone chasing me). I headed back to the house knowing what I needed to do.

I called Simon, but didn't hold my breath because I was still panting from the run. When he answered, I practically screamed, "You're supposed to be with Sandy, at a meeting in Macon, but you're not—because he lied. He's going to Melissa's."

"What are you talking about, DC? I mean, yeah, I was supposed to go to the meeting, but I didn't. Sandy went without me."

"You're lying to cover up for him. She called and left a message."

"He and Melissa broke up three months ago. I know for a fact he isn't seeing her."

"Then explain the call."

"Who knows? She's a nut case."

"Then find Sandy, wherever he is, and tell him I'm getting in a cab, going to the airport, and getting out of here."

"DC, stay put. Don't go anywhere. I'll find Sandy and everything is going to be okay. All right?"

"You've got an hour," I said, figuring that was how long it would take me to shower, pack, and get a cab.

SIMON AND JOANNA WERE AT THE front door, minutes after I got out of the shower.

"Where's Sandy?"

"He'll be here in a few hours. I talked to him. He's leaving Macon soon," Simon said, looking at his watch.

"Let's go get some dinner and wait for him," Joanna suggested.

"I couldn't eat if you put a gun to my head."

"How about a margarita?" Simon suggested.

"How about a pitcher?" I said at the restaurant.

True to my word, I didn't eat a thing, although a little lime-pulp from the margarita offered some nutritional vitamin C, I told myself as I slipped into one of the most lucidly drunken states I've ever been in (and I'd been drunk in several states including Florida and Tennessee, which coincidentally bordered Georgia).

Joanna and Simon tried to calm me, but the more I drank the more of a mess I became. They finally decided we needed to get back to Sandy's. *I might be embarrassing them,* I thought, but didn't really care much, as I stumbled past the bar to the exit.

Sandy greeted us at the door. I searched his face for guilt, but in my condition—seeing double—just made him look two-faced. Even in my angry, drunken state, I didn't lose the irony in that.

"Where in the hell were you?"

Before they even crossed the threshold, Simon and Joanna took this as a cue to leave.

"Like I said, I was at a business meeting."

"Bullshit," I said, stumbling up the stairs to his bedroom, as he followed behind me.

I pressed the *play messages* button on his answering machine. There were no new messages, according to the computer voice.

I looked at him, confused.

"I already played it, DC. It doesn't mean a thing. I wasn't at Melissa's."

"Why would she call then?"

"I don't know. She's a twisted bitch. I told you about her slashing my tires. Maybe she knows you are in town, or saw me leave and left that message for you to hear."

I fought to find what little logic I could grasp in his answer, because I wanted something to hold onto. I settled for a seat on the toilet, and held onto the side of the bathtub for balance. He stood in the doorway.

"If you were at a family business meeting, why wasn't Simon with you?"

"It really wasn't that important for him to be there. He only handles legal matters for us, and this wasn't about anything like that."

I pulled up my jean shorts and washed my hands. Still wobbly, I tried to look Sandy in the eyes and read the truth, but realized I didn't know him well enough to tell if he was lying. *Yet, I'm thinking about marrying this guy?* I also knew that if we didn't get past this, it would be over. My instincts told me I couldn't just drop this, and my adrenaline continued to surge, combining with the tequila.

I came up with a plan.

"Okay, let's put an end to this argument. Let's call Melissa and find out what she has to say."

To me, this was sound logic.

"DC, I told you she's twisted. If she left that message, she obviously wants to break us up, so she'll say anything to make that happen. She's nuts."

Good counterpoint, I thought, wishing I hadn't drank so much, as the alcohol seemed to add to my confusion. Then it hit me.

"Okay, let's call your dad and he can tell me about the meeting."

"Hey, this is crazy. Let's not get my dad involved in this. First of all, you've never met him and for a good reason—he can be a son-of-a-bitch, and secondly, you're drunk."

I started crying and headed downstairs to the couch. I pulled my legs up and put my arms around them, hugging myself for comfort. Sandy sat next to me and stroked my hair.

"I'm sorry, but I just don't believe you, and if I don't believe you that means I can't trust you and I can't marry you," I heard myself saying. I was crying so hard I was practically hyperventilating.

"All right DC, I'm going to tell you something. I'm going to tell you where I really was tonight because I do love you and I do want to marry you. It's something I needed to tell you eventually, but...."

Sandy looked at me as if for the very first time, and with all the innocence of a lamb said, "I was on family business in Macon but a different kind of business. I was making a drug deal."

"What are you talking about?"

He's making this up, like somehow a drug dealer is better than a cheater? Why is he doing this? It doesn't make any sense.

I felt myself starting to sober up.

"It's part of our business, and it's the most profitable."

"I don't believe this!"

Sandy stood up, pointed toward the stairs and said, "Oh yeah? Then why do you think I keep all of those guns under my bed? Go look. See for yourself."

I made my way up the stairs looking for a punch-line to a joke; to call Sandy's bluff, but not to find what I least suspected to be there—an arsenal of guns. My heart leapt into my throat and I was speechless for a minute until I saw him on the stairs.

"What kind of drugs?" I asked, as if it mattered, holding the stair-rail tightly as I descended.

"Coke. But, I don't actually hold any—I just make the money transaction. Somebody else holds and distributes it."

"You mean, sells it," I said.

Sandy read my lips, and then my psyche.

"C'mon, you've never done coke?"

I read this as a bad attempt at justification. Having made a lot of bad attempts at justification throughout my life. I considered myself an expert.

"Sure, I tried it a few times. You know, 1980s Dallas club-scene. But this is different."

"Did you really think I made this money by selling used furniture? How do you think I bought this house? How did you think we were going to be able to afford the houses we're looking at? If you want this kind of lifestyle, you are just going to have to accept some things."

"How can I possibly marry you and have your children, knowing you're a drug dealer?"

"Do you think Joanna questions where Simon got the money for her Mercedes, or even cares?"

I was hypnotized by his voice. I didn't move, I didn't say a word. He mistook this for acceptance and pulled me toward him, hugging me. I felt like part of me had just died. My body was stiff. Rigor mortis was setting in.

IT HIT ME THAT I DIDN'T KNOW THIS MAN AT ALL. I was afraid of what else I didn't know, what else he had done, or what he was capable of doing.

What if he thinks I will break up with him, and he can't let me go with what he's told me? What if he tries to hurt me, or worse....

I decided to play it cool, not let on how I really felt.

"Sandy, I'm exhausted. This is just so, uh, so much to comprehend. I love you too. I just need to think about this."

I wondered how good of an actress I was. Good enough, I guessed, because he hugged me tighter, and I pretended to hug him back.

"Do you mind if I sleep on the couch?" I said.

"If you're going to be tossing and turning all night over this, go ahead."

It struck me odd that he didn't offer to sleep on the couch and give me the bed. Then I remembered that this wasn't the guy I thought he was.

"There are two guest rooms, you know," he offered.

"No, the living room's fine. I might watch some TV," I explained. Really thinking, *I want to be as close to the door as possible.*

I woke up like one always does after something terrible happened, hoping it was just a nightmare. But I was on the couch and the reality hit me. I didn't think I was being overly dramatic as I planned my goodbye to Sandy at the airport.

"I think I'll be okay with it," I told him. "I just need some time to think."

On the plane ride home, I made plans to move to a new apartment complex and change my phone number.

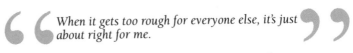

When it gets too rough for everyone else, it's just about right for me.

—Denny Stanfa

J U S T
S H O O T   M E

WE WERE AT THE GOLDEN PARACHUTE, a very exclusive members-only Dallas nightclub. "Just shoot me," I said to my best friend, Jamie. "If I'm that old and still hanging out at bars, just pull the trigger and put me out of my misery."

I was pointing in the direction of two 40-ish women, all spandex, lace, and Tammy Faye Baker make-up. The necklines of their outfits were so low they appeared to be having a cleavage contest (which I wouldn't be entering).

"Really," Jamie agreed. "Shoot me, too. It's pitiful how desperately they're trying to hang on to their youth."

"Or pick one up for the night."

It was the eve of my 27th birthday. I'd been living it up for five and a half years in Dallas, the land of no commitment. As my 30s approached, I was afraid I'd be living it down for the rest of my life in revolving door relationships, with heavier make-up and a camouflaged heart.

I played with the olives in my martini. (Jamie and I usually swilled beer out of bottles at the not-so exclusive Dallas clubs.)

I thought about Jack, my on-again, off-again, long distance soulmate who'd told me he loved me *more* like a friend. Then I briefly agonized over the rebound relationship that followed Jack: the only relationship where I almost got married—into the Greek Mafia.

Some other "M" words floated around that thought. *Mortality: Dad's diagnosed with lung cancer and here I am smoking.* I put out my cigarette. *Motherhood: Will I ever have children?* From death thoughts to birth thoughts. *What in the hell do they put in martinis anyway?*

More martini. Martini's, wasn't that the name of the bar in It's a Wonderful Life, *where Jimmy Stewart contemplates the mess of his life?*

"Had enough?"

I knew by Jamie's dimpled smile she was referring more to the superficial atmosphere than my intake of alcohol.

"Let's go to Jack-in-the-Box," I said, "and spit in the clown's face."

"But there are plenty of clowns you could spit at here." Jamie grinned. I detected some bitterness in our voices in the midst of our banter as we walked toward the valet station.

"Even the birthday party girl has to eventually call it a night," I said, frowning like a sad clown.

Home alone. I was thinking too loud to sleep. *Sometimes there's a fork in the road; sometimes it's a Russian Roulette revolver. Put down the gun and walk away, dummy. Party's over. Time to settle down. It's 1987, there's some scary shit going on, namely AIDS. Plus, the timing couldn't be better—get away from the boss from hell.*

Within a week, I requested a job transfer out of Dallas. The packaging company I worked for was used to controlling transfers and was therefore stunned by my request. I told them that it was for personal reasons. They did have an open sales territory in Virginia. What did I think about Richmond? It was a ten-hour drive to my hometown and family in Toledo.

I desperately needed to be closer to them, especially with my father's illness. And Richmond was also only an hour and a half from the beach. That's all I needed to know.

After selling corrugated boxes for five and a half years, I knew you couldn't make a move without one. Lots of them, I determined. My old boss (the good one, not the one from hell) wisely expressed to me on several occasions, "Life ain't nothin' but a cardboard box." I was getting the picture. He also had imparted some southern wisdoms to me that stuck with me, such as "Don't piss on me and tell me it's raining."

The transfer came through in November of 1987. A midwinter move to a climate with actual seasons caused me to get my heavy coat out of mothballs. Not knowing a soul in Richmond, I thought it best to keep my heart in storage.

To say I was on the rebound would be putting it lightly. I'd hit the backboard so many times I was deflated. New game ball. New ball game, but this time I hoped it would be a slam-dunk.

It turned out the game wasn't basketball. It was racquetball and it was a soft lob, not a slam-dunk. The apartment complex I moved to had racquetball courts and a clubhouse, like my Dallas apartment, but the tone of the place was much more subdued. There were married couples and families. The atmosphere fostered different conduct than the "all adult" complexes, which had been deemed discriminatory and could no longer exclude children.

Richmond, overall, was a much more proper place for a young lady. But having not been properly introduced to society (although I was sure Mom and Dad were still planning that debutante ball, back in Toledo) I hung out at the bar. At the apartment clubhouse, that is, near the racquetball courts.

Within a few weeks, I'd eased my way into an honest-to-God clique. The group was composed of about ten fellow residents. They were all single and looking, like I was. We got together on weekends to party, either at the clubhouse or another Richmond drinking establishment.

David was one of the guys in this group. He was four years younger than me and very cute, in a fresh-faced kind of way. He was from rural North Carolina and had a soft innocence about him that was appealing. He traveled quite a bit for his job as a bank examiner. I got to know David better as we started playing racquetball without the group.

One of the girls in the clique, Samantha, told me, "DC, he's got a major crush on you. It's so obvious."

I shook my head. "Sam, David is so nice and sweet that I don't want to date him. I'm afraid I'll hurt him."

Then I had an epiphany, of sorts.

"Wow, did you just hear what I said? I'm afraid I'll hurt him. I've never said that before about anyone. I don't think I've ever thought it. I've only ever been concerned about myself getting hurt. That must mean I really care about him."

David was so different from the type of guys I'd dated in Dallas, so refreshingly different. Almost a complete opposite of Sandy. Not worldly, but grounded. Not dynamic, but secure. Not wealthy or materialistic, just real. David and I were already good friends, and that is the best way to start a romantic relationship, or so I'd been told by friends and family who'd seen my combustible streak with "hot" romances.

So I lit a new torch for David, although he may not have set my world on fire.

Most important, he isn't going to ever burn it down, I thought.

The next group night out, while he was scanning the bar for someone to dance with, I asked him. A fast dance, then a slow dance. We turned up the heat on the dance floor to Madonna's "Crazy For You." It was the song we chose for the first dance at our wedding a year-and-a-half later.

IT WAS SUPPOSED TO BE A SIMPLE BEACH wedding, but Hurricane Hugo changed all that. Sure, I could have gotten married in Toledo—the traditional hometown thing—but having narrowly escaped from there in the early 80s, less than a decade later I wasn't nostalgic enough to give it serious consideration.

Then there was David's hometown: Conover, North Carolina. It didn't have a hotel or a banquet hall—to speak of. Although there were quite a few fish camps in the area, places where you neither camp nor fish. They were restaurants.

Richmond was too old-south-stuffy for both of us. So eventually we decided on Myrtle Beach, South Carolina, for several reasons; plenty of choices for accommodations, driveable proximity for his family in Conover and our friends in Richmond. My family and friends in Toledo were mostly seasoned travelers—and a trip to the beach for my wedding (which few people thought would ever happen) sounded good to everyone.

Although my sister Lori had just gotten married in July and it was probably a strain on my parents, both financially and emotionally, David and I set the date for November 4, 1989. With Dad's cancer and latest prognosis we really couldn't wait, or there was a chance he wouldn't be able to walk me down the aisle.

Anyone who has ever planned a wedding, especially one several hundred miles from where you live, knows how time-consuming and tedious it is. We did it before computer Internet/website services were standard for such an event. In just two trips, we figured out locations for the service, the reception and guest rooms—all three at the North Myrtle Beach Hilton; got a minister who'd perform a beach-side service; and chose a florist, a photographer, and a saxophonist (the only music at the service—my choice).

The invitation read: *Come away with us to the sea, the sand, the sunshine and the autumn breezes. Share in the beauty of God's creations. Share in the joy of our celebration.* Little did I know how powerful autumn breezes can be along the Atlantic shore. On September 22nd, one of the worst hurricanes in a half-century hit Myrtle Beach.

Hugo's autumn breeze clocked in at about 115 mph, causing $5 billion in destruction and killing sixty people. As devastating as it was to the area, my main concern was the wedding and 125 out-of-town guests (many of whom had purchased non-refundable plane tickets).

The phone lines were understandably down for nearly a week. When they were back up, a security guard—who refused to give me any information—answered the phone at the Hilton.

A week later, I was finally able to speak with the food and beverage manager, Barbara. She told me that the hotel did sustain some damage, which was still being assessed. She wouldn't get into any specifics, but she was "pretty sure" they'd be open by November 4th. I reminded her that David and I and others in the wedding party were coming in as early as the first, which was less than a month away. I also told Barbara that we needed confirmation on the menu items, and oh-by-the-way, the guests put down room deposits but had not had received written confirmations, as had been promised.

Unlike Barbara, I was not "pretty sure" about anything. I called our photographer and asked her to do us a favor: take a drive over to the Hilton and let us know what was really going on. The photographer reported back that day that she couldn't get near the place because of the police barriers.

I immediately phoned Barbara, who then admitted that maybe the damage was more extensive then they'd originally thought.

"We feel like some of the rooms will be ready, but aren't sure how many. We will have to relocate the ceremony, since the deck and pool area won't be re-opened by your wedding date." Barbara was sweet, but robotic at the same time: the Stepford employee.

David and I took off for an unplanned Myrtle Beach

trip—three weeks before the one planned. Some buildings in some areas weathered Hugo pretty well. The Hilton was not one of them. When Barbara led us around for a first-hand look, I was shocked we weren't required to wear hard hats. The place looked like a war-zone. She was right, the ceremony would have to be relocated, because there no longer was a deck, nor a pool, nor even a pool-bar.

Who'd want to stay here, even if the rooms were open, let alone get married here?

Barbara was understanding and assured us she would help relocate everything and we'd get all of our deposits back (as would our guests). After a round of phone calls, we found condos available at the Radisson, much nicer than the Hilton hotel rooms, and they negotiated some great prices for us—given the situation. There was also an outdoor deck for the ceremony. It was not exactly overlooking the beach, like the one at the Hilton—which may have saved it from destruction. The Radisson didn't have a banquet room available for the reception, but helped us secure a banquet hall a few miles from the resort.

For all the initial anxiety, things appeared to be well in place two weeks before the wedding. We just had to phone each guest to give them the details and hope we didn't miss anybody.

The wedding itself went about as smoothly as most weddings, with a few standard glitches. Some good friends from high school—Amy, Robin, and Kim—got stranded for a day at the Atlanta airport and missed the bachelorette party. On the golf cart ride from the condo to the ceremony, my hat wouldn't stay on my head (damn autumn breezes again) which delayed the wedding about ten minutes. A quick-thinking Sue (one of my bridesmaids) stabbed holes in it with scissors and secured it to my hair with a dozen bobby-pins. Then our ring-bearer (David's 5-year-old nephew) ditched his duty half-way down the aisle.

But these were little idiosyncratic burps, the kind that make weddings even more memorable than they would have been otherwise: the look-back-and-laugh-at-it stuff. Some of my wilder friends danced on tables, and of course I had to take part in that.

Sunday morning, David and I changed our Florida honeymoon flight departure to Monday. It had been an exhausting wedding, with the re-do of everything and we just wanted a day to chill. His family left by lunchtime. My family and some of my parents' friends were staying until Monday, as was their original plan.

What happened next was in what I'd categorize as you-can-never-look-back-and-laugh stuff.

We were going to dinner, several carloads of us. The car David and I were in made a left-hand turn off of Highway 17—a four-lane road, and the main drag in Myrtle Beach— into the restaurant parking lot. The car directly behind us in the turning lane, my Uncle Carl's, didn't make the turn with us. We parked behind the restaurant, which obscured our view of the road. As we got out of our cars, we heard a horrendous crash. David and I ran faster than the rest of the group toward the road. My uncle's car had been rear-ended by a pickup truck. My panic intensified as I noticed the car, now a twisted accordion, was still moving, slowly, dangerously crawling into the two oncoming lanes of traffic. David ran into the road, as it was apparent my uncle was too dazed to control the car. He opened the door, reached in, shifted into low gear, turned the steering wheel, then pushed the car to the brim of the road.

My mom jumped out of the car, blood flowing down the front of her face.

"Oh my God, I think your Grandpa is dead," she said to me, then screamed to the rest of the group, now on the side of the road. "Get an ambulance!"

I took her place in the car to check on everyone. She had been sitting next to my grandparents in the back seat. My grandfather, my mom's father, was to my immediate right. He was unconscious, and blood was coming out of his left ear. His breathing was labored. My dad was in the front seat with my aunt and uncle. He turned around.

"What happened?" he asked.

"Are you hurt, Dad?"

"No."

Uncle Carl (Grandpa's brother) and Aunt Mary were alert and talking by now, and I could hear Grandma faintly from the other side of Grandpa, though I couldn't see her.

"Jimmy," she said, and repeated it several times.

Jimmy was her nickname for Grandpa, whose real name was Bruno.

"Alma, are you all right?" Aunt Mary said, looking back at us.

Just as I was trying to remember any bits of the first-aid training I'd had in college, the rescue squad arrived. We found out later that someone witnessing the accident called 911. Though time seemed to crawl, the response time was only around four minutes.

At the hospital Mom was treated in ER. She had a gash in her scalp that was stitched up, and a lot of nasty looking bruises. They checked Dad's vitals and determined he was, miraculously, completely uninjured. We all felt that God spared him from being critically injured because he was already battling a terminal disease. When God can be found in the middle of a tragedy, it is a miracle. As the weeks and months of his illness went on, we continued to see more mini-miracles in our midst. It helped if you were looking.

Most of Grandpa's bones on the left side of his face were broken, including his jaw. He also had several broken ribs. But Grandma was the most severely injured. She had broken ribs and a broken neck. Mom and I were called into a room to talk with a doctor, who explained the surgery they were going to do. He told us they'd have to drill holes in her skull to fit her with a device called a halo: a stainless steel appliance that looked as though you were wearing a small walker on your head.

Uncle Carl and Aunt Mary were not seriously injured but

were admitted for observation of back and neck pain, while the driver of the truck walked away without a scratch.

"You did do a blood alcohol check on him?" I asked an ER nurse as he walked out the exit. She didn't answer, which pissed me off, and was an indication they had not.

Mom and Dad, my sisters and their husbands, all stayed the week. The honeymoon was postponed indefinitely. Aunt Mary and Uncle Carl were released on Monday. Grandpa Bruno refused pain medication after they performed his surgery; wiring his jaw shut. The next day, the stubborn old German insisted on ambling down the hallway to see his wife, Alma, who was in ICU.

By Tuesday, Alma's condition had worsened, she developed pneumonia and almost died. They put her on a respirator. My mom and dad, my sisters and their husbands, along with David and me, rented a house as everyone extended the stay in Myrtle Beach—at least for a few more days, and for some of us even longer. My typically funny and sarcastic family did its best to keep the mood light, even with the gravity of the situation.

One night, we talked about Grandma and some of her quirks. She often mixed up words or phrases, supposedly by accident. Once, she told us about a TV program on the "luckiest monster." We were perplexed until we checked *TV Guide's* listing on the Loch Ness monster. She delivered another classic at Christmas time when my mother put out the decorations. "Gloria," she said. "That's a beautiful activity scene."

In Grandma's absence, my dad came up with a good one— summing up the accident, and his own tribulations: "You know, every cloud has its silver lightning."

We all took turns going to the hospital. Grandpa was getting antsy because he couldn't get to see Alma as much as he wanted to: the ICU allowed brief visits for immediate family three times a day. Bruno was released from the hospital Friday, and by that time, the family had come to some important decisions.

Grandma was not improving, and Mom had to get Dad

back to Toledo for his chemotherapy. Everybody else had to get back to work. In a way, I felt responsible for the accident. If I hadn't chosen a beach wedding, it wouldn't have happened. I talked to David, and then called my boss. I decided to take a leave of absence from my job and stay in Myrtle Beach with my grandparents.

The next few weeks were a sad, repetitive blur: taking Grandpa to the hospital and ICU, where we held Alma's hand while she fought for breath and life. I shopped for food and fixed meals for me and Grandpa, which was challenging, considering he couldn't open his mouth. Everything he consumed had to be drinkable—through a straw. Baby food worked, and some vitamin supplement drinks. I prided myself on coming up with his favorite: Spaghettios in a blender. Sometimes it's best to chop up things you must consume, like medicine and painful memories, both tough pills to swallow.

Most nights while Grandpa watched TV, I walked the beach, wondering what the hell was happening in my world, and why. Betrayed by my beloved beach. My guilt over the accident continued to grow. *If I'd just had the wedding in Toledo, it wouldn't have happened.* As I walked, I talked to God and looked at my footprints in the sand, thinking about that story—where Jesus said He was with you during all your troubled times, and you said, "Lord, but there were only one set of footprints in the sand," and He said, "They were mine. I was carrying you." And I argued, "What size are your feet Lord? These are clearly size 9 ½ womens."

My fun-loving, outgoing, beach-loving self transformed into someone else, someone I wouldn't normally hang around with—given a choice. I didn't want to talk to anyone. (Which was perfect, since Grandpa or Grandma weren't talking either.) I answered David's calls when they came but had little to say, even to my husband. Luckily my friends left me alone. What could they say: "How's the honeymoon?"

Just before Thanksgiving, Grandma's condition was stable

enough to have her flown, by medical plane, to a Toledo hospital. Grandpa and I flew commercial, and David flew in from Richmond for the long holiday weekend.

With Grandma in the hospital and Mom having to take care of both Grandpa and Dad at home (Dad was getting weaker from chemo and the cancer was still spreading), I realized what an insurmountable situation she was in, and knew what I had to do. Being an only child, Mom had no siblings to help her. Both of my sisters had full-time jobs and Sherry had a five-month-old baby to take care of. Mom was already on a leave of absence from the University.

"I'm staying," I told David. "I'm moving back in with Mom and Dad for a while."

"For how long?" he asked.

"Until Grandma is out of the hospital, and Grandpa can drive again."

While I knew David wanted to start our marriage out together, he was stoic in his reaction to my decision. Which made it a lot easier for me.

"Do what you have to do," he said, hugging me.

From what the doctors told us, it could be a couple of months before Alma would be well enough to be released, and she'd have that halo on for even longer.

I asked him if he'd consider moving closer to Toledo. He really didn't want to do that, but when I told him that Hospice had been called in for my Dad, he knew what that meant.

"When he dies, I have to be closer for my family."

Neither one of us was crazy about living in Richmond, although we'd made some pretty good friends there. I'd come to an awareness over the years how transient most relationships were—people moving in and out of my life, as they so often had. The importance of family had taken on a new dimension with Dad's cancer and "The Accident," as it came to be known. I convinced David to work on a transfer. David worked as a bank examiner for the Treasury Department, so as long as it was a major city, he could put in for relocation. We considered Pittsburgh and Cincinnati, both within a four-hour drive of Toledo.

Grandma was in a rehab facility but came to our Christmas Eve celebration at my parents' house for a few hours. She arrived in an ambulance and was wheeled into the living room on a gurney, sporting a red bow on her metal halo. She was happy to be there, and we all were a little more festive as a result.

David took vacation between Christmas and New Year and flew to Toledo. We drove to Pittsburgh and Cincinnati, on separate weekends, scouting out a new possible hometown. Pittsburgh was colder and snowier than Cincinnati, and Cincinnati was also a quicker drive to his family in North Carolina. Our decision was made. It was just a matter of time before the transfer would come through, David assured me, because after that Charles Keating thing, Cincinnati really needed bank examiners.

I officially established residency in Ohio and resigned from my job in Richmond, the first week of January. I filed for unemployment and starting getting the Cincinnati newspapers to look for a job.

Something other than selling boxes, I thought. *It's time for a new career.*

My mood got darker and matched the Toledo weather as the worst of winter kicked in. I began to spiral downward into a full-blown depression. Mom, on the other hand, was strong and kept her mood upbeat, especially in front of Dad. The amazing woman made several visits to Grandma each day, often taking Grandpa with her. I alternated and shared a lot of visits, as well as transporting Grandpa to some medical appointments so she could spend time with Dad. I knew their time together was growing limited.

By mid-January, we had a healthcare hat trick: Grandma was released from the hospital, had her feeding tube removed, and Grandpa's jaw was unwired. Living with my parents again conjured mixed memories. Growing up, I couldn't wait to leave. Liberated from Toledo almost a decade earlier, I recognized now, home is neither a prison to escape from nor a day spa to return to. It is the only revolving door to love that you need.

When David and I talked on the phone at night, I'd close myself in the bedroom and cry—telling him that I could never do this—take care of a husband of thirty-five years while he was dying. I told him I could never love anyone enough to do that for them, and that I wanted a divorce. We had this same conversation, in one form or another for weeks. David was patient with my neurosis and even diagnosed it.

"You're just depressed. You don't mean what you are saying."

He also urged me to talk to a Hospice grief counselor, which I did. The counselor suggested that I take some time for myself, and start working out again—running and playing racquetball. I joined a local gym. Exercise, and working up sweats, helped exorcise some of the demons trying to take hold of me.

The first weekend in February, I flew to Richmond to help David pack. The Cincinnati transfer came through, and we were—at least David was—moving. This alone helped lift my mood a level above catatonic. Dad's cancer was still closing in on his vital organs, but the discontinuation of chemo gave him back some strength. He and Mom came to Cincinnati the following weekend to help us move into the apartment. She joked that he "let me drive for once." We laughed, because with the morphine he was taking, he had no choice.

We had a leisurely, enjoyable weekend as the movers did most of the work (and we didn't have much to move to begin with). Mom and I put away dishes while the men watched college basketball on TV.

David started work on Monday, and I went back to Toledo with Mom and Dad. By now, I'd regained some of my own strength. I knew I was being too self-focused about the situation, and along with the rest of the family, I refocused on making Dad's last days the best they could possibly be. I also recognized the gift I had been given. If not for The Accident, I would not have been spending these last months with him.

Though Dad's appetite had diminished, we went out to eat at all of his favorite restaurants, acting as if everything were normal. But during a family counseling session with Hospice, we were encouraged to confront the situation. We all, including Dad, reluctantly but cathartically, shared how we were really feeling. We were scared, but our faith grew. We held onto each other and to the hope of being with each other in the next life.

We had a birthday party for Dad on March 2. He was really excited about it. Amidst his pain, and likely his certainty of what was to follow, he was happy to have all of the people he loved together. Friends and family brought presents, acting like everything was going to be okay, although we knew otherwise.

My dad, Denny Stanfa, died early in the morning on March 13, at home, and in the arms of my mother. My sisters and I, who had spent the night there, had the privilege of seeing him cross over into the next world. At the end, although his eyes were closed, a smile came across his face, and I knew he was seeing something wonderful.

THE TIMES

BETHESDA NORTH HOSPITAL   MAY 22, 1992

Baby Hedrick Bounces into Presidential Forefront

CINCINNATI, OH—A new United States presidential candidate was announced today.

Cori Lynne Hedrick, weighing **6 pounds, 14 ounces,** and **19 1/2 inches long,** entered the presidential and human race at approximately **3:46 a.m. today,** a welcome and long-anticipated entry for many concerned.

Being a newborn and a female are two firsts that many political experts consider to be major advantages. "This candidate has virtually no past for the media to pick apart, no controversy. She's perfect," said **Daryl Gildenblatt, M.D.,** who delivered the baby.

The parents, **David and Denise (D.C.) Hedrick** agree with the predicted success of their child's campaign. "This country is deep in doo doo. It's time for a change. It's time for Cori," said David.

When asked about Cori's viewpoint on domestic and economic policies, D.C. replied, "I'd say that she favors a hands-off approach at this point. If she could talk (and you know she'd be incapable of telling a lie) she'd say 'Mommy and Daddy will take care of it.'"

Despite a Congress full of crybaby tactics and the infantile attitudes of other presidential candidates, there seems to be no question that cute and cuddly may be the deciding factor for Cori Lynne and this year's election.

223

> *This is a trading world, and men, women and children,
> who cannot live on gravity alone, need something to
> satisfy their gayer lighter moods. He who ministers to
> this want is in a business established by the Author of
> our nature.*

—P.T. Barnum

R E V E N G E
A N D
M A K E - U P

I SAT IN A DIMLY LIT HALLWAY IN A CUSHIONED folding chair, doing head rolls and deep breathing. These exercises were to tame down the flutters in my stomach so that my breakfast wouldn't fly away. I'd experienced similar stage fright before giving speeches in college speech class many years earlier. Of course, twenty fellow students were a little more forgiving and a lot less imposing than a studio audience of 200.

Laura, a producer for the show, told me to follow her into the "green room" with the five other guests. There we were briefed about how the taping would go, and each of the guests was coached on the angle or spin of their particular story.

"Denise, you're feeling very angry about the way men have treated you," said Laura.

Suddenly I could hear my own heartbeat and my shoes began to feel too tight. "Wait a minute," I interrupted. "My story was more about having fun. You know, turning the table, a game. I explained this all in my phone interview."

"Denise, we're trying to get the audience in touch with a feeling they can relate to, so can you give me some anger?"

"But, Laura, you see, I was watching the show a couple of weeks ago and there was this number to call if you had an interesting story. So I called and they booked me. I didn't realize it was going to be about anger."

"It's not. It's about revenge."

The other guests didn't say a word. They just listened intently. I choked back some bile that had made its way into my throat.

Laura took an exaggerated breath, then exhaled an exasperated let's-not-be-difficult-now sigh. "When we review the call-in stories, we group guests together under a show topic that fits best. We felt yours was in the revenge category, like these other folks."

I looked around the room at a collage of people, older, younger, and diverse in appearance. The black girl with the platinum blonde wig and feather boa caught my eye. I'd seen her in the make-up room. I wondered how her story was similar to mine.

"The other producer, I forget his name, assured me that we could plug the movie script my sister and I wrote. She's in the audience. That's the main reason I wanted to be on the show," I continued, hoping she'd finally understand.

Laura was obviously tired of my whining, but she still tried to be accommodating.

"Okay, when you get on stage, point her out to me and I'll cue Jerry and the director."

On that cue, Jerry entered the green room.

"Hi, I'm Jerry. How is everybody? Listen, don't be nervous. Be yourself. When it's your turn, just tell me your story. We're here to have some fun."

Yeah, fun, now we're talking, I thought, as we were led on stage.

I'd seen a couple episodes of this show during the past several weeks of maternity leave. Unaccustomed to being home, and with my newborn sleeping most of the day and being awake most of the night, I became bored by the recycled plots on the soaps that I hadn't seen in more than ten years. Luke and Laura, still, or again. Daytime talk shows seemed to have changed quite a bit since Merv. This Jerry Springer Show aired in Cincinnati and was syndicated to some other stations around the country. How tough would it be to be a guest? I had a pretty entertaining story—and an ulterior motive: my script.

I had one more week before returning to my job selling corrugated boxes to business and industry. I wondered how my boss might feel about me taping a TV show while out on leave. I certainly hadn't called him to find out.

I was seated to Jerry's immediate left, and the other guests were lined up in chairs to my left, in order of appearance. The platinum blonde black girl next to me was now donning some dark sunglasses that almost covered her face. As microphones were put into place, the audience was escorted in. I saw my mom and sister, Sherry, who'd driven down from Toledo, and my husband, David. My neighbor was baby-sitting our little girl for a few hours. My mom and Sherry were excited about my appearance on the show. My husband was supportive, yet apprehensive. David did see it as an opportunity to market the script, having weathered my frustration after a different window of opportunity had closed.

That window originally opened a few years earlier when I'd written Bob Greene, human-interest author and syndicated columnist, hoping he would help me get a magazine article about our *GQ* beach scam published. He said he couldn't help directly with the article, but I agreed to let him use our story in one of his columns. He used my real name and the city I'd lived in at the time (Dallas). I started getting all kinds of weird phone calls, including a couple of "producers."

Unsure of the right moves, I hired an entertainment attorney and sold an option for $1 to a writer's guild signatory to represent me in Hollywood and pitch the story. The option expired with no progress. In the meantime, I had moved to

Virginia and met and married David, but never gave up on a movie about our story. Now in Cincinnati, with no Hollywood connection, my husband was about to share some local limelight. He certainly wasn't crazy about the story itself, even if it had happened before we met.

When everyone was seated, Laura came over and asked which woman in the audience was my sister. I pointed her out. Sherry waved as Laura whispered something to Jerry.

Jerry stood up. The audience quieted. "This is a very special episode for us. This is the last time the show will be taped in Cincinnati. In two weeks, we'll be moving to Chicago. With the show's popularity, twenty-seven more stations have picked us up for next season. I want to take this time to say thank you to my great staff and crew for the great success. Some of you are going with us, and others have chosen to stay in Cincinnati. God bless you. We'll miss you and Cincinnati."

I didn't know if it was my unbalanced hormones from pregnancy and childbirth or the sincerity in his voice, but I was touched.

What a nice guy, I thought.

I'd heard all about Jerry Springer during the three years I'd lived in Cincinnati. He was an ex-anchorman and ex-mayor. There was this little scandal where he'd paid a prostitute by check and got caught.

So a guy is paying for sex. That's pretty up-front commerce if you ask me. He knows the goods are for sale and for what price. He gets the goods for which he has paid. I wouldn't necessarily get caught up in the method of payment unless the prostitute didn't accept checks, which may be a better business practice anyway.

I thought about all the lecherous men who tried to acquire the goods when they were not for sale, from us "non-professionals," with cheap liquor and cheap talk.

Who's committing the real crime?

The director was into the countdown when I finished my mental defense for legalized prostitution. As Jerry began the intro to the show, I felt those flutters in my stomach again. From my point of view, Jerry's nose resembled the toucan on the cereal box. I used it as my focal point for relaxation as I'd learned to do in Lamaze. My original Lamaze focal object, a colorful plush toy, was nowhere in sight. As I looked toward the monitor, Jerry was saying, "So today you're going to hear some revenge stories that are going to knock your socks off."

I was really regretting the fifty pounds I'd gained during the pregnancy, although I'd dropped almost twenty since Cori was born. I mentally added back ten for the camera. Once I saw myself in the monitor, I decided the purple suit jacket camouflaged most of it, and the make-up person had contoured my cheeks to minimize the weight gain on my face. My new-mommy, under-eye, sleep deprivation circles were all but gone due to the magic of makeup.

"Five years ago, after being dumped by yet another boyfriend, Denise Stanfa was fed up with the way men were treating her and was determined to make them look like fools. So she and some friends posed as talent scouts for *GQ* magazine. Denise, tell us about your scheme."

"Well, Jerry, I'd like to preface this by saying that I'm not at all malicious or angry."

I smiled at him, the camera, and the audience in that order.

"Sure, sure," Jerry said, playfully. I was getting a little more comfortable.

"What happened with our scheme was, well, it was actually a scam. I had been single and dating, and during that experience I had been lied to and scammed myself. I was planning a beach trip with some friends and thought it would be fun and entertaining for my friends and me to pretend we were with *GQ*. But the revenge part was more like a game. You know, evening the score."

"Was there a specific group of men you targeted?"

"We decided to appeal to the vanity of really good-looking

men at the beach, you know the type that wouldn't usually pay any attention to me or my friends. The kind of guy that is really self-absorbed, the male equivalent of a bimbo."

"So, how did the men react when you asked them if they wanted to model for *GQ*? How did you pull this off?"

"Well, after we'd picked out a prospect, I'd approach him and hand him a fictitious *GQ* business card, which I guess made it somewhat authentic. Then I'd have him come with me to where our cameras and everything were set up at the beach. It was pretty amazing though, 'cause I never really expected these guys to fall for it so completely. But they did, hook, line and sinker."

First there was a smattering of laughter, and clapping, which grew into official applause from the audience. I was both relieved and grateful for the response, and really excited to tell them more. I looked up at the monitor to see a close-up shot of the fake business card I'd used. Muffin Hardgrove, VP of Talent. The *GQ* logo was a cut and paste but looked pretty good, even under the scrutiny of the close-up.

The next shot was a group photo of the girls, taken in front of our rented beach house. We were dressed up for a night out and also looked pretty good. A series of photos followed, about eight of the dozen or so men we'd photographed. Although their faces were obliterated by lawsuit-proof blue dots, their buff physiques were evidence that we really had picked the best at the beach, real *GQ* material. The predominately female audience gasped, whistled, and applauded their approval of the men we'd scammed.

"So for the past several years, all these guys have been buying *GQ* magazine, thinking their picture might be in it?" Jerry pondered out loud while looking toward the audience for a reaction.

"Yeah, I guess so," I said, shrugging my shoulders.

"You mean, I'm not going to be in *GQ*?" Jerry flipped his fingers through the sides of his hair in a mock, modeling gesture. The audience laughed.

"Maybe on the cover some day," I said, smiling, eliciting a few more laughs myself from the audience.

I answered a few benign questions from the audience, and then Sherry was asked to stand up.

"What do you think about this scam?" Jerry asked her.

"Well, I'm her sister and I was in on this scam with her. I thought it was pretty amusing. Also, Jerry, we've written a screenplay about this that we're trying to sell...."

Great, there's our plug, the reason we're here.

Then we broke for a commercial. Even though this was taped, they tried to keep the timing as real as possible.

"Welcome back. Now we're going to hear another story of revenge. When Sasha Epstein found out her boyfriend was married, she plotted and carried out a plan of drastic revenge. Sasha, tell us your story."

Sasha's story was a drastic contrast to mine—as stark as the contrast of the platinum blonde wig against her dark brown skin.

"Well, Jerry, I'd been celibate and minding my own business when this cable guy comes to my house. Then he pursues me with flowers, wining and dining, the whole nine yards. But then I done my investigation, I found out he was a minister. Come to find out, brotherman's also married."

"Hold on, hold on." Jerry feigned total shock, speaking to Sasha but looking out at the audience. "You mean to tell me he's a cable guy *and* a minister? Ya mean God doesn't lay cable on Sundays?"

The audience roared at Jerry's comment.

"Uh huh. So, he comes in like the devil, deceiving me. The Lord says, 'Vengeance is mine.' But I said, 'Excuse me Lord, let me take up your slack!' So to get back at him, I lie to him and tell him I'm pregnant and need money for an abortion. I take the money, and me and my girlfriend go to Vegas, skinny!"

The audience hooted over that one, too. Sasha was a hit.

Then she told Jerry and the audience about conspiring to get the minister/cable guy's wife fired from her job. She also revealed other vengeful deeds against co-workers and neighbors, putting urine in coffee and sugar in gas tanks. The audience was going wild. They were screaming at her as Jerry went to the audience for questions.

The show aired a few days later. I critiqued my performance to be about a six on a ten scale. Good creative content. My delivery should have been better, having majored in communication and been in sales for over a decade. I came across a little too glib, which I attributed to nervousness.

Juxtaposed to Sasha, I was also unforgivably boring. But I decided boring is better than psycho any day of the week. There was only one real glaring error, though not mine. The "plug" had apparently been pulled on our screenplay plug. My sister Sherry's comment had been edited out, I'm sure for "time" purposes. I was not blind to the humor in the irony. The scammers get scammed. Karmic justice, Jerry Springer style, prevails.

IN THE WEEKS THAT FOLLOWED AFTER, I returned to work, and word had gotten around the office from some second-shift plant employees about my appearance on the show. After some prodding, I brought the tape in for co-workers to watch during lunch.

An unexpected phone call came two weeks after the show aired. It was Laura, one of the Springer producers.

"Denise, I didn't go with Jerry when the show moved to Chicago. I took a job in New York. I'm now a producer for Geraldo. We're very interested in doing a similar show to the one you were on, only we'd want you to bring a couple of your friends and your sister to be on the show with you. Also, we'd like to track down some of the guys you scammed to appear on the same show. The idea is, they'll respond to having been scammed."

Geraldo. This is really the big-time.

I became pretty excited, and naïvely pictured our movie finally being made.

"Wow. Uh, let me think. I can call my sister and friends and see. When are you planning on taping this?"

"In a couple of weeks. But it's really important to get a couple of the guys on, too, or we have no show. Geraldo wants the confrontation."

I got Laura's number and told her I'd call her back, even though I knew we were probably sunk. As predicted, sister Sherry was the only one to agree to go on with me. The other girls who hadn't written a script had no incentive to be a part of a daytime sideshow. It wouldn't have been prudent for their marriages and careers that had taken off since the *GQ* scam. I knew my husband would really balk at this opportunity to market the script. And it wasn't exactly my dream to get on the talk show circuit. (Now, David Letterman, after the movie was actually made, *that* would be a real ticket.) But Geraldo was a national show, and who knew what movie connections could be made with this exposure?

The real show killer turned out to be lack of organization. Sherry and I could not locate the fake talent release forms that we had the "models" sign, which contained their names and addresses. We'd both moved a few times since the *GQ* scam and pitched a lot of excess baggage along the way. I made a brief, yet futile, attempt to contact one of the guys through his previous employer. Unfortunately, the manager at The Rusty Rudder, a famous Dewey Beach bar, had no idea how Brock (last name unknown) the bartender, could be reached. Anyway, I doubted that even good-natured Brock would agree to be humiliated on national television.

The last and most unsettling phone call came from a producer from the Sally Jesse Raphael show, who'd gotten my name from the talk-show circuit guest list that had taken on a life of its own.

"This may be a bit of a reach, but in your profile it says you have a sister. And we're doing a show on siblings and breast size. Is it possible that one of you has larger breasts than the other and there's some jealousy about that?" asked the producer.

I couldn't contain my laughter.

"You want us to come on the show to talk about our breast size? You're right. You're reaching."

How low would I go to hold the hand of fame? From where I sat in my little house in Cincinnati, with my infant daughter asleep in the next room, it was much too far of a reach, I thought as I hung up the phone.

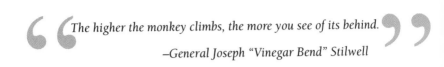

The higher the monkey climbs, the more you see of its behind.

—General Joseph "Vinegar Bend" Stilwell

JUST SHOOT ME AGAIN

J UST FAST-FORWARD LIFE'S MOVIE, and press the play button during a marriage counseling session three years later. Although many friends and family had told us that once we'd survived the wedding disasters and me living with my parents for four months afterward, we could get through anything, I was starting to think our oppressive beginning was an omen.

"David and Denise, I don't know what more I can do for you. You're just two different people with extreme differences in expectations of your marital life. Denise, what attracted you to David in the first place was the security he offered, and now you're saying you're bored."

The clarity of the counselor's words was terminal. I had mistaken security for love. I married for the foundation of Maslow's pyramid of human needs and was now seeking self-actualization—which was way up on top of the psychology model.

"David, what attracted you to Denise was that she was a doer and a go-getter. Now you're resentful of the time she devotes to her job, friends, and activities outside of the marriage," said the third therapist in three years, as our three-year-old daughter

Cori played blocks on the floor, occasionally glancing up at the low-volume Barney video.

"Would you want your wife to be on the Jerry Springer show?"

David made a good point. The defining moments that led to the end of our marriage had seemed to pile up quickly after that. I remember him saying, "the apple didn't fall too far from the tree,"(in reference to my free-spirited, fun-loving mother), and me saying "ditto," referring to the idiosyncrasies of his own family. Once we began attacking each other's roots, our little branch of the family tree broke in two.

IT WASN'T WHAT I'D CALL A BITTER DIVORCE, relative to horror stories I've heard. Beyond the inherent pain, there was hope for our daughter Cori's future, and we were gallant in our efforts to work together on custody and other issues, for her sake. During the marriage we had regular verbal fights in front of Cori. After the divorce proceedings began, we could have won a bite-your-own-tongue contest while she was in the room.

No one in my family had ever divorced. Many of them were Catholic, and some stayed miserably together so that they would be assured to spend eternity with the object of their misery. So, having no frame of reference for being a divorced mom at the age of 36, I reactivated the angst I faced a decade earlier in the dating world. Only this was Cincinnati, not Dallas, and all of my friends were married now, except me. The dating world, at my age, was a very small planet with alien creatures.

In my New World, there were no invitations from neighbors or other married friends; I was now on the market and a prime husband-stealer. Planet-single-and-pushing-40 had an intense gravity, which increased my fear of falling flat on my face in all aspects of life. I took as much control as possible over what I perceived to be in my control. I read twenty self-help books on divorce and single-parenting and emotional healing in the first six months. Then I thought about writing one.

On Mommy-days, Cori was the center of the universe for me. On the three Daddy-days of the week, I couldn't stand to be home without her. On those days, I became a workaholic and those nights a workoutaholic. Yet there was still empty time and more of Maslow's needs to be met. But where did one go to meet those needs, the Maslow Hierarchy of Needs Bar and Grill?

After more introspection, meditation, and contemplation, I decided to go to the place that had been a magical source of healing many times before: the beach. My two sisters and our core group of friends were happy to accompany me in my post-divorce time of need. It was the twentieth anniversary of my first spring break, and the girls still did an annual beach trip, although not always in Florida.

Fort Lauderdale was a sweet tropical release from cold, harsh reality. It was not exactly spring; it was early February. Even better to escape the frigid north during its peak. Lounging in the sun, telling stories, re-hashing memories of high school and other beach trips was as cathartic as six years of psychotherapy. It was a safer, warmer world, even if it was only for a week.

Since my sisters, friends, and I had married, we'd eliminated a longtime compulsory exercise from our beach trip events—looking for men. However, on the second day in Lauderdale, my friend Janet made an announcement. "OK, girls, we're going to find DC a date."

I didn't protest. They were looking out for my best interest, as always.

Although the responsibility of motherhood had reined in my wilder horses, my animal instincts were butting up against the gate, trying to break free. We dressed up for dinner, which meant no jeans, and arrived at Mr. Bliss in some semblance of style, or so we thought. This bar/restaurant was a hot spot for 30-and-above singles, and came highly recommended by the concierge. Upon entering the bar, it was obvious we were underdressed —or overdressed, depending on how you looked at it.

The female patrons, standing and modeling in Mr. Bliss's bar, were attired low on the upper deck and high around the lower deck. In other words, there was a high skin-to-spandex ratio. The men were all pushing 50 or older, various stages of baldness and paunch camouflaged by loud sport coats and deep tans.

"Just shoot them," I said to my group, as we did the first lap around the bar.

Lori, my older sister by a year, and Sherry, the 34-year-old "baby sister," appeared more out of their element here than I did. Of course, I was no stranger to the superficial singles scene, having done it in Dallas a decade earlier. After one drink and an eternity of silent stares into the abyss of the crowd, a vibrating device rescued us, notifying us that our table was ready.

"Oh my God. They all look like prostitutes," said Sherry.

"Not all of them. Some look like professional models." Sue's pronouncement was accompanied by a slow wink.

Janet, not to be outdone, cut to the chase. "A bunch of coke whores and nose-candy daddies."

"But high-class," I added, dryly.

I mentally flashed back to the Golden Parachute in Dallas ten years earlier, and the 40ish looking women there. And now here I was in the sequel.

The one-time ingénue, now too old to reprise her role, returns as the ingénue's mother.

Lori said, "I felt invisible in there, in my cute little sundress, since I wasn't showing any T or A."

"I'll bet if DC were to take off her leggings and strolled in just her jacket, through that bar, no one would even notice," Janet said.

"Are you kidding? DC's got those long, toned runners' legs we'd all love to have. If she takes off those leggings, she'll be noticed," was Sherry's comment.

Then Sue said four words that have caused me trouble ever since the onset of Catholic repression: "DC, I dare you."

The daredevil was in me since I could remember. It sprouted horns and a forked tongue and got fierier as I grew older. In the quest to entertain and get an approval fix from my friends, I had often sacrificed myself up for the disapproval of nuns, parents, and other governing authorities. Sometimes it was worth it.

On this occasion, the governing authority would have been the bar or restaurant manager. I calculated my risks to be minor, including the risk of self-embarrassment. My friends would tell you I never learned the meaning of that word.

While savoring the last bites of key lime pie, Sue wasn't giving up on the dare.

"Five bucks is what I'm throwing in. Who's with me?"

"For what?" Lori asked.

"For DC to take her pants off and waltz through Mr. Bliss's Brothel, that's what," Sue clarified.

"Oh yeah, I'm in for another five," Janet sweetened the pot.

"I gotta see this, sis," Sherry said pulling a five-dollar bill from her purse. "Double or nothin'." My wise older sister Lori made the offering unanimous, with an inspirational adage often used by our deceased father.

IN THE LADIES ROOM, JANET STOOD outside of my stall.

"Just throw me those pants over the door. I'll hold onto them until we're outta here."

I was feeling a little wine-buzz and laughed as I pulled my seashell printed leggings off. I had a matching shirt under my nautical blazer. The jacket was double-breasted with gold painted buttons. It barely covered my ass.

"What the hell. Here's my shirt, too."

I was cracking Janet and myself up as I tossed my garments over the bathroom stall door. I exited, sporting my buttoned-up jacket and little else.

"What 'cha got under there, girlfriend?" Janet inquired.

"A running bra and panties," I said, as I checked myself in the mirror. Janet was laughing so hard I didn't know if I could keep a straight face to complete my jaunt.

Sherry, Lori, and Sue were ringside, standing on the elevated perimeter of the bar area, which provided eagle-eye-view. I descended four steps into the arena of skin. I scanned the crowd. The lions were devouring bleu cheese-stuffed Martini olives, while we Christians were standing in glib judgment, taunting the lions for our harmless self-amusement.

I sauntered and scoped, not looking for but not avoiding eye contact. I passed a woman in a white, body-hugging, see-through spandex gown that seductively advertised her thong underwear. Many pairs of eyes were fixated on the ad, trying to read between the lines. *Will blow for blow,* I thought was her not-so-subliminal message.

Janet was right. Nobody gave me a second look. Few people gave me even a first look, which left me a little insecure and wishing I had on heels instead of flats, more fitting for my new look. I caught Lori's eye as she and the others were convulsing in laughter at the spectacle I was causing for our own party, which was invisible to the rest of the bar patrons. The challenge now was to control my own laughter as I completed my three-and-a-half minute loop around the bar.

Janet had my pants ready, in hand, as we ran out of the bar. I began slipping them on while Sue started the rental car.

I was laughing so hard I thought I'd pee my pants before I had them back on. "What do you have to do to get a date around here?"

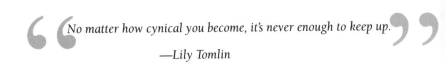

No matter how cynical you become, it's never enough to keep up.

—Lily Tomlin

ZEN AND THE ART OF TABLE DANCING

THE SECOND DAY OF THE "TRIP OF THE LOST LUGGAGE" was about as delightful as being awakened by a mariachi band at dawn on New Year's morning. It was an experience I could do without, and that's just what we were: without. In Acapulco, Mexico, without our stuff, except our carry-on bags. And without a clue regarding the whereabouts of the lost luggage.

While I'd experienced baggage delay before (that's what my under-eyes look like after too much tequila), the airlines had always delivered it within a day or so. This time, it appeared to be a complete luggage lobotomy.

Our Continental Airlines flight from Cincinnati to Houston had been canceled due to mechanical problems. So we hustled over to a Delta flight, arriving in Houston in plenty of time to make our Continental connection. While my friend Karen and I had a leisurely lunch, discussing our divorces and exes—our "bitter halves"—the baggage handlers must have been busy doing the same, or watching another "Surprise, Honey, I'm Really A Man" episode of Jerry Springer. Quite possibly, they were not putting our bags on the Acapulco flight.

What were we thinking, placing our confidence in the airline industry to actually get our belongings AND us safely, without incidence, to the same destination? How could I complain? After all, *WE* arrived safely at the gate, along with the other passengers who prematurely stood, despite the flight attendants warnings, to gather their carry-on luggage and cling desperately to it (well before the three-bell signal). It's a good thing we did, too, or I'd have been stuck in the beautiful Acapulco sun without the fleece jacket I so carefully packed in my carry-on (under the-it-was-cold-when-we-left-and-it'll-be-cold-when-we-get-back theory). But we were away from the frigid weather in a paradise on earth. It was also difficult to complain because I couldn't speak the language.

My foresight and planning weren't as bad as it sounds. I did pack my own carry-on with a bathing suit and a pair of pink shorts with a beer stein emblem. I also threw in one of my many Put-In-Bay T-shirts and an extra pair of undies. Apparently, Karen was never a Girl Scout. Or was that "always prepared" slogan a Boy Scout thing? She didn't even pack a bathing suit in her carry-on. When I reviewed her cumulative carry-on inventory and noted the large VOID area, she explained, "I wanted to have room to take back the shit that I buy." Little did she know how brilliant that decision would prove to be.

On day one, we already made the first of many purchases that would follow. The two gift shops at The Mayan Palace were resplendent with clothing items you wouldn't see outside a tropical resort community — you know, Resortwear. Karen and I were exhausted from lying perfectly still in lounge chairs by the pool. We had no energy to go into the city to shop for anything else (I was still laboring under the assumption there WAS something else). We were not exactly thrilled with our choices, but we came away with two similar, knee-length, faux-batik frocks, uh, sundresses. We ate lobster, drank tropical drinks, and blended into the palm trees at the resort on night one. The plan was to lie low until the next day when our luggage and real identities showed up.

So by the evening of day two with still no luggage, libations in hand, we remained pool-side well past sunset, still in bathing suits, performing self-executed liquid lobotomies and trying to make room for new identities. In our new lives, we could only wear Resortwear.

My new identity greeted me with a tequila shooter and an attitude as cynical as Dennis Miller after a tax audit. I began ranting.

"What's with this Resortwear anyway? This stuff was not dreamed up by your typical fashion designers. You wouldn't see a skeleton on heroin walk down the runway in such cruel clothes. All these white or beige, cotton or linen, embroidered and gilded gunny-sacks sell for an average of $350 a yard, if I'm converting the pesos correctly."

"Our bar bill today is probably up in that area," Karen interrupted. "So I'm sure your math calculating skills are at their peak, DC."

"Anyway, who'd wear these things outside a resort? Unless you've joined the resort cult and sold all your belongings for margarita salt and a cabana boy named Ricco. Resortwear might as well be called Last Resortwear," I said, wrapping a beach towel around my bare legs.

"So, as a last resort, we're going to have to continue wearing this crap," Karen added, "And paying ridiculous prices to buy it."

My cynicism was turning to sarcasm. "Oh, we'll get some use out of the clothes after this week. I'm sure I'll look hot at my kid's soccer games in it. Or maybe I'll pick up some cute guys cruisin' the grocery aisles at Kroger."

Karen was laughing at my suggestion.

"Right, like I'll ever get another use out of that flowing white gown I bought last night."

"Karen, those dresses we bought were beige."

"Oh, sorry," she grumbled. "I must have been thinking about my wedding dress. Oh, well, same idea, you get it. The Resortwear was actually more expensive than my wedding dress. At least I got laid the night I wore my wedding dress."

Karen's new identity was humorous, yet slightly confused.

By day three, I was anticipating cashing in on the movie rights for the *Up in Smoke Luggage Vacation* starring Chevy Chase, and Cheech and Chong.

"Karen, I'm going down to talk to the concierge," I said, removing my running shorts, underwear, and bathing suit from the balcony railing of the five-star resort where they had hung to dry after I hand-washed them for the zillionth time. "Maybe he's heard something from the airline," I said, as if I might believe it.

"And I'm going to get my virginity back soon, too," she said.

Apparently she had awakened on the cynical side of the bed.

JUAN GREETED ME LIKE AN OLD FRIEND. No, let's make that a hotel concierge expecting a big tip.

"Ah, *mi amiga, si, si*, good news from Continental. Your bags have been found. They are at the airport and will be delivered this afternoon."

I was stunned.

"*Gracias*. Please let us know as soon as they get here."

I ran to tell Karen.

By happy hour, Karen and I were three Pina Coladas to the wind and wondering where the afternoon and our bags had gone. She did the fourth check with Juan and came back with further news.

"You got a full drink, Deece?" she inquired as she returned to the pool bar.

I nodded, anticipating the worst.

"Well, they found my bag. I took it to the room. Unfortunately, yours is still missing."

"I've been talking to some people here at the bar," I said, ignoring this latest piece of news. "They're telling me we really must go see the cliff divers. I didn't get a chance last time I was in Acapulco."

I was quickly moving into my denial phase.

"If it makes you feel any better, someone stole most of the clothes out of my suitcase. They even took my socks."

"Why would it make me feel better if someone stole your socks?"

I signaled the bartender for another round.

"The airline representative told Juan that they'd pay us back for the replacement value of whatever was stolen, up to $300."

She was trying to cheer me up. I sat, sipping and doing a mental inventory of what I had packed.

I sighed. "Three hundred dollars won't cover the cost of my shoes."

"How many pairs did you pack?"

I shrugged her off. "That's not the point. Replacement value? I packed most of my favorite fun clothes, like the BITE ME sweatshirt with the little fish from Lake Travis. And how about that T-shirt from the Cincinnati half-marathon? I'll never run that far again."

Now I was ranting.

"Maybe the airline can hire somebody to run it for you next year and give you the shirt."

"Don't get me started on what they'd have to do to prove they had new lucky underwear. Replacement, my ass. What about the sentimental value?"

"Like those Betty Boop shorts you wore when you pushed your way onto the stage at the Danger Brothers show in Put-In-Bay?"

"Then again, there are some things we're better off not reminiscing about," I said, studying the back of a pack of matches.

Karen stood suddenly, her face focused in determined desperation.

"Maybe we can make some memories out of this Resort-wear after all," Karen suggested. "Let's go party."

We pieced together mixed and unmatched outfits out of Karen's non-stolen garments, made another Resortwear purchase at the gift shop, and hit some Acapulco night spots. We ended up at a Mexican Chippendales show where we discovered why there are obscenity laws in America.

BY DAY FOUR OF THE STOLEN, never-to-be-seen-again luggage that apparently preferred a separate vacation, I was blaming myself, and everyone else. The fate of my bag and its contents was sealed when I so carelessly locked the damn thing. If I hadn't, the custom agents that usually steal the contents of tourists' luggage would have been able to swiftly rummage through it, like they did Karen's. Instead, they had to take it to the secret hiding place where they pick the lock.

Of course, that's just a small part of the operation. It's really a big conspiracy. Everyone is in on it. In addition to the customs agents, the hotel, the chamber of commerce, the Mexican government, Resortwear designers, Charlie Sheen, and perhaps even my traveling companion, Karen, have all worked together to pull off this heinous crime.

Let me explain: The customs agents make out on the cash they get for the goods at the black flea market and then give a little kickback to the Mexican government, as if they needed more bribes. The hotel, restaurant, and shop-keeping members of the chamber of commerce are in deep clover with the now-necessary purchases of tacky attire. Charlie Sheen was on a movie on the WB channel when I woke up, and, well, he just can't be trusted. I need to start making some notes, get this figured out on paper.

It's beyond me how Karen managed to hook up with the other people. I mean, after four trips to Mexico, she still can't even ask where the bathroom is in Spanish (after mas cervesas es muy necesario). However, I know she's always coveted my cute clothes. I'll just have to keep my eye on her. As for the airlines, they're in on it for the sheer entertainment value. The stories they must hear. "Sir, you should know better than to pack your erectile dysfunction medication in a checked bag. That's why God invented carry-ons. Yes, it will be a disappointing honeymoon, won't it?"

In the midst of my paranoid pondering, Karen splashed water onto the raft I'd been floating on.

"Whatcha doin?" she asked.

"I have just come to the conclusion that my entire warm weather wardrobe now consists of eight items. Six of them have Mayan Palace Acapulco printed or embroidered on them. It's such a lovely logo that I'm considering having it tattooed on my butt."

I must have sounded pretty wired because Karen suggested a drastic move.

"Let's go, like, look for a Wal-Mart or something."

I felt a tear welling up at her unselfish gesture.

So Karen and I ventured out in a Mexican limousine (a VW cab) in search of non-Resortwear.

"Is there somewhere we can buy clothes?"

"Si, senorita, La Plaza Grande," the cabbie answered, beaming with local pride. "Have you seen our fabuloso cliff divers?"

"No, but we saw a guy stumble off a pretty steep curb last night. That was entertaining," I answered, deadpan.

La Plaza Grande should be re-named La Plaza Nada. 'Cause that's just about what I bought there. I had never recognized how tiny Mexican women are, at least the teeny weenie *chicas* that live in the city and shop at La Plaza. The rural women in the hillside farming communities are just as short in stature, although a lot more chunked up on burritos.

Picture them either making their own clothes or shopping at the flea market and buying larger sizes abducted from well-fed tourists. Picture Consuela Maria Conchita Rodriguez and her four bambinos (under the age of five). Consuela has hand-washed the few articles of clothing her family possesses and is hanging them on a line to dry. She is wearing a T-shirt that says "INFIDELS WORLD BEACH TOUR 1984," which has a list of famous beaches on the back. She is also wearing my golf shorts and golf shoes. She has a cotton footie (also mine) stuffed in the toe of each shoe. They may not be a perfect fit, but the functionality speaks for itself. The soft spikes help keep her grounded, and as she stretches to pin another garment to the line, she doesn't slip or slide on the angling hillside.

I'm no giant. But at five foot six and a half, clothing size 8 or 10, the largest sizes at La Plaza were too small on me. And forget shoes. I wear a 9 ½, and the largest size at any of the shoe stores was a 7 ½.

So what exactly did I buy? One pair of butt-binding underwear, ditto on a pair of shorts, a Gecko T-shirt, and a pair of men's flip flops. After four hours of sun and alcohol, I clenched the few garments I now possessed, knowing that I would much too soon be hand-washing and hanging them to dry.

BY EVENING ON DAY FOUR, I felt myself slipping down fashion hill. Karen must have sensed it. Despite suffering acute shopping trauma, Karen made a wise and important decision.

"Tequila shooters, now!" she screamed to the Acapulco streets.

For those of you who are following closely, you'll remember Karen saying something about making new memories out of Resortwear. The mission was in full swing. Margaritas in hand, Karen and I toasted to something, maybe even twice. As I looked around the bar I saw no sign of Charlie Sheen, and I decided maybe Karen wasn't in on the conspiracy after all.

We were in a downtown Acapulco restaurant/bar named Carlos and some American name. These places, a dime a dozen in any Mexican resort area, serve cheap Mexican food, then trap you into staying by having the waiters entertain. The waiters then get the audience in on the act, blowing whistles to eardrum-popping music in order to hypnotize the masses. The Conga lines get going and the waiters pour a little tequila down your throat for free so that you keep entertaining yourself and others, and they can take a rest. Then they charge you whatever they feel like the rest of the night for drinks, because no one's sober enough to figure out the bill. This is an uncomplicated, fairly straightforward scam. Like the free lunch theory, I've learned, there is no such thing as free tequila.

It isn't a complicated conspiracy, except maybe the table dancing. Unless you've been to one of these places, it's not what you're thinking. They don't actually employ female table dancers, just the more-than-willing audience members. Once it's understood that the management and staff encourage the patrons to stand up on tables and chairs to dance, well, they just do it. It's beautiful. We get to exhibit our talents and the waiters get to rest. Another bonus the "friendly staff" enjoys is helping the female patrons up and down from tables, grabbing whatever body part is most handy.

Karen and I watched as some waiters were looking up the short skirts of two blonde girls they had just placed atop a table.

"You know, it does look like fun, and I could use the exercise. But it's just not much of a challenge in a place like this."

"Really?" Karen seemed interested in my opinion, so I continued.

"The places to dance on tables, or bars, for that matter, are those which really frown on the idea. You know, uptight, upscale places. Unless you risk being obtrusive, disruptive, or thrown out, why bother?"

Karen knew where I was headed with this. "So, you're looking more for the extreme form of the sport? You sound like you may have some experience."

We had wandered through a few popular watering holes and come upon a lovely little Mexican Bistro overlooking the bay. A four-piece band was playing a catchy little tune.

"Unbelievable view!" I exclaimed to Karen, as I swayed to and fro toward an unoccupied table. "We'll have an even better view on top of this."

I didn't even bother to push the white tablecloth aside as I stepped from the floor to the chair to the tabletop. Karen snatched the silverware and handed it to a waiter.

"C'mon," I beckoned for Karen to join me, with my favorite vacation mantra.

"We'll never see these people again."

The crowd roared. The band picked up the pace. My cute white linen top and skirt from the Mayan Palace was the perfect costume for the show. I was Jennifer Beal without the welding. I was Jennifer Grey without the Swayze. I was drunk, wired, and delusional. But most dangerous of all, I was falling in love with my captors. The bandleader tipped his sombrero in my direction and shouted, "Where are you from?"

"Proud to be a Buckeye," I shouted back, suddenly feeling patriotic to my Midwestern roots.

As I cha-cha'd and dipped my shoulders to "The Girl from Ipanema," I saw a shot glass with an arm connected to it, out of the corner of a blurry eye.

"Do you know where Fremont, Ohio, is?" asked a middle-aged man in aviator glasses and a flowered Resortwear shirt.

My mantra had once again failed me. I downed the shot of tequila and took his hand to steady my descent from the table.

"Uh, thanks. Yeah, my boss is from Fremont."

"What's his name? I probably know him. It's a small town."

"I'm sure you do," I answered, deciding that I wanted to give no further details.

I was looking for Karen to rescue me. She appeared like an angel with a Corona and a smirk.

"Geez, DC, didn't they inform you that as a member of the witness protection program you shouldn't make such a spectacle?"

The morning of day five of the Maybe-It's-Not-Lost-Just-Kidnapped-Luggage, denial phase of the vacation, Karen suggested we go look for a nudist resort. I was too hung over to argue against such sound logic.

We found ourselves roaming a stretch of beach, past scores of tourists and beach vendors. I scanned the horizon for anything familiar, including a hint of my past identity.

"Keep a close eye on the surf, Karen. Maybe something will wash up on the shore."

I had a glazed look in my eyes as I watched the beach vendors suspiciously to see if they were already selling my garments and calculated how much I might spend to re-purchase them.

"DC, get over it. There won't be a magic message in a bottle instructing you on how to retrieve your luggage. It's gone," Karen said, with tough love and little compassion.

We ended up at The Princess Hotel.

"So is this a four or five star resort?" Karen wondered out loud.

"I guess it depends on the planetary alignment and the size of the payoffs to the people who vote on those things," I said, peppered with cynicism.

"I think it should depend on how many bars are in the hotel, you know, rate them a four or five bar resort. It'd be good advertising," Karen said.

Despite the security guards on our tail, we made a beeline to the gift shop, holding out some hope that there might be some more normal clothing to purchase there.

"It's the exact same shit as the Mayan Palace," I announced, distressed.

"Well, at least they have Acapulco Princess printed on it instead," Karen commented, as if it mattered. "You need to calm down," she added, patting me on the back.

She was right as usual. We exited the shop. With shoulders slumped in defeat, I declared, "That's it. No more wasted time shopping on this vacation."

The security guards at the Princess were actually pretty insecure, as it turned out. They continued to follow us, unsure of our intentions. Finally, one asked us our room number (we didn't have the colored plastic bracelet that identified us as part of this particular cult).

"We're not those kind of girls," I said. "We don't give out our room numbers to strangers."

Karen laughed. The security guards gave up and took off, probably because they didn't understand English.

We slipped into one of the poolside bars at the Princess and were immediately embraced, literally, by an American man in his mid-50s who looked like he might have forgotten to sleep for a few days. "Lovely, lovely ladies, what'll you have? Anything, anything at all, it's all on me."

The words spit from his mouth like an underwater machine gun blast.

"Anthony Palmetto, Dubuque, Iowa, at your service," he said, as he dribbled kisses on our hands, an act which is supposed to prove that someone is a gentleman because he is pretending to treat you like a lady.

Personally, I've never bought the routine. Especially when the drill is done in a bar. Speaking of drills, it turned out our benefactor was a dentist.

"Help me celebrate, ladies. How about some champagne, or a margarita?" Anthony threw a couple of hundreds on the bar, just in case anyone was missing his generous display.

"I'm DC, and this is Karen."

"Correction, Negro Modelo and Pina Colada," Karen said, pointing at herself, then me.

The bartender nodded and quickly went to his task.

"Celebrate what?" I inquired, while wondering, *and for how long?*

By the looks of him, it was three consecutive days, or perhaps a lifetime, with a few hours of shut-eye slipped in through the years.

"I hit for $230 grand in Vegas Friday night and hopped a plane here as soon as I was sure I had run my streak." He then proceeded to run a new streak with his mouth. "You see, that's important. Too many people don't understand that about gambling. You don't cut your losses at a limit or quit while you're ahead. That's for amateurs. You have to ride out the streaks, the ups and downs. It's a rhythm. It's a roller-coaster. It's a wild ride. You can't just get off somewhere in the middle."

Just as I thought this guy would never stop talking, Karen jumped on his train of thought.

"Wow, $230 grand! So you must be a professional gambler."

Attempting to look mysterious, Anthony cocked his bushy gray and brown eyebrows over patriotic eyes (yes, that's red, white, and blue, comrades).

"I'm a dentist by profession and a gambler by necessity," he unfurled.

As Karen and I imbibed our liquid anesthetic, I poured more metaphors in my mind. "You mean you're a dentist in order to support your gambling?"

"Almost right. I'm a dentist for a living. But I live to gamble. If I didn't gamble, I wouldn't feel alive. I have a large, respected practice in Dubuque with two associates. But I'm not a hypocrite and my patients stick with me. Even through an unfortunate FBI sting that put my face on every newspaper cover in town."

He paused for a moment, I think to blink for the first time since Vegas. I thought *I* was wired the previous night. This guy *WAS* the wire, sizzling.

"I won't go into the details of that little mess. But with the support of the community and a few well-connected Italian friends, I beat the rap and kept my good name."

Karen and I were nodding for him to continue at this point. He was the electric company looking to unload some high voltage. We were plugged in.

"The feeling I get when I gamble…Well, sometimes my

heart just stops. I can be up $50 grand or down $100 grand. It's a total rush. I HAVE TO HAVE THAT FEELING!" he said with an exclamation point, throwing back the remainder of his 151 rum. "Ladies, you gotta understand. Vietnam really fucked me up. When you're crouched down in a minefield with bullets whizzing past your head, well, it's a horrible fear. But now I crave that feeling, and gamblin' is the closest thing to that same rush."

Karen and I exchanged looks of painful amusement, like we might have during the Nixon resignation speech.

"C'mon ladies, another drink?"

He ordered another round.

"Having a good time?" Anthony asked.

"Yeah, pretty good. Except my luggage was stolen," I said, surprised that he'd ricocheted back to the present moment.

The conversation must always come back to me, no matter how interesting someone else's story.

"That's too bad. C'mon, whaddaya say, let's go. I'll buy you new clothes, anything you want."

I heard sincerity in his voice, even though he was talking louder and faster.

"But, first, we should all go to my room where there's lots of little lines and mirrors." He was attempting to wink at us for agreement in some Popeye-gone-mad, cartoonish manner.

"You are kidding, right?" I asked, rhetorically.

Karen shook her head in disbelief and signaled me with a thumb toward the beach. "I think this ride is over, time to get off," was her whispered response, as she quickly finished off her drink so as not to waste any alcohol, *our* drug of choice.

Anthony immediately tried to redeem himself from his miscalculation of our characters.

"Now, I don't do this stuff in the states. I could lose my practice. But it's everywhere down here. I mean, I'm a good dentist. I don't believe in braces for braces sake. Too many people have been talked into them and end up with serious T.M.J. I also don't believe that white teeth are necessarily the healthiest teeth. A good, green set of teeth that can still chew a corn-on-the-cob is O.K. by me."

He might have been waiting for an amen at the end of this barstool sermon. We didn't give it. Redemption with dental advice. Well it was O.K. by me, but I won't be judging at the pearly whites (gates, that is).

"Did I mention that I'm being comped tickets for the Streisand show for New Year's at the MGM?" he asked, finally, in desperation.

Usually up for more of the story, I wasn't sure I wanted to witness full-fledged shellshock this early in the day. Besides, I hadn't been mistaken for a coke whore for quite some time (like, ever) and I was just a bit antsy.

"Anthony, hon, thanks for everything. But it's arts and crafts hour at our hotel," I said, looking at my naked wrist for a watch.

"Yeah, we're going to paint porcelain fish. It's just something we've been wanting to do," Karen added.

On the walk back to our hotel, I was aware that my little luggage problem was nothing, relatively speaking.

"Who do you think we should call first, the DEA, the IRS, the FBI, or the Dental Association of Dubuque?" Karen wondered aloud.

"That was funny, but, also sad," I said.

"Kind of like your golf game," said Karen.

As usual, she was right.

WHILE I SLEPT, I WAS VISITED BY THE WAL-MART Fairy. He looked like Dustin Hoffman. He placed several nice crisp Hanes high-leg cotton panties under my pillow. But when I awoke, my mouth tasted like cotton and the panties were gone.

I concluded that either it was just a dream, or I had eaten

them. Unless the fourteen Coronas I consumed the night before had anything to do with anything. As I lay in bed, underwear dreams gave way to T-shirt fantasies. Let me explain: My problem with most T-shirts is that they lack originality. I mean, "Hard Rock Cafe," "Hard something else Cafe," "Something, Something Resort or Bar," and so forth. Even those that have catchy phrases "One tequila, two tequila, three tequila, floor" are mass-produced on demand, by the hundreds or thousands. That's how my friends and I got into the business of designing and making our own T-shirts for commemoration of special events and vacations. We came up with original shirt designs, in limited editions of fifteen to twenty, max.

As I lay in bed, paralyzed with thoughts of never-to-be seen-again, original design, limited edition T-shirts that had been packed in my luggage, I made a bargain with God. Although I was excited at the possibility of a new design, a limited edition of one T-shirt that read "My mother spent my inheritance on Resortwear and all I got was this lousy T-shirt" for my daughter, I asked God to get me back my luggage. In exchange, I would quit making fun of other peoples' lack of originality in pre-shrunk cotton outer-garments.

I bolted out of bed with tremendous conviction and a minor migraine. Gathering up my Mayan Palace-acquired garments and devoid of clean undergarments, I placed everything except my running shorts and T-shirt in a Mayan Palace laundry bag and called for the valet. I decided to go for a therapeutic run to sweat off the alcohol and stop sweating the whole lack of clothing issue. Even though I'd have to remain in my bathing suit all day until my laundry was delivered.

Karen was doing laps in the pool when I returned, getting rid of her own alcohol accumulation and presumably making room for more, but I decided to do my lapse outside of the pool. I needed to start looking on the bright side. I'd survived all but two days of my vacation with or without certain essentials. And I knew I could turn this negative into a positive.

I had experience doing just that. Like table dancing, it required equilibrium, attitude, and balance. On this fine day, my balance was a little off. So I played it safe by lying motionless on a lounge chair, poolside, and philosophizing to Karen.

"You know, I've been thinking, there's a reason why this happened."

"Searching for meaning in a senseless crime?"

"Something like that," I said, softly. "Do you think I'm materialistic, Karen?"

"You're not materialistic, you are a unique freak."

I opened my eyes and sat up at her proclamation.

"Go on," I said.

"Your self-absorption isn't about the same icons as the truly materialistic people. You place a higher value on being different rather than being the same. You could care less about the Tommy Hilfiger or Calvin Klein or Liz designer stuff you could easily replace. I've been listening to you drone on for days about the one-of-a-kind stuff at some out-of-the-way place that nobody else is wearing."

Karen was borderline psychic by now.

"Like the T-shirts I designed for all the girl trips?"

"Exactly."

"Wow, I'm a creativity snob. How can I be a creativity snob when all I've written is T-shirts—okay, and a screenplay that went nowhere."

It was a relief to admit my sin out loud.

"You've written some pretty funny answering machine messages," Karen said.

I glanced over at the book I'd been reading, by far the best thing I had purchased from the Mayan Palace gift shop— *Island Of The Sequined Love Nun* by Christopher Moore—and thought how cool it would be to write such a great, funny book.

"So there is some kind of lesson I need to learn from this."

I searched the pool area for a Zen master to appear.

"You have the knowledge, now what will you do with it?" asked a gecko in the grass. O.K., maybe it was Karen, or maybe it was the pool boy. Perhaps my equilibrium was a bit off.

"Maybe you're supposed to open up a line of one-of-a-kind, unique Resortwear clothing that you could sell next to the lost luggage claims at the airport."

"Or I could start a support group called Luggage Lobotomy Association of America, or Resortwear Addicts of America."

"How about having a Resortwear burning party when we get back to Cincinnati?"

Karen shut her eyes and leaned back in her lounge chair. She was pretty smart, all right.

I had one last fantasy about Mayan Palace sponsoring a tabletop dancing tour of the world—me dressed in their Resortwear. Ultimately, I knew the party was the way to go.

Ironically, through further Zen contemplation, I understood that I had to lose my wardrobe to find my true identity. Some people may see me as chronically cynical. But without my old wardrobe, I had become a more tackily attired, chronic cynic who once thought "Life ain't nothin' but a cardboard box." I knew better now. Life ain't nothin' but a burlap sack, 'cause it's what they're wearing in resorts around the world. Then I thought, *there's a fiesta tonight, and I've got just the thing to wear. That is, if my laundry makes it back...*

In the meantime, I might just start writing that book. Wonder if I've got any funny stories to tell?

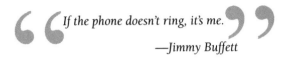

If the phone doesn't ring, it's me.
—Jimmy Buffett

A FLING WITH GRAVITY

THE JOLT AWAKENED ME, snapping my head up then down. Bobblehead, I thought, amused. Eyes open, I renewed my bearings and thought something else. *A little turbulence or mechanical problem with the left engine?* Neither. I was convinced the plane was caught in God's throat and that was a hiccup: a symptom of His laughter from watching me the past two days.

I noticed the gray-haired man, suit and skin to match, wasn't shaken either. Another bump, whether in the air, or along life's road, was just a reminder that gravity would get us eventually, one way or another. A brief interruption of the crossword puzzle was all it was for Mr. Gray. But two days in Minneapolis and some crosswords had me puzzled and battling gravity roller-coaster style. We'd had a silent ride to the airport— tension building like an overstretched bungee cord ready to snap back. I was surprised I could have dozed off at all, now that *I* had snapped.

"Don't email me or call me," I had said, staring at the wrinkled black leather duffel Rory had set on the curb.

Don't give him anything but indifference, I thought. But anger stepped out in front first, guarding, then slamming all emotional doors.

Now, nothing more could escape. Nothing else could get in. Left with one solitary thought—alone again, naturally. A mental karaoke performance of the Vonda Shepard re-do of the Gilbert O'Sullivan classic song helped hermetically seal out the pain. I could almost laugh. A good humor seal. What a cheesy song. What a cheesy moment.

Get over it. Get over yourself.

After about fifty failed relationships, including one that lasted approximately thirty minutes and took place in a closet during a Dallas toga party when I was 24—which explains it—I could no longer suffer from a broken heart. I just added a new layer to the shell around it. When my heart turned entirely to stone, I thought, I'll just skip it across the water for my further amusement.

What happened this time?

It wasn't as if I thought Rory and I would get married, but neither did I expect the weekend to go from chased to chaste.

LIQUID LOBOTOMY: THAT'S WHAT MY FRIEND Karen called it when you drink so much you forgot things. The mind, like a lone ice cube melting into a different state of being, not gone, just becoming something else, morphed into its surroundings. My problem was that sometimes I remembered too much, replaying scenes over and over. So routine was this brain exercise that over the years I'd developed brains of steel—cold and numb. I probably wouldn't have felt a frontal lobotomy. The liquid lobotomy didn't work, either.

As a matter of fact, the ONLY thing fuzzy about that last night was how Rory ended up on the couch—and I in the bed—when I started out on the couch, assuming he was in bed. The solitary thought of being solitary again bungeed back: Why did I always end up sleeping alone? Well, maybe not always, but for most of my life.

As far as I could see, I'd done nothing to deserve that fate, except maybe the time in the ninth grade when Linda Marks and I put a dead rat in a box and wrapped it up like a gift for Mona Phillips. I couldn't still be paying for that thirty years later, could I? Was it bad judgment agreeing to come to Minneapolis in the first place? No, that wasn't it. Saturday was good. Hell, Saturday was fantastic. *There's nothing wrong with me. He's the one who's whacked.* My post-mortem relationship mantra.

My tongue searched my mouth for moisture. The bottle of water in my Elvis carry-on bag was too far of a reach, and the task of extracting it from under the seat, poking and prodding through its contents, was way too tedious to consider in my wretched state. I sat and thirsted in martyrdom for all the women of the world who had been backhandedly and undeservedly slapped by male rejection.

Especially when we were such Good Sports.

SATURDAY, WHEN RORY OPTED TO GO to the Twins game instead of a nice dinner, I was agreeable. I didn't even complain about the nacho cheese dripped on my sleeve by the guy to my right. And on Sunday I'd actually acted enthused about going to the Adam Sandler movie.

"You know, I've been thinking that's what life is all about, about love and having THAT kind of relationship," Rory said.

He was in a deep philosophical, ethical, and religious funk over the moving movie experience. I was thinking that Adam Sandler relied perhaps too heavily on the expletive "Oh shit" before or after every episode of physical comedy, which detracted from the lack of story-line depth. I was also wondering if Winona would get convicted on those shoplifting charges. But, then, we all process the arts differently.

On the drive back to his house, Rory explained how God had spoken to him through the movie, showing him that the lovemaking we'd enjoyed Saturday night was wrong. I think that's when Rory decided we should sleep apart. Sunday guilt I understood, being a recovering Catholic, but this was too much. It was beautiful yesterday and ugly today?

"The least you could have done is to reach this moral epiphany tomorrow after I'm on the plane," I'd said, not knowing what else to say.

We both looked out the car windows for cue-cards. His read, "This doesn't have anything to do with you, it's me."

This cue-card has gotten around. I've heard it read before. I've even read it myself. This time, I was hoping for a Happier Gilmore ending.

I had met Rory three years before, almost to the day, on vacation at a lake resort in Minnesota. I was with my friend Karen, and Rory was on a golf weekend with some buddies. Our last night there, we were in the resort bar. Rory's group had been playing golf and drinking all day, not necessarily in that order. He was the cutest, and at first I thought, also the quietest. His golf cap was on backwards and he had dimples-to-die-for, of game-show-host proportions (one of my many men weaknesses). When one of the guys dared him to dance, he did. Just got out on the dance floor all by himself and moved. The boy could move. I made my own move when he sat down at the bar. An hour and twenty minutes later I hated to leave, but we had to drive several hours the next morning to catch a flight. Sure, they'd invited us back to party at their condo, but there were twelve of them and two of us. It didn't take a mathematician—or a prude—to understand two divided by twelve was a negative number. Karen kissed her "date" goodbye, and Rory further impressed me with a game of tongue-twister.

I never expected to hear from him again. Why would I? He lived several states away, and we both shared custody of our kids with exes and had so many other things going on. But he called and emailed, and I called and emailed back. There were lulls when one of us was dating someone else, and then we'd both be dateless for a while and swear to figure out a way to get together. The biggest problem was, we had our kids on opposite weekends; singles today know, for the most part, that custodial incompatibility trumps geographic undesirability.

One weekend (around the first anniversary of our meeting) I was supposed to meet him in Chicago when my ex had our daughter on vacation. It wasn't as though I just blew it off. Rory was going with a group of guys to a Cubs game anyway. It wasn't as if he'd be alone, I'd told myself. Another opportunity arose the second year of our correspondence. His ex was taking their daughter over Thanksgiving weekend. I was finally flying there (he was paying). The day before I was to leave, my grandfather died.

But when Rory's ex got remarried, she asked to change weekends to match her husband's visitation schedule (stepfamilies get complicated). We no longer had an excuse not to get together, so we planned my long-awaited trip to Minneapolis. Some of my friends couldn't believe I was going. Karen wasn't one of them. She thought my impetuousness was cool (but she wasn't around when I stole my parents' car in junior high and hit a few parked cars, either).

"Do you remember what he looks like?" she asked.

"Not really, but I know he was cute," I told her.

"He had a hat on when we met him. Do you think he has hair?" asked Karen.

"I don't know, but as long as it's not a comb-over or a toupee, I don't care."

SO WHEN, EXACTLY, DID GOD start laughing?

It had to be when I got to baggage claim Saturday morning and Rory wasn't waiting, as I imagined, with a bouquet of flowers.

No flowers.

No Rory.

In the half hour I waited for him to arrive, as other passengers were met, retrieved their bags and exited, I imagined a lot of things. I imagined several men to possibly be Rory, as I couldn't be exactly sure what he looked like. One was not very attractive, wearing a wrinkled T-shirt. He also had a very big nose (which he picked like a scratch-off lottery ticket). But, he did have dimples, like Rory's. I wondered how much I had to drink the night I met him.

Oh my God I hope that's not him.

That's probably when God laughed, when I first invoked His name. And then I thanked Him when the nose-picker wasn't Rory.

After waiting over twenty-five minutes, I imagined that he chickened out for some reason and wasn't going to show up at all. What would I do? The possibility turned into a romantic comedy/drama as I wrote the movie script. *Sleepless in Seattle* was one of Rory's favorites. This would be *Dateless in Minneapolis*. I would contact a local TV station and get the ear of a sympathetic reporter, telling her all the details of the three years of correspondence, the sheer romance of it all. Then how I'd been left at the baggage claim. The camera would be angled to my good side, and when I teared up, the men of the Twin Cities would come to my rescue. There'd be phone calls to the TV station, offers from gorgeous leading men-types to take me out, or take me in.

As I was picturing the final scene in my daydream—

Leading Man moves to Cincinnati—Rory sheepishly appeared from around a corner. When I told him about the screenplay in my head, he laughed and looked sideways at me.

"So I showed up and ruined your ending. Now how are you going to write the story?" he asked.

"Well, we'll have to wait and see what happens. That's what I told a couple of my friends who thought I was crazy to come here," I said.

His smile wrapped around my doubts and hid them like a magician's cloak. What tricks could he have up his sleeve?

A hard lemonade for me and a beer for him later at a pub near the stadium, and I was caught up in the familiar rhythm of our conversation, which usually took place over the phone. The added dimension of physically being there, smelling his cologne, connecting with his eyes, and watching his expressions aroused familiarity, which created a feeling of almost instantaneous intimacy for me. I was sure he felt it, too.

"How's the story going so far?" Rory asked, as he inched beside me at a stand-up table at the outdoor bar.

That's when I felt the first flush of lust.

"So who do you want to play you in the movie?" I joked.

"I'll have to get back to you on that, but I do want to choose my name: Rory Hansen," he said.

"Sounds like a hockey player," I said, shooting him my You're-Cute-and-Funny-So-Why-Don't-You-Kiss-Me look, which may have been a little off because he held my hand instead.

Is it just me, or do professional sports delay the progression of emotional intimacy in our culture? Sure, there's the occasional public marriage proposal flashing on the JumboTron, but that's for show. I can't recall being at a baseball game or basketball game where couples talked, held hands, or exhibited other PDA's. Probably why they came up with the Kiss-Cam—which I'm sure was invented by a woman.

So it was a tad disappointing to sit through nine innings without going to first base.

Back at Rory's condo, we fell back into the rhythm of relating, first on the back patio and then on the couch.

"Do you want to watch *Sleepless in Seattle?*" he asked. Before I could answer he gave it a second thought.

"You know, I haven't even kissed you yet," he said.

Mind-reader, I thought. The kisses started sweet, then turned into a playful bobbing-for-tongues contest.

"We probably don't need a movie," he said, as he took my hand and led me upstairs.

THE MEMORY OF A NOW absent tongue. Tongue party of one, stained, revealed remnants of last night's wine, which no longer satisfied. I could have spit. Instead I reached for the Elvis bag, *Where's that damned water?* I had a sip, then an epiphany of my own. *Elvis, he had that, what? Madonna/Whore complex.* Which, as I understood it, was having some sacred infatuation with one's mother (the Madonna symbol) and having some unmet needs for the love of her, as an infant. Fear of intimacy may develop as a defense against allowing those early hurts to become conscious. Sexual contact between lovers can trigger the Madonna/Whore complex sufferer's need to get away from an intimate emotional and physical relationship that he associated with pain. The lover is subsequently sexually rejected: viewed as a whore.

Maybe that was Rory's story. How else could you explain going from John Holmes to Billy Graham in less than twenty-four hours?

BY SUNDAY MORNING I'D DECIDED I had a new boyfriend—long-distance but a boyfriend nonetheless. He'd rolled over to hug the side of the bed instead of me when he woke. As I rubbed his back gently, he remained frozen. This was not the kind of stiff I hoped to wake up to.

"I have a terrible headache," Rory moaned. "Too many beers."

I did a mental calculation of five beers in eight hours, spaced hours apart with only one at the game. It didn't add up to hangover, especially not for a guy who'd bragged about tailgate parties beginning at dawn for his beloved Vikings. He was from up "Nort." *The boys up here can drink,* I thought. So when I went to the bathroom and came back to find him up and fully dressed, I was more certain something else was up.

"How about we go to breakfast and then I drop you off at Mall of America to shop for a few hours? I need to go into the office," he said, avoiding eye contact.

"On a Sunday? You're going to work on a Sunday?" I asked. At breakfast, he barely ate. I thought, *maybe he really isn't feeling well.* Looking for some sign of recovery, or the guy I was with the night before, I said, "Last night was great."

He looked at me briefly, then stared at his omelet.

"DC, I feel kind of guilty about that. I'm not sure we should have done that," he said. "Remember I told you about the last girl I dated? I've been thinking she was right, you know, to wait."

"Yeah. The 28-year-old-virgin," I said, a little too sarcastically. "I didn't realize virginity was contagious." He was trying to tell me something, I thought.

Listen.

"Hey, never mind. We'll talk later. I need to get to the office," he said.

I initiated a small kiss before I jumped out of the car at the mall. He kissed me back, which I took as a good sign. Three hours later, when he came back to get me, I hoped it would be the yesterday Rory, the last night Rory, not the morning Rory—the Hot Minnesota Twin not The Cold One.

The plan was to play nine holes of golf. I mean, I'd dragged my clubs up from Cincinnati. But Rory decided we'd go to the driving range instead. I kept my Good Sport face on. His body language said Cold Rory, and his lack of flirtation put an exclamation point on it. He still claimed to be hungover. Not naïve enough to believe this and experienced enough to have gotten the cold shoulder after short meaningless relationships, I couldn't chalk this up on the same board. Three years, for God's sake. Wasn't that SOMETHING?

What about the sex? To me it wasn't sex, it was making love. You know the difference. Okay, maybe I was a little overly enthusiastic, but it had been MONTHS since the last time. Maybe I'd come off as too experienced and the sex was TOO good. So good that he felt bad, dirty, guilty. Most men I've dated would say, yeah, that's when you know you're doing it right. But for Rory it may have triggered the Madonna/Whore thing.

I HAD HOPES THAT THE MOVIE WOULD lighten the mood. Dark movie theater, some good laughs, a little hand-holding, and…I was sooo wrong. Rory seemed to enjoy the movie all right, but he might as well have been alone, and I suspected he wished he were. It was as if the right side of his seat (next to me) was the mouth of the river Styx and he'd perish in its abyss if he got near it (or me).

On the ride to Rory's, the car served as a confessional. He told me about not being very religious before in his life, but now thinking that sex should be more sacred: saved for a real relationship like the one Adam Sandler was having with Winona Ryder in *Mr. Deeds.*

Sex only in a real relationship?

I reminded him that he'd told me over the years that he would never get married again.

"You broke up with the virgin because you said she wouldn't have sex unless she was married, yet you didn't want to marry her or 'be a monk the rest of your life.' Which is it? And by the way, I thought, until today, that we did have a real relationship."

I was raising my voice. As hope fell, my voice inevitably rose.

Back at Rory's, I helped myself to a bottle of wine, opened it, and escaped to the back patio where I chain-smoked in silence.

He's been begging me to come visit him, and we talked about the sex thing several times. He knew very well where this weekend might go, and it did, and it was great. So what in the hell is he doing?

Rory sat cautiously across from me at the patio table. I smoked and stared and told him just what I'd been thinking.

"I'm sorry. I don't know what to say except for I'm being honest about how I feel," he said.

"No, I think you were being honest with how you felt last night, and gave into it, and now you're scared, for some reason," I challenged him with my tight-lipped look.

A bumper sticker came to mind: *If You Can't Stand The Heat Don't Buy A Lap Dance.*

While I was inventing bumper stickers, he read that same old cue-card. "This has nothing to do with you (inserting an improvised, you're great!). This is about me and something I'm going through," he said.

"Bullshit! That nice guy routine doesn't fly. You're just being an asshole today, I mean, completely caught up in yourself and how you're feeling. Have you for a moment thought about how I might be feeling? I'm feeling terrible. Yesterday I was on cloud nine, and you helped put me there. Today, I wish I'd never come here. I feel totally rejected and emotionally lower than I've been in a long time. And it's your fault!"

I paused for a second to catch my breath and to see the look on his face. I thought he was afraid I might throw something. Instead I stood up, stomped out my cigarette, and pointed a finger in his face.

"Rejection is rejection, even if you want to put God in the middle of this. This isn't about what happened last night. You think what we did last night was a sin? I'll tell you the real sin—spending an entire day at this distance without so much as holding my hand. Especially after what we did last night. THAT is a much bigger sin!"

"IT'S 68 DEGREES AND CLOUDY in Cincinnati. Flight attendants, please prepare for landing."

The pilot's voice reminded me of the matter-of-fact pilot Peter Graves from the movie, *Airplane*. I imagined him coming on next with a line from the movie, "Have you ever seen a grown man naked?" Back to self-amusement.

Another good sign. I'll get over this in a week, I think. A bad sign. That kind of resilience must mean I'm jaded; my heart of stone is made of jade. Could be a good Aerosmith lyric.

Life's a bitch and then you become one. And I must be. My last words to Rory, there at curbside, were stinging wasps. "Thanks for the story," I'd said, doing my best Rizzo-to-Kenickie impression, as though that's all I'd come for and had never felt anything more. It was an attempt to belittle. Thereby, I effectively became little. I tried to hide my last brief glance at Rory, but the sadness in his eyes caught me. His stoic dissonance was a sign I'd ignored. "Take The High Road," it read.

The pilot braked. The sound was loud and high-pitched, like God clearing his throat. And here I was, urging him on.

Go ahead, I'm listening. Speak up.

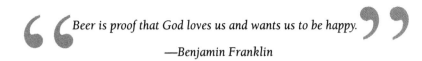

Beer is proof that God loves us and wants us to be happy.

—Benjamin Franklin

H A S H I N G I T O U T

WHEN I REFLECTED UPON THE EVENTS surrounding my divorce, I could see that humor wore a mask that rendered it almost invisible. In retrospect, the only thing the least bit funny about this and a few other truly tragic life episodes was the comic magnitude of my own self-absorption.

Guilty, party of one. Please sit me at the pitiful table, by myself, in the dark, while the rest of you happy couples go about your merry married way.

I managed to keep both the house and my self-pity after the divorce.

Good attorney.

In the years following the divorce, I tried to reach out to the universe and get my arms around my New World so that it would all revolve around my young daughter and me. The telephone remained as silent as that guy from Penn and Teller—the one who doesn't talk. The universe seemed to put me on hold while it took other calls. Perhaps I needed to learn to expand into the world, instead. But how?

On the advice of other people who had as little clue as

I did about how to be successfully single again, I attended a singles charity event. I quickly concluded the charity must have been for a cure for male-pattern baldness and potbellies and was a perfect testament to the fact that most, if not all of them, should have just stayed married.

While I hadn't fantasized that my single-again life would be Melrose Place, I was mortified by the prospects at my ripe-old age of 36. I would have had a better time visiting a convent, where I could have at least tormented nuns with bawdy stories and off-color jokes. Instead, I was forced to be pleasant, watching 60-year-old men flirt with 25-year-old women in inane conversation. Bad script. Could use a rewrite.

A few comments about the bar scene: The bands start too late, and the older I get, the louder they are. Did I mention that I also like a chair to sit in after a long day? On the other hand, the freelance nature of the bar is preferable to an event (let's say, singles for charity) you paid to enter while being forced to wear a HELLO MY NAME IS name tag. (which stipulates 'we're in the same club, you have to talk to me').

In a bar, you have every right to ignore or walk away from any individual you find irritating. At such an "event," this behavior is frowned upon, especially by the people who organize them—because it is the only way they can get people to talk to them.

Take Parents Without Partners. Sounds like a fun organization. I really shouldn't judge. I'm sure there are some lovely people in this group. But I'd suggest a name change, like Potential Sex Partners Whose Kids Are At The Exes A Lot. It's all about marketing, after all.

Here's some other worthless advice on meeting eligible bachelors. I received it from a happily married coworker: "Go to church."

"I do go to church," I said. "The only other single person in my age group is my ex-husband."

"Try a different church."

"Yeah, I could go back to the Catholic Church. At least the priests are single."

It was dear old mom who finally came up with a workable plan.

"Get involved in an activity you like, and you'll meet other people with the same interests."

I was already in a girl's racquetball league, where we did some socializing. But all the women were married to husbands who had no single brothers or friends to fix me up with. I checked.

Another activity I enjoyed since college was running. *Running after boys, running off-at-the-mouth, running from the truth.* Then there was the physical kind. I did that some, too.

On the weekends Cori was with her dad, I renewed my 5K and 10K race participation (abandoned sometime during the marriage). At these charity events, the runners kept pretty much to themselves, or to the other people they came with. Somewhat disappointed after not making any connections to potential new friends or, God forbid, "dates," I didn't give up.

I sincerely hoped this form of exercise would lead to horizontal exercises, in which I had not participated for a year and a half.

As a result of the charity runs (sounds like diarrhea for people who want to lose weight), I began receiving a newspaper published by a popular Cincinnati running store. Bob Roncker's Running Spot listed all upcoming events and running groups. The running/walking groups included a mall-walking club for seniors, a gay and lesbian group, and a marathon training team. One group, however, advertised itself as "a non-competitive, 3-5 mile, fun running club." Looked like the perfect tree to climb, though SCH4, the name of the group, meant nothing to me. Some inconsequential acronym, I assumed. The important thing was that the next scheduled run for SCH4 fit into both my work and my parenting schedules.

SEVERAL DOZEN PAIRS OF RUNNING SHORTS identified the wearers as members of this group, as they milled around the parking lot. Several grabbed cans of beer out of a cooler, which was on the back of a pick-up truck. I checked my watch, thinking I must have missed the run, since beer drinking (in my experience) follows the event, not vice versa. A tall guy with a silver footprint earring carried a clipboard and wore a whistle around his neck, which gave him some air of authority, so I approached him.

"The paper said the run starts at 4. Is that right?"

"Thereabouts," he said. "You must be a virgin."

I laughed at what I thought was an off-the-cuff metaphor.

"We'll get going soon. What's your name?"

"Uh, DC," I said, glancing around at a few faces that had entered into my peripheral view as he wrote on the clipboard. I found it curious that everyone wore whistles.

"I'm A.V."

I didn't laugh, as it was not a very original joke. Often, people introduce themselves by their initials after I have introduced myself by the nickname I've had my entire life.

The mild 70-degree June day was perfect running weather. A light cirrus screened the sun as A.V. blew his whistle and yelled, "Circle up, you wanks."

The crowd slowly moved, forming a sloppy amoeba.

Wanks? What the hell are wanks?

The girl to my right was bent over, greasing up her legs with what appeared to be sun block. She looked up at me. "Want some?" she said, offering the bottle.

"Ivy Block?"

"Yeah, there's going to be a lot of shiggy," she said, as if I knew what that was. Before I could inquire about "shiggy," the shrill sound of the whistle diverted my attention.

A.V., the attractive lanky drill-sergeant, stood in the middle of the ring of runners with another guy, sort-of Woody Boydish (beats Woody Allenish). Neither wore wedding bands. I'd learned to spot a ring-of-gold a football field away. Ringdar. I'd worked on this skill since the divorce. Combined with Gaydar, these two surveillance techniques can quickly help sort out ineligibles or at least the honest ones—some married men don't wear a ring, for obvious reasons.

"Virgins, front and center!" commanded A.V.

I didn't budge.

"C'mon, all first-timers, to the middle."

I did a quick 360 and saw a curly-haired guy walk into the center of the circle. "You, DC, get over here."

I complied. The military tone of the scene continued as A.V. and "Woody" marked the parking lot with chalk and flour, then talked in code.

"We are the hares for today's hash run. We will be marking the trail to lose and confuse the rest of you. Follow the marks we make and you'll eventually, hopefully, catch up with us at the end, where they'll be much rejoicing and beer."

His smile hinted sarcasm.

"This is a check," Woody said, pointing at an X he'd drawn. "This indicates the trail can go in 359 degrees in any direction."

After several other marks, including arrows and code words like back-check and boob-check, I lost interest in the instructions and busied myself by checking out the crowd.

The age range was 25 to 40. The gender ratio was 70/30, heavy on the male side. Good odds for me, I thought. I had to wonder what kind of pseudo military-type exercise this was. Luckily, there was no mention of paint-balls. I'd heard they can hurt. I also noted, despite some military similarities, there were no weapons, nor any crew cuts in the group.

"Clock starts now," yelled A.V., as he and Woody ran off in opposite directions spattering handfuls of flour.

The rest of the group loosened up the circle, but didn't

follow the guys. The girl with the Ivy Block came over and introduced herself to me.

"Hi, I'm Mystic Blow," she said.

Then a guy with earrings in both ears offered his hand to shake mine.

"I'm Red-Hot-Chili-Pecker," he said.

I was now officially blown away.

"Could one of you tell me what exactly is going on? What kind of running group is this, anyway?"

"It's a drinking club with a running problem," said Red-Hot.

"It's fun. Just go with it, you'll see," Mystic Blow encouraged me.

Red Hot yelled, "Song mistress, please."

A blonde 30ish woman moved into center-circle and started singing a song that had arm and leg motions to it.

Soon everyone had joined in singing, jumping up and down, flailing his or her arms around.

"Father Abraham had seven sons, seven sons had father Abraham and...."

It didn't turn out to be a religious song. The song finished and whistles blew from all around me.

Mystic said, "The hares' ten-minute head-start is up. C'mon, let's go. Run with me. I'll make sure you don't get lost."

We ran from the parking lot toward a building on the campus of Northern Kentucky University. The pace was slow enough to carry on conversation without losing my breath. Mystic quizzed me. "Those aren't brand new running shoes, are they?"

"No, about a month old. I just don't run that much, a few times a week."

"Good, 'cause new shoes are a crime. You'd have to drink out of them later."

I could tell by the tone of her voice she wasn't kidding.

"It's all right, we're usually nice to virgins."

We followed flour droppings like they were yellow bricks

that would take us to a magical place. The dollops of flour led through the University quad and into the library. Several runners ahead of me blew whistles upon entering the building.

"On-On," someone shouted.

Running through the library hallway, I looked sideways at Mystic.

"What's going on?"

"It's okay. We're on true trail. That's what On-On means."

"True trail?" I was going to need further clarification, and Mystic was getting used to it.

"Yeah, as opposed to being on a false trail. The hares WILL try to lose us, you know."

We ran up and down some stairs and then exited the library opposite of where we'd entered the building. Mystic pointed out a chalk marked X on the sidewalk. Runners were scattering in all directions.

"It's a check. Remember? Trail can go anywhere," she said.

And by this point, I was sure it would go somewhere interesting. We heard whistles coming from a wooded area several hundred yards away.

"It's the FRB's. Trail must go into the woods," a medium built guy with a pointy nose and ponytail said as he passed us.

"What are FRB's?" I asked my interpreter, Mystic.

"Front Running Bastards. The fast runners."

I felt an adrenaline rush as we took off toward the woods.

I get it. It's a game, I thought, just with some code words and stuff. Nothing too weird.

I was finally putting it all together, like stuffing the hay back into the scarecrow after the flying monkeys got him. Nothing too precise, just a general idea that it all fit somehow.

We came to an abrupt stop at a thick wall of trees. The foliage, bushes, and ground vines made it difficult to see anything that resembled a path. Ducking under low branches and stomping down pricker bushes (that's what we called them as kids) challenged me to use muscles I wouldn't need on an ordinary run.

Mystic and I arrived at a creek bed where clear flour marks on tops of stones rising out of the water indicated the trail blazed right through the water, and that we would surely follow.

"This is some serious shiggy," Red Hot said, as he stepped into the creek.

"Leave it to Anal Vice to lay this kind of trail."

I paused before stepping into the mucky stuff. "Mystic, please translate. Shiggy? Anal Vice?"

"Shiggy is off-the-road crap, like this," she said, pointing at the muddy ground. "Anal Vice is one of the hares, the tall one."

A.V., an abbreviation for another dirty sounding nickname.

I plunged my Nikes into the calf-deep, slow-moving current.

Halfway across, a petite blonde in front of me slipped on a submerged rock and did a full on-her-butt wipeout. I helped her to her feet, losing my footing, and then regaining it. She was laughing, vocal evidence she was unhurt.

A few hundred feet past the creek crossing, flour spots along the tree line led to an opening, *an escape from the shiggy.*

I tilted back my head at a 90-degree angle to accommodate the view of the same angle of a one helluva Kentucky hill. Whistles beckoned us from its summit. I looked back at the forest, which now seemed like a safe refuge. Mystic, once again beside me, smirked. "On up."

We climbed on all fours, grabbing tree trunks and rocks and digging in our heels to help us ascend rather than ass-end.

Nearing the top, several of the men reached down to pull us weaker ones (that would be me) up to level terrain.

"Beer near," said a cute guy wearing a bandanna.

There was more than a hint of sarcasm in Mystic's voice as she translated, without me asking. "That means beer is near."

Panting, sweating, I followed her to a gathering of fellow runners crowding around plastic trash bags filled with cans of beer. There were also a couple jugs of water and plastic cups. I went for the water.

I found a flat rock to sit on, drank most of my cup of water, saving some for my thorn-torn legs, rinsing off little trickles of blood, which revealed remaining scratches.

"There goes that leg modeling job I had lined up this week," I said to no one in particular.

A round-faced, round-bodied, 30ish guy looked up at me from his spot on the ground.

"Really?"

My laughter was evidence I was joking.

"Good one," said a woman standing behind me. "I'm Sucks." She held out her hand to shake.

"So, do we just walk back to our cars? I'm not sure if I want to go back the way we came."

"Don't worry," Sucks assured me, "we won't be going back the same way. We're not done yet. We're just taking a break."

The remainder of the "running game," as I continued to think of it, lasted another forty-five minutes. There was some standard on-the-road running, as well as a good stretch of railroad tracks, then "true trail" through a golf course.

"Pay no attention to the no trespassing signs," Mystic told me. "They don't apply to Hashers."

WE ENDED UP IN A SMALL TAVERN where the bar owner must have been expecting us. Pitchers of beer were already on tables. We'd run on and off for nearly two hours. I was exhausted, but in a good way, like after sex. I checked with Red Hot.

"Is the running really over? This isn't just another break?"

"Yep, the running is really over. Only drinking will henceforth be required. After all, it IS a drinking club with a running problem."

Mystic was in close conversation with A.V., so I decided to pick Suck's brain. She was very nice and easy to talk to. When she told me she taught school, I was a little surprised.

What is a sweet girl like you doing with a bunch of renegades?

She gave me a brief rundown on the group, which turned out to be international in scope. She said Hashing had its roots in Kuala Lumpur around 1938, and was dreamed up by some bored military personnel. She admitted Hashing was one of two social outlets since her divorce a few years earlier.

"I also belong to Mensa, which is way different from this group. Being a single parent, it's hard to meet people. The Hashers are a bunch of mostly professionals, who really know how to have fun."

Sucks said her "mother-given name" was Kathy, and gave me the scoop on the group. She pointed out some decent dating candidates and warned me of a few players. She summed up her advice in one memorable sentence: "Careful, the odds are good, but some of the goods are odd."

"CIRCLE UP," YELLED RED HOT, with the now familiar accompanied whistle.

Again, a human amoeba formed amidst bar stools, tables and chairs.

"No sitting in the circle," Red Hot admonished two lollygaggers.

"Hares, front and center."

A.V. and the "Woody" guy, now known as Vomit Dog, sauntered into the middle. (Sucks had filled me in: very cute, very single, very young).

"What did we think of this trail?" asked Red Hot.

There were shouts from all around the room.

"Not enough poison ivy."

"Not enough hills."

"Not enough shiggy."

The comments were all opposite of what the trail really was.

Sarcasm, which I well understood.

Red Hot started a song, which everyone immediately joined in, to the tune of "Happy Trails." The refrain was "Shitty Trail," and the lyrics included phrases like "I would rather drink my beer than hash your shitty trail."

Then, A.V. and Vomit Dog had to guzzle beers for "hare crimes."

Next thing I knew, I was being summoned to the middle again.

"Okay, virgins. First, tell us what your name is and who made you come today," said Red Hot, full of innuendo.

After telling the group my name and explaining that no one made me come, they laughed.

"Too bad, but the night's not over," said Vomit Dog.

The other virgin, a guy named Mark, said he'd made himself come, and got even more laughs and mock-sympathy.

We were instructed to guzzle our respective beers after a song was sung in our honor. "Here's to the Hashers, they're true blue," and on with some off-color lyrics. It sounded like an English drinking song.

I hadn't chugged a beer since college. Afterward, when I was congratulated and welcomed into the group, I wondered why I hadn't. The buzz of the beer, the exhilaration of the run, plus the camaraderie of the group, had gone to my head.

"You guys are crazy," I said to A.V. and Vomit Dog. "I'll definitely be coming back."

"You think this was crazy? Wait until you experience the Red Dress Run," A.V. said.

"We'll have, like eighty hashers running through downtown Sin City in red dresses," Vomit Dog added.

Several people were dancing on chairs and what little floor space remained. Vomit Dog took my hand and pulled me toward the jukebox.

CHUMBAWAMBA'S "TUBTHUMPING" was playing. As I listened to the lyrics—"I get knocked down but I get up again"—I thought, *Yeah, I sure do.*

As we danced, we shouted conversation over the song.

"What do you do for a living?" Vomit Dog asked.

"I sell empty boxes."

"I'm sure there's a helluva Hash name in that somewhere."

"That's scary."

"Don't worry, it's all good."

And for the first time in a long time, it felt like it was.

E P I L O G U E

MY OLD FRIENDS, JANET AND SUE, found the loves of their lives but retain a healthy skepticism about men—in general. Jamie lives in Nashville with her husband, who shares her intolerance of stupidity. Karen remarried but opted for a traditional wedding gown rather than Resortwear.

My sister Sherry continues her writing career as PR director in Toledo, and has two teenage boys. She was either guilted into—or inspired by me—to write her first novel, then anted up with another book (She says Guilt; I say Inspiration.)

Sister Lori became a lawyer and practiced, with reasonable disgust, for two years before returning to social work. She and husband, Mike, have a young son.

Gloria, AKA Gramma Glo, undeterred by the passing generations, remains cool as both grandmother and mother. She quit working as a secretary after Denny died, and went on to sell flowers, then books, travel the world, and volunteer for various non-profits. Glo continues to worship at Catholic Mass, although she still has issues with the Church, which she'll gladly tell you about.

I continued dating—in serial monotony fashion—a chain of fools, including a guy who once was mistaken for dead and woke up in a body bag at a 1980s rock concert. I began to see my choices as an indictment of my own intelligence, and finally, by the grace of God—meaning more luck than brains—found a good man who cured me of bad boys. It took a police chief, no less.

I live in Cincinnati with my teenage daughter, Cori, who has thus far disproved that old "payback" theory.

I still hang out with my sisters, and along with Sue, Janet, and the other girls take beach trips. We still make T-shirts for some occasions.

I remain friendly with Jack, the Zen boyfriend, who became a gazillionaire and lives in California with his wife and kids.

As for the football player friends in college, I recently gathered my courage and emailed a few of them, hoping for a reunion some day.

We know what happened to Jerry Springer, of course.

On the other hand, Mr. Put-In-Bay Disappearing Act, Brian Callahan, was never heard from again.

DC Stanfa's abilities in salesmanship led to speaking before both social and professional events where her topics include *From Bold To Sold: Getting What You Want By Being A Shameless Opportunist.* Her engagements—built around humor and the importance of self-esteem—draw from her own experiences at surviving high school, the Catholic church, datelessness, and the Jerry Springer Show.

Born and raised in Toledo, Ohio, DC insists she grew up after college in Dallas during the 1980s, an experience she refers to fondly as "the destructive and reconstructive years." Her maverick spirit is revealed early on in *The Art of Table Dancing: Escapades of an Irreverent Woman,* when she—as a mere seventh-grader—goes toe-to-toe with the church, and continues through a chronicle of crazy-but-true stories revealing how imagination and perseverance may carry one through. From Toledo to sex in the Big City, DC manages both an epic escape and a remarkable transformation. Armed with sarcasm and a pen, she proves truth is funnier than fiction.

DC is active in Cincinnati based Women Writing For (a) Change and was featured in an interview for *In The Tank,* a documentary program on PBS. She lives in Cincinnati with her daughter, Cori, and two cats, the requisite writerly minimum.